TAKING THE TRANSFERENCE, REACHING TOWARD DREAMS

TAKING THE TRANSFERENCE, REACHING TOWARD DREAMS

Clinical Studies in the Intermediate Area

M. Gerard Fromm

KARNAC

First published in 2012 by
Karnac Books Ltd
118 Finchley Road, London NW3 5HT

British Library Cataloguing in Publication Data

A C.I.P. for this book is available from the British Library

ISBN 978 1 78049 056 4

Edited, designed and produced by The Studio Publishing Services Ltd
www.publishingservicesuk.co.uk
e-mail: studio@publishingservicesuk.co.uk

www.karnacbooks.com

CONTENTS

ACKNOWLEDGEMENTS

Some of the chapters that follow have been previously published in slightly revised form elsewhere. I am grateful to the publishers for their permission to include them in this volume.

Chapters One, Three and Eleven were previously published under the same titles in *The Facilitating Environment: Clinical Application of Winnicott's Theory*, which I edited with Bruce L. Smith in 1989. They are reprinted here with the permission of International Universities Press. Chapter One was first published in *Resolving Treatment Impasses: The Difficult Patient*, edited by Theodore Saretsky in 1981. Permission for reprinting here comes from Rowman & Littlefield Publishing Group.

Chapter Two first appeared in *Psychoanalytic Psychology*, 12, in 1995. It is being reprinted with the permission of the American Psychological Association. Chapter Six was first published in *The Embodied Subject: Minding the Body in Psychoanalysis*, edited by John Muller and Jane Tillman in 2007. It is being reprinted here with the permission of Rowman & Littlefield Publishing Group. Chapter Nine first appeared in *The American Journal of Psychoanalysis*, 59, in 1999. It is being reprinted here with the permission of Springer Netherlands.

In Chapter Four, extensive quotes from Mehler and Argentieri's paper, "Hope and Hopelessness: A Technical Problem", published in the *International Journal of Psycho-Analysis*, 70, in 1989, are reprinted with the permission of John Wiley & Sons Ltd. In Chapter Eight, extensive quotes from Marion Milner's 1957 *On Not Being Able To Paint* are included with the permission of International Universities Press. Lyrics to Van Morrison's 1991 song "See Me Through, Part II" from *Hymns to the Silence*, quoted in Chapter Twelve, are included with the permission of Hal Leonard Corporation.

The clinical work reported here draws on years of both presentation and attendance at the extraordinarily rich case conferences of the Austen Riggs Center and on years of conversation with teachers and colleagues at the Center. Their names are too numerous to mention but I do want to recognise the mentorship of Ess White and Martin Cooperman, the clinical leadership of Edward Shapiro and James Sacksteder, the scholarship and inspired teaching of John Muller, and both the brilliance and the friendship of Francoise Davoine and Jean-Max Gaudilliere. I am extremely grateful to have travelled this path with all of them.

I also want to thank Lee Watroba, Executive Assistant of the Erikson Institute, for her ever upbeat support and ever careful project management. I especially thank Maryjane Fromm, whose good sense about life, whose care and understanding of me, and whose honesty and sophistication about people have made her my best supervisor over the years. Finally, I am enormously indebted to my patients for joining me in such difficult but intimate work and allowing me to learn and grow along with them.

M. Gerard Fromm, PhD, is currently the Evelyn Stefansson Nef Director of the Erikson Institute for Education and Research at the Austen Riggs Center in Stockbridge, MA. He also directed the Therapeutic Community Program at Austen Riggs for many years, where he is a senior psychotherapist and supervisor. He is certified in psychoanalysis, and is on the faculty of the Massachusetts Institute for Psychoanalysis, and the guest faculties of a number of other psychoanalytic institutes. He is also on the faculty of Harvard Medical School and the Yale Child Study Center, and is past President of the Center for the Study of Groups and Social Systems and President-Elect of the International Society for the Psychoanalytic Study of Organizations. Dr Fromm is a member of the Academy for Critical Incident Analysis and the International Dialogue Initiative. He has presented and published widely, including the edited volumes *The Facilitating Environment: Clinical Applications of Winnicott's Theory*, with Bruce L. Smith, PhD, and *Lost in Transmission: Studies of Trauma Across Generations*.

To my patients

Intermediate space

"One of the aims of this game is to reach to the child's ease and so to his fantasy and so to his dreams" (Winnicott, 1971a, p. 115). What a lovely description of an easy interplay between two people, leading to the communication of, even the creation of, inner life. Winnicott was a theorist of the unnoticed obvious, as much in this statement about his squiggle game as in his recognition of the eternal phenomenon of transitional objects. But it is also a commonplace of clinical psychoanalytic practice that no sooner is inner life contacted, and a beginning link made to the external world, no sooner do both parties realise that the behaviour that seemed so idiosyncratic actually has relational meaning, than something else happens: transference, and taking the transference becomes the new, vital, and risky clinical problem.

Symington (1986) puts it this way: "Each new patient . . . challenges the analyst to further his emotional development. . . . It is for this reason that I have stressed that the most difficult matter for the analyst is to 'take' a transference" (p. 321). I might re-frame this by saying that the patient engages the person of the analyst to further his or her emotional development, and that this intimate process necessarily pushes toward the development of the analyst. Symington argues that the trouble stems from the fact that "the transference is a distorted truth about the analyst" (p. 321). I would set aside the question of distortion and highlight those powerful moments when highly charged histories intersect. However one accents this challenge, it is fundamentally about trust: "There is the patient and the analyst . . . but there is also a process. This is the third term in which trust is ultimately placed" (Symington, 1986, p. 324). This process, of course, takes place in a space, a setting, formed by two parties, their task and the boundaries around them; Winnicott was the first to give words to this setting and to the in-between or intermediate space that might develop, should things go well.

This book reports on clinical work in that intermediate space, perhaps the space between reaching toward dreams and taking the transference. Most of this work took place at the Austen Riggs Center, a small psychiatric hospital in which quite troubled patients are offered intensive psychoanalytic psychotherapy in a completely open and voluntary therapeutic community setting. Some of the clinical vignettes report on my own work and some on the work of other therapists, with patients for whom I was in a different role—for example, supervisor or community consultant. To protect confidentiality, all of the patients' stories have been disguised and some have been made into composites. Within this protection, they are nevertheless meant to convey the actuality of the therapeutic process, in the recognition that the data from such intensive work can be of enormous value to other patients and therapists.

Within a broadly psychoanalytic frame, Austen Riggs has a long history of theoretical pluralism—from its origins as a centre for ego psychology through its era of interpersonal work with more psychotic patients to its more recent engagement with contemporary ego psychological, neo-Kleinian, Winnicottian, Lacanian, and relational ways of thinking. What holds this conceptual diversity together, and indeed allows for thriving cross-fertilization, is its being completely grounded in clinical data. The twice-weekly, two-hour, in-depth case conferences, which so often report the entrenched difficulties, genuine traumas, and profound suffering of patients, their families, and even their therapists, are nevertheless also exhilarating experiences of learning from the clinical encounter. And we are all in it together; all of us on the staff treat patients, all of us struggle, and all of us learn from each other and from our patients.

This book is, to some extent, a record of my learning—influenced quite deeply, as is already evident, by Winnicott's work. It seems to me something of a mystery as to why a particular theorist speaks to one therapist more than to another. For whatever reasons, Winnicott's work speaks to me, meaning that it resonates with what I hear from and experience with my patients, and it helps me make sense of things. In fact, this is what led to an earlier volume, co-edited with Bruce Smith, on clinical applications of Winnicott's theory (Fromm & Smith, 1989). "Application" was perhaps a poor choice of words. Erikson (personal communication) once said that as therapists, "We need a history and we need a theory, then we must forget them both and let each session stand for itself." Theories can never be "applied" in psychotherapy; in fact they must be forgotten to be useful at all. Yet somehow my patients often seem to be speaking Winnicottian to me, completing a squiggle that he started, so to speak. In the treatment situation, the accuracy of what I am hearing is ultimately up to the patient; in this book, it is up to the reader.

Winnicott is associated with the Middle School or the Independent Tradition of British psychoanalysis. In a sense, he was a theorist of the middle in a number of ways, especially as his major concept of transitional space (1951) describes an intermediate area, an in-between space, an arena of play, which mediates the inner and outer worlds. In a more pragmatic and political sense, he was always in the middle between the factions represented by Anna Freud and Melanie Klein within the British Psychoanalytic Society (Rayner, 1991), and, as I have argued elsewhere (Fromm, 1989a), he was in the middle theoretically, insofar as his ideas build upon both ego psychological and object relations concepts.

As an ego psychologist, Winnicott was centrally concerned with the effects of the real environment on the developmental processes of the child. Following Freud's theoretical shift after, and really in response to, the First World War, Winnicott too wanted to name normal developmental processes, to explore the effects of trauma, and to study the "protective shield". From his work with children and families in what he called his Psychiatric Snack Bar, he gave us as a quip his most basic frame of reference: "There is no such thing as a baby"; there is "a *baby and someone*. A baby cannot exist alone, but is essentially part of a relationship" (1957, p. 137). It is probably this emphasis on the two-person frame of reference, no matter how things might appear, that has proven most valuable to both clinicians and parents. The clinical work reported in this book is grounded in the idea that *there is no such thing as a patient; there is only a patient and a therapist.* Beyond the recognition that patienthood is a role, not a person, this perspective insists on taking seriously both the generative potential space that may develop between patient and therapist and the unconscious dynamics—one might say the systemic properties— of the twosome.

Ever the optimist, and also the realistic observer of resilience in children, Winnicott believed that the developmental arrests we see in our patients not only stem from, but also record, the early breakdown of the environment and make it available in potential form for renewed development. He called this "the freezing of the failure situation" (1954a, p. 281) and, building on Freud's idea of the repetition–compulsion, he felt that the person damaged in his development would naturally seek and move toward re-integration if the new environment proved reliable. Paradoxically, the cornerstone of his clinical practice turned out to be the therapist's unreliabilities or failures (1955–1956). From the two-person point of view, any major resistance or setback in the work with a very disturbed patient must reflect that person's response to an actual or threatened failure in the holding environment. As Adam Phillips writes, "people are only ever as mad as other people are deaf" (1996, p. 34). The more ill the patient, the less he will be able to perceive the failure as "out there". Thus it is incumbent upon the therapist to think what the patient cannot think, namely, about the "out there", the other, primarily himself. This is the challenge of taking the transference. In his seminal paper on "Hate in the countertransference" (1947), Winnicott describes the psychoanalyst as studying, on behalf of general psychiatry, not only primitive stages of development but, more importantly, "the nature of the emotional burden" (p. 194) treatment personnel must learn to bear.

As an object relations theorist, Winnicott appreciated Melanie Klein's contributions, especially her elaboration of the dynamics of projection and of persecutory and reparative systems. Following Klein, who was following the Freud of the death instinct, Winnicott needed to come to terms with aggression, or as Green (1999) elaborated it, "the work of the negative". An early effort in this direction came from Winnicott's extensive contact with delinquent children, whose lives had been seriously disrupted by the war and who led him early on to link the antisocial tendency to deprivation, the loss of a good environmental provision late enough for the child to recognise that something "out there" had happened, but early enough for the memory of the deprivation not to be sustained.

The two primary expressions of the antisocial tendency (1956a)— stealing and aggression—Winnicott saw as directed toward mother and father respectively. They both represented a hope that had come dangerously alive in a new, potentially reliable environment, a calling to the environment to become important again, and to see that the delinquent child is seeking people rather than things. Winnicott (1969) also argued, as one of his most enduring and important themes, that at some point the patient would move from "relating to" the therapist as a subjective-object to "using" the therapist for what he uniquely had to offer. This would be accomplished through aggression, through the patient's pushing the illusion of the intermediate area to its boundary and then some response from the therapist that established his "out-there-ness" and survival as separate, as non-retaliatory, as having something like clinical expertise to offer from this now more objective position.

Many of the studies in this volume include an exploration of aggression as a pivotal moment in the clinical encounter, one that adds its own degree of risk and challenge to the task of taking the transference, and one that so often needs the support and consultation of others to become clinically transformative. Within this set of considerations at the edge of the intermediate area, I also find links to the work of Lacan (1977), my understanding of which comes largely from many years of conversation with the Lacanian Clinical Forum, led by John Muller, and from the work of Francoise Davoine and Jean-Max Gaudilliere (2004), who find trauma at the heart of psychosis. Perhaps one could say, a bit too neatly, that the clinical work reported in this volume takes place in the space between Winnicott and Lacan (Luepnitz, 2009; Kirshner, 2011), between the "laws" of mother and father, between the *Nom (Non) du Pere*, to be sure, but the *Oui* (We) *de la Mere* (Fromm, 2009) as well, between what one reaches for with another person and what one must take in the process of receiving them.

CHAPTER ONE

Impasse and transitional relatedness

Throughout its history, psychoanalysis has necessarily and usefully concerned itself with problems related to impasse—for practical clinical reasons as well as for theoretical ones. Impasse is a situation of no movement, and hence of a failure or at least a partial failure of therapeutic results. The patient remains, in some fundamental way, unchanged in his suffering. The analyst is disappointed, frustrated, doubting, and fatigued. To the extent that we still live in a culture of narcissism, the analyst may feel more than passing disillusionment and more than passing concern—for the patient's continuing troubles as well as for the way those troubles seem to accuse him, as if their existence, in and of themselves, is the enduring responsibility of the person who, at one point, wished to help in understanding them.

On the other hand, it has indeed been the experience of impasse in analysis that has provided the clinical data and impetus to push our understanding of human development beyond whatever its then current confines might have been. An early example comes directly from Freud (1905e), whose deeper consideration of the impasse in, and the unexpected termination of, Dora's analysis led him to see the centrality of the transference, at first as a major if now recognised obstacle to the treatment. Here, knowledge of the transference as resistance evolved from impasse. Bird's (1972) discussion of this issue emphasises Freud's redoubling of this process; that is, with further reflection, Freud turned the impasse of transference-resistance into the knowledge of the transference as the major vehicle of the treatment. "Then, in what seems like a creative leap, Freud made the almost unbelievable discovery that transference was in fact the key to analysis, that by properly taking the patient's transference into account, an entirely new, essential, and immensely effective heuristic and therapeutic force was added to the analytic method" (Bird, 1972, p. 269).

There are innumerable examples of this dialectic process, of impasse leading to discovery, throughout the development of psychoanalysis. There are also ways in which this dialectic has divided the analytic community: for example, around the issue of analysability. Should analysts risk the inevitable experience of impasse, failure, perhaps harm to patients and the profession that eventuates from working at or beyond the borders of clearly understood psychopathology? Rather, should not analysts conserve themselves and their standing in society by accenting psychoanalytic work with patients whose pathology has been documented to be clearly accessible to analytic investigation and influence (Rangell, 1975)? On the other hand, how are we to learn about and help those deeper troubled areas of human experience if not by risking ourselves and our methodology in an effort to bridge the communicative gap between two people (Green, 1975)?

These questions, among others, flow from the experience of impasse (A. Freud, 1976). Data with which to address them have been accumulating slowly over the past several decades, as analysts, sometimes overly optimistically, sometimes out of sheer necessity, have found themselves presented with patients whose suffering was intense and yet whose ability to engage in analytic work, as traditionally defined, was severely limited. One pervasive trend in this work has become quite clear: that an interactional dimension, defined broadly, must be taken into account in understanding the power, and therefore also the vicissitudes, of clinical psychoanalysis (Greenson and Wexler, 1969; Winnicott, 1971a). André Green (1975), in a major paper outlining his understanding of changes in analytic practice as reflective of the severe psychopathology currently seen in clinical work, made this point emphatically:

> Problems of indications for analysis [can] be approached from the point of view of the gap between the analyst's understanding and the patient's material, and from that of the evaluation of the mobilizing effect of the analyst's communication on the patient's mental functioning, i.e., on the possibility . . . of forming an analytic object (a symbol) by the meeting of the two parties. (p. 18)

Consistent with this effort to illuminate the dyadic nature of psychoanalysis is the concomitant effort to illuminate impasse as an interactional phenomenon. Langs (1976) has emphasised this point of view in his work on the bipersonal field, as has Gorney (1979) in his thorough discussion of a particular kind of impasse, the negative therapeutic reaction. Will's (1964) definition of chronicity fits equally well the interpersonal phenomenology of impasse; that is, that a stereotyped presentation meets a stereotyped response. Curiosity, revelation, and change itself are casualties of this stereotypy; nothing new seems to happen. Both parties to the treatment seem fixed in their image of the other. The fundamental processes of the analytic relationship—attachment, revelation, change, and separation—are aborted. Indeed, the impasse may have to do with the particular phase of the patient's relationship to the analyst and to the treatment; that is, the impasse may have as its major motivating force the avoidance of a particular experience, with its fantasy elaborations, in relation to the analyst. One thinks here of the paranoid patient for whom beginning feelings of attachment produce intense turbulence, or the patient for whom the idea of termination assumes catastrophic and growth-inhibiting significance, a domino effect in reverse.

To the extent that an impasse in fact aborts a treatment, one sees a progressive, insidious devaluing of the analyst and the analytic experience by the patient. When the treatment comes to an actual end, there is no process of separation or grieving. Rather, there is only the depleted termination of a tiresome non-experience. Nothing differentiates this treatment from the amalgam of the patient's life so far; hence, there is nothing new to be lost. To the extent that the analysis once held hope for the patient, there is, after the aborted treatment, only the defensive warding off of its absence and the dissociation of whatever in it might have mattered. The all too frequent outcome of unresolved impasse is an elision of the patient's entire experience of the treatment.

Frame and medium

If we consider the psychoanalytic impasse from an interactional point of view, rather than solely in terms of the patient's intrapsychic structure, the question of the analyst's contribution to it is necessarily raised. Apart from a simple intrapsychic (countertransferential in the strict sense) focus on the analyst, one might approach the analyst's potential contribution to impasse by considering her contributions to the treatment in general. The technique of clinical psychoanalysis can be described in any number of ways. One such description would accent two primary functions for the analyst: the establishment and maintenance of the frame, and the offering of a medium. These important concepts have been developed elsewhere (Balint, 1968; Khan, 1960; Langs, 1976; Milner, 1952) and can only be sketched briefly here.

The frame refers to the boundedness and structure of the analytic situation. It has to do with all those technical prescriptions and "arrangements" for the treatment that securely establish the rhythm of the work, the privacy of the setting, and the constancy of the analyst. Insofar as the establishment of the frame presupposes the analyst's knowledge (e.g., of the conditions for benign regression and for transference development), this action reflects the analyst's authority and professional identity.

The offering of the medium differs from and complements the concept of frame. The analyst as medium offers himself—his empathic responsiveness and total mental functioning—to the patient. His purpose is to receive the range of impressions the patient is trying to convey, the range of self and object images, and of affect that at any given point constitute the experiential, transferential level of the treatment. The concept of medium connotes the process level of the treatment, the level of resonance. As the frame of the treatment fades into the background, the analyst as emotionally responsive medium becomes its foreground. Countertransference in its broader sense has its place here, in that the feeling-reactions of the analyst can be seen as primary data with regard to the unconscious communication of the patient. The crucial factor in the treatment becomes the analyst's apprehending these countertransference feelings—containing them, analysing them, and, in some way, imparting their significance to the treatment.

The analyst's dual functions correspond to two modes of relatedness between analyst and patient. In establishing and maintaining the

frame, the analyst deals with the patient at the level of everyday reality (e.g., of fees and schedules). The mode of communication is linear,
logical, informative, and individuated. The analyst is, in a sense, the
emissary of reality, the professional solver of problems. Expertise is a
factor, and the distribution of authority is clearly imbalanced; the
analyst leads in setting the arrangements and the method, that the
patient accepts, more or less, and follows.

The analyst's actions in setting the frame, however, mark off a
space in which an entirely different kind of relatedness may occur.
The patient's efforts to contact and integrate the dissociated parts of
himself require a different communicative mode—associative, empathic, and merged in some way with the analyst as alter ego. Again,
the distribution of authority is imbalanced. The patient leads the effort
to communicate or to evade; the analyst follows. Ultimately, the accuracy of the analyst's interpretive activity rests with the patient to,
mostly unconsciously, confirm or not. This form of relatedness, called
into play via the analyst as medium, occurs, in Winnicott's (1951)
terms, within an area of illusion. That is, the question of the reality
status of the patient's imaginings and constructions of his experience,
including his experience of the analyst, is set aside unasked; in its
place is only the search for its personal meaning. From one perspective, this can also be seen as the area of transference experience, called
into play as a transitional phenomenon (Greenson, 1974; Modell, 1963,
1968) to comfort and to bridge a gap between present and past—so
that the patient can be someone and be with someone that he is no
longer and is no longer with.

The problem of impasse can be approached from this dual angle.
My thesis is that impasse in the analytic situation may at times be best
understood as reflecting a pathology of relatedness between analyst
and patient, and that this pathology may occur in one of two forms,
deriving to some extent from the analyst's two technical functions.
Pathology is perhaps too strong a word, for the pitfalls to be discussed
are inevitable and importantly a part of the ongoing work of the treatment. However, I want to stress the truly debilitating impact on the
entire treatment if these differing forms of impasse are not grasped by
the analyst and worked with. A guiding conceptual structure for this
discussion will be Winnicott's work on transitional phenomena (1951)
and his later discussion (1969) of the distinction between relating to
and using the object.

Of particular importance with a first kind of impasse are Winnicott's (1951) early formulations regarding illusion. "The mother ... by an almost 100 percent adaptation affords the infant the opportunity for the illusion that her breast is part of the infant. . . . Omnipotence is nearly a fact of experience" (p. 238). Eventually, of course, disillusioning processes occur, and, bit by bit, the infant comes to know and integrate reality as represented primarily by mother's separate person and the particularities and vicissitudes of her care. This cannot occur successfully, however, according to Winnicott, without "sufficient opportunity for illusion" (p. 238) in the earliest stages of post-natal life. Winnicott sees this gestating experience as the foundation of an individual's sense of creativity and of robust connectedness to the world. "In another language, the breast is created by the infant over and over again out of the infant's capacity to love or (one can say) out of need" (p. 238). Khan (1971) goes on to apply Winnicott's notion of illusion to the analytic situation, focusing in particular on the problems in working with those patients who seem incapable of developing and sustaining the illusional aspect of analytic treatment without serious discomfort.

Defeating processes

There are some treatments that seem to come to a particular kind of impasse. As described thoroughly by Cooperman (1969), this impasse has two distinct clinical characteristics. First, the progressive development of the treatment and of the treatment relationship is interrupted or even reversed by the behaviour of the patient. Second, the therapist "experiences a loss of good feeling" (p. 7). In place of feeling cautiously optimistic, the therapist feels "thwarted, often anguished, helpless, frustrated, lost, angry, hurt, and even, when the interference is precipitously introduced, as though physically struck" (p. 7). In short, the therapist feels, and in fact is, defeated in his wishes for, and efforts toward, the growth and development of his patient. He is hit by the patient where he, to some degree in fact, is vulnerable, that is, in his basic identity as a therapist. That the patient is also defeated in her defeating of the therapist is both true and beside the point. For the moment, change toward more satisfying ways of living has become an irrelevant consideration (perhaps also an impossible one, given what

will be discussed as the precipitant for the attack); it is more important for the patient to have her illness than it is to have her therapist.

Dr Cooperman offers several detailed clinical vignettes to illustrate
his essential point that "a patient may destroy the therapy in order to
defeat the therapist, regardless of the price he pays in doing so" (1969,
p. 27). Others (Fromm, 1978; Langs, 1976; Searles, 1975) have noted the
patient's effort to set right a treatment course thrown off by the misunderstanding or the personal reactions of the therapist; under certain
circumstances, patients may well feel inclined to destroy a treatment
course as well. The degree to which this is a conscious *vs.* an unconscious effort is a secondary issue; in fact, Dr Cooperman's data are
quite striking for the awareness and articulateness his patients
displayed about the defeating process. One patient reported "that I
was right about feeling about to be struck, [that] he had been debat-
ing about whether to strike back at me by continuing to come to
sessions, going through the motions, not making any progress, and
leaving after several months. He then went on to note that he had
done this to his previous therapist" (p. 9). Another patient responded
to Dr Cooperman's formulation of his manic regression and its consequences as an attack on the treatment by gleefully noting, "that I
was exactly right . . . [that] to his wife and family he was now viewed
as the sick person to be cared for and I was an incompetent and un-
caring doctor" (p. 17).

Dr Cooperman goes on to describe three interrelated elements of
the defeating process: first, that it represents an act of vengeance for a
specific hurt felt by the patient to have been inflicted on her by the
therapist; second, that without attention to this hurt, the defeating
process escalates into a full-scale power struggle that may both diffuse
and escalate further as "splits" within the treatment organisation;
finally, that his patients' mode of being in the defeating process
mimicked behaviour of their mothers that they had felt to be hurtful
to them in their growing up. In effect, in getting back *at* the therapist,
they also seemed to be getting back *to* their mothers.

This description of impasse highlights what might be thought of as
the wilfulness of the patient (whose diagnoses in Dr Cooperman's
report range from characterological to depressive to psychotic conditions). Certainly, an adversarial situation is being described—in reality, as opposed to only in the patient's transferential life. The therapist
is being defeated in the only way he really can be, that is, via his real,

appropriate, and understandable stake in the therapy itself. Two elements in this mode of relatedness are exceedingly important: the reality level of the exchange and the separateness of the two parties. Dr Cooperman notes the latter to be the primary precipitant for the defeating process. "Each patient . . . described feeling hurt, humiliated, or badly used (narcissistically wounded), and rendered helpless by a considered and concrete act of mine which directly affected the arrangement of the therapy. . . . With each, I had arbitrarily forced into focus our separateness" (pp. 18–19).

In this context, wilfulness is exactly the point. The patient falls back on individual will, a separate will, for several reasons. In hurting because hurt, she both avenges herself on and mirrors the therapist. The injury is the therapist's separateness; the response is a display of the patient's separateness. But, at a deeper level, the patient's wilfulness may well serve to confirm the continued aliveness of a jeopardised self, a self that had been cautiously but necessarily giving over to the process of the therapy until being abruptly forced into separateness by the therapist. In other words, in the context of risky dependency, the patient reacts with a form of primitive omnipotence to the therapist's individuating actions, ordinary as those actions might seem from the outside. The function of the omnipotence is the reassertion of the delusion of control, when in fact there is an underlying panic—that the therapist has gone and taken with him the nuclei of ego functioning and evolving self-representations that had begun to develop within a beginning-to-be-reliable therapeutic matrix.

The basic fear in this emotional context is of psychic death, a fear followed immediately by the assertive reinstatement of the symptoms as both a comfort and a weapon. I once heard of a young man, the youngest of a large family, who, at a point in his adolescence when his ever tenuously held together family was finally fragmenting, as was his own psychic functioning, leaped in front of a subway train to his death. His motives, in retrospect, seemed to have to do, not so much with a wish to die, but rather with a wish to stop life. He seemed to desperately need to put himself in the path of events and of time itself, in a delusional effort to halt the inexorable. In doing so, he dramatised the killing impersonality of his life experience; he became a casualty in and of the real world.

The therapist's separateness, in effect, ruptures the area of illusion forming ever so subtly in the treatment (Khan, 1971; Winnicott, 1951);

in Searles's (1976) terms, the therapeutic symbiosis is damaged. The patient is forced to operate on either the level of delusion (i.e., on the level of a brittle denial of injury and an assertion of magical control), or on a totally depleted reality level, a reality into which the patient now feels helpless to deliver herself. Whatever was being brought to life in the treatment—Winnicott would encourage us not to ask by whom—left with the individuating therapist, leaving the patient feeling without any capacity to create, from within herself, anything which would join her in a living way with the external world.

In another language, this form of impasse having to do with defeating processes can be described as following from an action by the therapist along the frame of the treatment, that has as its primary negative effect a severe perturbation in his offering himself as medium. There is an assertion here: the therapist has exercised his legitimate authority—to be the separate person he is, to set and manage the arrangements of the treatment. But this clear shift in a mode of relatedness disturbs, even shocks, the other mode of relatedness having to do with the medium of the treatment. Action on the medium has been given over to the initiative of the patient. Hence, there is a sense of mutual betrayal in the patient's response to the therapist's initiatives. It is as though, in Lewin's (1954) terms, the therapist has jarred into painful wakefulness and harsh reality a patient who had been, until that moment, using the therapist and the therapeutic situation to move toward a state of quasi-sleep and a necessary dream. If the therapist misunderstands or devalues the importance of his patience in allowing the patient the use of the medium, then that phase of hesitation (Winnicott, 1941), preliminary to the patient's comfort with the illusional aspect of the treatment and requiring the initial constancy of the therapist, cannot come to completion. Once the area of illusion has been established, traumatic disillusionment becomes a possibility, from which the treatment cannot recover without the considerable turmoil of the defeating process.

The way out of such an impasse seems to be the way in. Winnicott (1971b) puts it in the following way for the abandoned child: "It is a matter of days or hours or minutes. Before the limit is reached the mother is still alive; after this limit has been overstepped, she is dead. In between is a precious moment of anger . . ." (p. 22). Drs Cooperman (1969) and Bird (1972) concur in the belief that the hope for the resolution of the impasse (and for its transformation into crucial analytic gains) lies in helping the patient get hold of, and allowing oneself to receive, the deep and live anger toward the therapist for the perceived injury. Bird (1972) puts the technical issue very clearly:

> Significant success, however, can be counted only if the response [of the patient] leads to some rather detailed chapter and verse discoveries as to how and why the patient's malicious intent against the analyst was actually developed and carried out . . . [including] how much it was retaliation for attacks made on him by the analyst. (pp. 292–293)

In essence then, the kind of impasse typified by the defeating process reflects an abrupt and premature separateness of the therapist and a disturbance in a healthily developing transitional relatedness. The frame of the treatment intrudes arbitrarily on the function of the medium. The logical consequences to disturbance in the transitional sphere threaten: delusional power or psychic death in a vacuously experienced reality (Green, 1975). Reparation and resolution can occur if the rage within the relationship can be contacted, contained, and worked through openly and specifically. The hoped-for outcome here is renewed trust, in the engineering sense; that is, having to do with a new appreciation of, and perhaps a new level of, the therapist's and the relationship's capacity to withstand stress. Such a capacity can now become an important background condition for a continuing and deepening analysis.

A case of derealisation

There is another kind of interactional impasse, the characteristics of which can be described along the dimensions of relatedness and technique just discussed, though with quite a contrasting configuration. In order to do so, a vignette will be offered as clinical data, one that was reported in the literature many years ago. In 1955, Victor Rosen published a paper entitled "The reconstruction of a traumatic childhood event in a case of derealization." (Excerpts from Dr Rosen's paper, originally published in Vol. 3 of the *Journal of the American Psychoanalytic Association*, 1955, are included by permission of Theodore Shapiro, MD, who was the Journal's editor at the time this chapter was first written.)

In essence, the paper is a marvellous illustration, as Dr Rosen intended, of the importance of the reconstruction of the traumatic fixation, in this case occurring at about the age of three and a half. Along the way, Dr Rosen also makes the point that identification may serve as a means for binding the overwhelming affect associated with traumatic experience. The vignette is summarised here in some detail because it also offers a striking illustration of an impasse and its resolution.

The patient, a professional man in his late twenties, came into treatment having recently begun to feel depressed, suicidal, as though he were fragmenting, and full of bizarre bodily sensations. Dr Rosen describes the patient's feelings of "fullness in the head", "twisting" and "choking" sensations, and "feelings of being transected through the diaphragm" (p. 212). The symptoms appeared after the patient's fiancée, upset with his unpredictable and often violent fluctuations of mood, broke their engagement. The patient lost interest in his work and embarked on a series of casual affairs, during which he developed the recurrent fantasy that his sexual partner would subsequently be found strangled and he would be accused of the murder.

The patient was the younger of two brothers. His father was a successful businessman, unhappy with and bitter toward his sons for not coming into the family business. He alternately bestowed and withheld money in an effort to control them. He also suffered from a paralysis of his lower limbs during the patient's early childhood. The patient's mother is described as jealous and possessive. She would at times become seriously depressed and at other times violently rageful. The children were put in the middle of the marital strife and expected to declare their loyalty toward one or the other parent. The patient complained about both his mother's seductiveness toward him and her depriving him of maternal care.

This patient was seen by Dr Rosen face-to-face, three times weekly, for approximately four years. The underlying diagnostic picture was thought to be schizophrenia. A particular technical problem in the therapy had to do with the patient's feelings of unreality and his negating all interpretations.

> He did not feel that what was said really applied to him. He felt that the therapist confused him with other patients. He said in this regard, I never know whether something belongs to me or to someone

else. . . . Occasionally, during treatment, he could not tell whether some idea had been transmitted from him to the therapist or vice-versa. (pp. 213–214)

During his second year of therapy, a series of puzzling but critical developments occurred. The patient began to recall incidents surrounding the discharge of a beloved nurse in his early childhood:

> the only one who had 'understood' him . . . 'the one witness in my behalf.' . . . There were recurrent references to recollections of 'some horrifying experience which occurred while I was looking down the long dark hall of our home as a small boy.' . . . The patient felt that he had been 'a witness to something that changed my life.' . . . At the same time he increasingly neglected his job. He felt that earning a living was unreal and that the money he was paid was 'make believe.' He began to neglect his bills and finally stopped paying for his treatment altogether. (p. 214)

Dr Rosen describes the patient at this time as manifesting "a sullen glowering expression", as "in moody silence", as "provocatively disparaging the treatment", as "slyly destructive", and as "making attempts at intimidation" (p. 214). At one point, the patient, in a menacing way, spent the session opening and closing a large clasp knife, leading the therapist to comment that he was indeed being made to feel anxious by this behaviour; at that point the patient put the knife away. The patient would not discuss the failure to pay for treatment. "His behaviour seemed to indicate a hostile determination to prove that the treatment was all 'make believe' and that it would continue whether paid for or not. This determination was impervious to interpretation" (p. 215). Finally, Dr Rosen decided to discontinue the treatment until the patient paid his now three-month debt. Payment was made in two instalments over the next month and, while waiting for treatment to resume, the patient wrote what Dr Rosen describes as "bitter letters".

> I did not believe you really meant what you said, I thought that you would get the money from my father . . . I know now that I must help in the solution of my problem. . . . If I must wait too long, my faith in you will again be shaken. (p. 215)

When treatment began again, the patient produced provocative data, leading eventually to Dr Rosen's bold reconstruction. In reporting a stiff neck, the patient said, "it felt as if my head were being twisted from my body" (p. 215). He became depressed and suicidal. He had the fantasy that Venetian blinds he had been playing with were really "hangman's ropes", and he also felt that he was being given "permission" by his therapist to recall something. Following his report of a dream having to do with "a small chest like a trunk lying on the floor", Dr Rosen had the feeling "of many loose pieces in a puzzle falling into place" (pp. 215–216).

> I felt quite certain that the patient's mother must have made a suicidal attempt during his childhood which he had witnessed. . . . It also seemed likely that the neck symptoms, references to the rope . . . and the earlier fantasy of the strangled girl, refer to an attempt by hanging. (p. 216)

Dr Rosen's offering this hypothesis to the patient released "a remarkable and violent flood of affect. He was racked with convulsive sobbing in a most dramatic scene lasting about ten minutes. This session was a turning point in the treatment" (p. 216).

Following this reconstruction, the derealisation symptoms decreased and the patient showed an increased ability to use the therapy. For example, he was able to analyse the meaning of his withholding the fee in terms of his "identification with his father's punitive and seductive uses of his money" (p. 216). He was also able to bring into the work at this time complicated and disturbing feelings about masturbation. With his father, he confirmed the fact of his mother's suicide attempt, that he had indeed witnessed during his fourth year, and that had indeed been made by hanging. Dr Rosen writes:

> The discharge of the nurse a year later was connected with the episode, because the mother had experienced her presence as a constant reminder of the incident. Both the father and the nurse had treated any mention of the event on the part of the patient as something that he had imagined or as a bad dream". (p. 216)

He also adds,

> when I had suggested the possibility of his mother's suicide attempt in his childhood, the patient had felt as if I had not restored the memory but had merely given him permission to talk about something he had known in some way all along. (p. 216)

The capacity to use the analyst

The impasse in the treatment just described was clearly a very serious one, yet resolution occurred as well as striking analytic gain. From one angle, it looks as though, and in fact it may have been the case that, Dr Rosen's reconstruction was the crucial move in breaking the stalemate, releasing the impacted affect, and crystallising important memory and insight. From another angle, the way for Dr Rosen's reconstruction seemed paved by the patient's unconscious effort to represent the traumatic memory (e.g., in the Venetian blind fantasy and in the dream about the trunk). Moreover, the patient had felt a strange new permission to discover something and had found a startlingly new ability to use his own and the analyst's words. Critically important developments seemed to have been occurring in the patient and in the analytic relationship prior to the analyst's reconstruction. How might these changes be described and accounted for?

Following Winnicott (1969), one could argue that Dr Rosen's patient came to make the critical shift from relating to the analyst to using him. The former implies a subjective experience, a cathexis toward the other, the operation of projective and identificatory mechanisms, and some movement toward physical excitement and discharge. The latter implies the capacity to use the other for the properties of the other and not as a figment of the patient's subjectivity. In other words:

> The object, if it is to be used, must necessarily be real in the sense of being part of shared reality, not a bundle of projections. . . . [U]sage cannot be described except in terms of acceptance of the object's independent existence, its property of having been there all the time. (Winnicott, 1969, p. 712)

Dr Rosen's patient became able to find his analyst's independent status in the real world. In this new place, the analyst's interpretations, previously negated by hostility or diffused as unreal and as the analyst's mis-identification, suddenly had compelling power. Furthermore, in this new place, the self-comforting, self-aggrandising aspects of his masturbatory activity could, for the first time, become part of a two-party discourse. This level of relatedness—a relatedness reflecting the analyst's separateness and therefore his availability for use for his own properties—is in marked contrast to the level of relatedness earlier in the treatment. Prior to the analyst's achieving reality status for the patient, he occupied what might be thought of as a pathological transitional object status. In other words, the pathologic relatedness cultivated by the patient included dedifferentiation of self and object, a level of primitive omnipotence, a diffuse and pervasive aura of "make believe" without grounding in reality, and a talismanic possession of the analyst for purposes of comfort rather than work (and rather than genuine play as well).

The impasse, therefore, being described here in terms of pathologic transitional status has as major features to its configuration the properties of unreality (e.g., to words, fees, feelings, and bodily sensations) and of merger, or lack of separateness between analyst and patient. This is in marked contrast to the impasse characterised by defeating processes, the main properties of which seemed to be its reality level and the traumatic separateness of the two parties. The defeating process attacks the reality of the analyst for his perceived role in the premature loss of an illusion. Pathologic transitional relatedness forces an illusion to the point of delusion, and cannot contact reality.

From a Winnicottian perspective, Dr Rosen's patient worked with him, and vice versa, in such a way as to accomplish the reality groundedness necessary and preliminary to the capacity to use the analyst's reconstruction. In other words, "this interpreting by the analyst, if it is to have effect, must be related to the patient's ability to place the analyst outside the area of subjective phenomena" (Winnicott, 1969, p. 711). For Winnicott, the means of this accomplishment is the patient's destructiveness, and the accomplishment itself reflects "the positive value of destructiveness" (p. 715). If the patient destroys the transitionally held other, and that other survives, then the other exists in a world outside the projective invention and omnipotent control of the patient. Hence the other is real and available for use.

To put it paradigmatically, if the child tears the teddy bear to pieces, the life of that teddy, invented by the child in the first place, comes to an end. If the child acts similarly toward the mother, the mother will eventually say "Stop it now. That hurts." The mother's invented life will come to an end, in both the child's wish and in the fact that something will survive intact. That something is the mother's real life, a property of her own, now discovered by the child, though there all along, and potentially to be used and loved as a genuine other.

Dr Rosen's data offer compelling evidence for Winnicott's formulation, for it does indeed seem that the gap between relating to and using the object, or between the pathologic transitional status and the reality status of the analyst, was bridged by the patient's destructiveness and the analyst's survival without retaliation. During the second year of the treatment, anxious memory fragments begin to occur followed by an increased living out of feelings of unreality in his work life and in the analytic situation. There developed then a mood of unmistakable aggression and destructiveness. Words, for both parties, were useless (relatively), and action by both parties followed. The patient played with the knife; the analyst responded with his actual feeling. The patient refused payment and refused analysis of his non-payment; the analyst eventually discontinued the treatment. After payment and prior to the resumption of the analysis, that is, prior to the analytic work leading to the reconstruction, the patient wrote in his letters that words, in effect, had finally acquired reality status for him and that "faith" in the analyst was now a new and tentative development.

The major thesis of this section of the chapter is that the termination of the treatment was a critical event to the subsequent developments in the treatment; that the patient's push toward representing his trauma, the analyst's capacity to grasp it, and the patient's capacity to use a reconstructive interpretation might well have failed to develop entirely without the event which "place(d) the analyst outside the area of omnipotent control, that is, out in the world" (Winnicott, 1969, p. 714). This event was Dr Rosen's limit. It limited the patient's destructiveness, and it also recognised the limits of the analyst's tolerance and technical ability. It affirmed a separateness that told the patient that his fantasy of murder would not become real with the analyst, that the analyst would survive the patient's actual destructiveness. Indeed, from another angle, the patient had in effect compelled this separateness as if to find the "witness" who might separately and credibly testify to the reality of a past event on the patient's behalf. This witnessing followed in the reconstruction and in the patient's confirming with his father the fact of his having seen his mother's suicide attempt.

The pathologic transitional relatedness prior to the event of the limit can be seen, to some extent only retrospectively, in transference terms. The patient does indeed subsequently analyse his withholding of the fee as reflecting his effort to control the analyst through money, just as his father had done to him. Only after the reconstruction, however, can one also see the additional transference meaning of the patient's non-payment and the analyst's allowing of a debt; that is, that the analyst–father is buying the patient–son's silence about the critical event; hence, the patient's feeling of "permission" to remember following the limit. It is clear in this material that the patient suffered a dual trauma in his early childhood: one in witnessing the horrible event of his mother's near suicide, the other in damage to his developing ego functions through his father's denial of the event (and its meaning) as the child's "bad dream".

Similarly, one can in retrospect see the pathologic transitional relatedness as having as its pervasive background a diffuse maternal transference. In effect, the patient's withholding of fees says to the analyst: "you will not leave me; you are mine", as well as "your life (your livelihood) does not depend on me". The transference implications with regard to the mother's potential death and the son's sense of dread and terrified self-accusation are clear. Also, one can now see the significance of the precipitating event to his illness (i.e., his fiancée's breaking the engagement), and to the memory precipitating his destructive mood (i.e., of the discharge of his childhood nurse). The point I wish to emphasise, however, is that the transference could not be grasped for its genetic meaning until the analyst and patient could ground the treatment in reality. Until such a development, the data did not seem to exist for, nor did words seem capable of establishing, a usable understanding of the patient's behaviour in transference terms.

It might, however, be argued at this point in the development of clinical psychoanalytic theory that the data indeed existed for an understanding of the impasse in transference terms, and that the data was the transference itself, as perceived through the aid of the countertransference; in other words, that the transference itself was the patient's best effort at remembering. It might also be argued that the analyst's use of the countertransference data in actual interpretive work might have effected the development considered to be key to the thesis under discussion; namely, the analyst's coming to existence outside the patient's subjectivity while still in contact with the patient. What Dr Rosen effected in action (though, importantly, not through intention) might now be possible in words, through a disciplined yet imaginative use of the countertransference.

The disturbed form of transitional relatedness described in Dr Rosen's clinical vignette is pathologic insofar as it must be; there is no leeway within it, no play in the system. The area of illusion, in which true play may occur, has become an area of delusion. The patient does not keep the agreement not to ask a basic question that may take a number of forms; for example, did you (the patient) create the analytic situation or did you find it? Rather, the patient poses the question and insists that his subjectivity is its only answer. This solipsism is clearly not without its own anxiety; nevertheless, it effectively denies object loss by denying the object existence. To return to the analogy of sleep (Lewin, 1954), it is as though the patient is caught and catches the analyst in a "bad dream", diffuse in time and space; the analyst's function as awakener becomes eventually imperative to the establishment of an object relation and a reality in which to continue the treatment.

A healthy transitional relatedness facilitates an imaginative mastery and integration of the experience of absence. Pathologic transitional relatedness does not allow absence to be constituted as an experience. Rather, the object is totally present (totally possessed by the omnipotence of the patient), and simultaneously non-existent, as a distinct other; there is never absence, as such. It may be that the patient cannot integrate the experience of absence prior to his analyst's making a similar integration. Applied to Dr Rosen's data, this hypothesis would suggest that Dr Rosen's integration of his patient's absence from him (his terminating the treatment) might have been necessary to his patient's developing a similar capacity, a capacity to constitute in himself an experience of genuine absence, the traumatic precursors of which had been so devastating. As Green (1975) has reminded us, the capacity for thought depends upon an experience of absence. It is only after the absence that Dr Rosen's patient can allow thought to develop toward the memory of many real and potential absences.

To return to the technical language elaborated earlier, pathologic transitional relatedness represents a diffusion of the medium in a way that erodes or otherwise breaches the frame of the treatment. The technical problem becomes the restoration of the frame. The analyst can only offer himself as medium within some frame; outside the frame, the patient is unprotected, as is the medium itself, since the analyst's feeling-reactions to the demand come into play. The analyst as medium can be offered, but not conquered—at least not without extensive damage to the reality that surrounds the treatment and hence to the treatment itself. Once the frame is restored (accomplished practically in action, as Rosen did, or perhaps by interpretation from the countertransference), anxiety de-escalates and the medium is available again for development and communication at the experiential level.

The positive value of destructiveness

Two forms of impasse that are interactional in nature have been discussed in this chapter. They can be described as (1) the defeating process, and (2) the incapacity to use the analyst. Both reflect a disturbance of transitional relatedness. In the former, the patient attempts, consciously or unconsciously, to defeat the treatment because of the analyst's premature and injurious disruption of the area of illusion developing between them. The patient is traumatically separate from the analyst and stuck in a depleted reality. In the latter form of impasse, the patient cannot use the analyst as analyst because the analyst has not come to be placed outside the range of the patient's omnipotence. The patient is traumatically merged with the analyst and stuck in delusion.

In a language having to do with the technical functions of the analyst, the defeating process reflects a traumatic withdrawal of the analyst as medium via his arbitrary action along the frame of the treatment. The incapacity to use the analyst reflects an erosion of the frame of the treatment via the patient's burgeoning demand on the analyst's capacity as medium. Aggression is central to the resolution of both forms of impasse. In the first situation, aggression re-contacts the separating analyst and discharges the panic that otherwise would be deadened internally and at great cost to the patient. In the second situation, aggression is the vehicle for finding what, if anything, is left in (or better, as) reality after the invented object has been destroyed. It is important to keep in mind that both forms of impasse develop naturally—at some basic experiential level and outside the conscious intentions of both parties. If impasse were to be a strategy of the patient for some reason or even a technical move of the analyst, we would be dealing with a different kind of problem. Any gains that come from the mutual work of resolving the kinds of impasses described in this chapter assume their good faith, so to speak, even if they are also a challenge to survive and work through.

CHAPTER TWO

What does "borderline" mean?

Speaking of "the pathological side of my identity confusion", Erik Erikson wrote:

> ... (N)o doubt it assumed at times what some of us today would call a 'borderline' character—that is, the borderline between neurosis and psychosis. But then, it is exactly this kind of diagnosis to which I later undertook to give a developmental perspective. And indeed, some of my friends will insist that I needed to name this crisis and to see it in everybody else in order to really come to terms with myself. (1970, p. 742)

Speaking first

This chapter represents an effort to "come to terms" with the term "borderline". After an exhaustive review of the literature on borderline psychopathology, Michael Stone (1986) closes by saying, "I'm haunted by the dark suspicion that the subject has gotten [sic] out of hand" (p. 432). By that he means that: "The borderline literature has swollen to a size too vast to be digested by one anthologist" (p. 432), and certainly by any one reader as well. I would like to consider something further in this haunting: an unsettling impression that what we mean by "borderline" has also "gotten [*sic*] out of hand", except perhaps as the term "borderline" has become synonymous with something having "gotten [*sic*] out of hand". My comments will address only briefly the theoretical aspects of "borderline"; rather, my focus will be on diagnostic and treatment practice, and on the word "borderline" as an empty signifier and a complicated speech act within a clinical context.

A few years ago, I was a discussant at a clinical case seminar. After the presentation, and in the course of discussion, I asked the group of about a dozen professionals, a number of whom were quite experienced, how they would think about the patient diagnostically; I added, "And let's think about this without using the term 'borderline' ". As might be guessed, the group burst into laughter that seemed both anxious and relieved. But they then began to use clinical-descriptive terms that had precise meaning in the data of the presentation, and, even more importantly, with which the patient herself would almost certainly have agreed on the basis of her own subjective experience.

This is the place I would like to begin: with phenomenology and subjective experience. It is my guess that, no matter how vast our literature on this topic, no clinician has ever had a patient enter her office and declare "I feel so borderline today", while we have all heard people speak easily of "obsessing", or being "narcissistic", or feeling "depressed" or "manic", "paranoid", "phobic", "hysterical", or even "schiz-y". In other words, there seems to be no ready or obvious affective or action referent *in the patient* to which the word "borderline" gives a name.

Perhaps this observation means nothing more than that this term "borderline" has not really been in circulation long enough to acquire a meaning to those suffering with it. Or perhaps it only raises an old issue about the relationship of subjective experience to the disease condition. Cancer patients do not feel cancerous; they may or may not even feel ill. A schizophrenic patient may be neither feeling nor behaving in a "schiz-y" way to be accurately diagnosed; furthermore, diagnostic assessment on that basis might be utterly inaccurate insofar as it does not include recognition of a formal thought disorder. Indeed, one of the earliest and most clinically captivating papers of the borderline literature is Helene Deutsch's (1942) discussion of the "as if" personality, in which she states clearly that these forms of

serious emotional disturbance and impoverishment "were not perceived as disturbances by the patient himself" (p. 302). Perhaps then,
"borderline" patients do not have a complaint that would lead them
to speak to us with the kind of self-descriptive statement of feeling or
action referred to above.

Interesting as Deutsch's observation is, I will for the moment leave
these considerations of a condition-without-a-complaint and return to
the problem of a name, "borderline", without an obvious referent. It
seems to me that such a diagnostic action, whatever else it might do
at its most professionally sensible and helpful levels, involves the
clinician in telling the patient what he or she is, through a name that
can find no personal experience in the patient. It is, therefore, an
action that immediately shifts the locus of authority away from the
patient's potential complaint, with whatever experience of distress
may inform that, and into the expert purview of the clinician. At its
extreme, this diagnostic action says: "What you are—namely borderline—is something you do not, perhaps cannot, know introspectively
or experientially, but I can know *about* it".

Obviously, there are implications in this diagnostic action—
regardless of how silently it might be carried out—for the frame of the
treatment, insofar as this particular statement, and the imbalances
within it, seem to destroy from the beginning a genuinely psychoanalytic frame of reference, while at the same time inflaming desires
and expectations in the patient to be the continued intensified object
of the analyst's power. If this action is not merely a singular one, a
potential misalliance, but a paradigmatic one with these patients, can
there be an effective treatment? It was considerations like these that
led George Vaillant to entitle a paper "The beginning of wisdom is
never calling a patient a borderline" (1992).

By an analytic frame, I mean our structuring a relationship to the
patient's inner process within which we *receive* the patient's statement
or inquiry about himself, in the confidence that together we can come
to know him. This structuring of the relationship defines roles; starkly
and schematically outlining the locus of initiatives within this role
relationship. André Green (1978) wrote that: "No analysis is conceivable in which, after the statement of the fundamental rule, the analyst
speaks first" (p. 180). It is my impression that our act of naming the
"borderline" patient, with a label he or she cannot know first-hand,
is often in practice a kind of "speaking first", a form of therapeutic

misalliance, setting into motion anti-analytic processes, processes that too often lock the analyst into the position of, in Lacan's phrase, the one who is "supposed-to-know" (Lacan, 1977; Muller, 1992).

This admittedly idiosyncratic train of thought could be carried further! For example, this diagnostic action is most usually carried out by a man upon a woman. It could thus be seen as not only an act of professional imperialism, but also of gender politics. And indeed, many treatments of "borderline" patients in the long run come to look like disastrous marriages, with the patient alternately struggling to liberate herself from this meaningless name—the psychiatrist's name after all—while also attempting to extract her due for having accepted it in the first place. I vividly recall the absolute dread that a patient of mine, a mental health professional, felt about the possibility that I might think of her as "borderline"; by that term, she seemed to mean both "crazy" and "too much". But more than these meanings and more than her own anxious self-diagnosis, it was the power of my potential diagnostic action my patient truly dreaded, an action trans-ferentially embedded in her family's history of Middle Eastern culture, within which the social status of women was rigidly defined and deeply toned by the male's unconscious fear.

Where is the border?

There is more to be developed on this theme as it is actually practiced, but I would like to leave considerations of gender for now and return to the question of experience. It seems to me that the only *experiential* referent for the term "borderline" (unless we return to its grammati-cal use as a qualifier, as in "borderline psychotic") is not *in* the patient at all, but in the clinician. This experience may take the form of a puzzlement as to whether one is facing a neurotic or a psychotic phenomenon, but very often it is something more urgent, something of a real dilemma in the clinician's embattled psyche about whether he or she is meeting a need or a demand. In other words, the clinician feels on a frontier of some sort, placed there—indeed pushed there—by a force from within the patient and often dreadfully ill at ease with standing firm or with stepping across.

My point of view here echoes the words of Robert Knight in his classic 1953 paper on "Borderline states".

> The term 'borderline states' . . . conveys no diagnostic illumination of
> a case other than the implication that the patient is quite sick but not
> frankly psychotic. . . . Thus the label 'borderline state', when used as
> a diagnosis, conveys more information about the uncertainty and
> indecision of the psychiatrist than it does about the condition of the
> patient. (Knight, 1953, p. 1)

Nearly forty years later, George Vaillant (1992) wrote: "I believe that
almost always the diagnosis 'borderline' is a reflection more of the
therapists' affective rather than their intellectual response to their
personality-disordered patients" (p. 120). He adds, citing two studies:
"That, perhaps, is why up to 90% of patients diagnosed 'borderline'
can also be assigned another, usually more discriminating, Axis II
diagnosis" (p. 120).

It seems to me that the history of work with "borderline" patients,
notwithstanding the very helpful clarifications of Kernberg (1975,
1984) and Fonagy (1991), includes a substantial number of failed treatments that founder on this uncertainty, which either never really get
started or drag out to disastrous conclusion as one side or the other of
this demand–need dilemma is enacted. Vaillant (1992) described these
twin countertransference pitfalls as the therapist's punitive and defensive setting of limits, on the one hand, or the therapist's attempting to
be a better mother than the one he thinks the patient had, on the other.
Neither helps. In Lacan's terms (1977), the psychotherapy of the
"borderline", if it takes off at all, is a psychotherapy aimed toward an
imaginary order only, a psychotherapy of desired but illusory images,
cut off from and ungrounded in a larger symbolic order of task and
meaning, and hence with no place for both parties to become subjects
within a matrix of social reality.

From this angle, the act of diagnosing the "borderline" patient as
such is, at its simplest level, a statement that "this person has a borderline personality disorder because *that's where she places me*", that is, at
a difficult dilemma about a boundary. Without this countertransference awareness, the act of diagnosing borderline phenomena becomes
an act of projective identification by the clinician, insofar as it simply
exports an internal distressing quandary into another person for
purposes of relief and clarity. (Recall Erikson's need "to see it
in everybody else".) It misrecognises who has what problem within
this twosome, and thus invites self-estrangement in both. In Vaillant's
terms (1992), "immature defenses have an uncanny capacity to get

under the skin" (p. 120); "the epithet 'borderline' " (p. 120) is a doomed and disingenuous attempt to free the therapist from this "contagion".

One becoming two

Before carrying this point further, I should perhaps say that I do not believe that borderline psychopathology is a solitary entity, but rather a vast developmental territory, indeed between psychosis and neurosis, eventuating upon failures of development in a number of seriously psychopathological disturbances of personality. Rosenfeld's (1979) descriptive typology includes the psychotic character, the Kernbergian borderline with "hardly any mental skin" (p. 197), the "as if" personality, the traumatised patient, and the narcissistic patient with disguised psychotic anxieties. The patients he describes we recognise from our own clinical encounters, and, though there is considerable overlap between his groupings, there are also clear differences of emphasis in the forms of defensive operations, the kinds of affects struggled with and the transferences.

All of this I believe derives primarily from developmental failure within that vast area defined by Winnicott's work as the pathology of the twosome. In fact, a simple arithmetical schema of development runs throughout Winnicott's work: psychotic vulnerability has to do with that phase of life within which the un-integrated infant comes, with the help of the as-yet-unknown holding environment, to achieve "unit status", becoming one person; neurotic illness has to do with that phase of life within which the passions of a twosome must be modulated by and re-organised to include a fundamentally important third party. In between zero becoming one and two becoming three is one becoming two, in fact a broad area of potential enrichment and failure, each form of the latter, as Tolstoy put it, unhappy in its own way.

This is the area of personality disturbance, of defences against anxiety learned so early in life that they have become fabric to who and how a person is. Their relative immaturity pains others more immediately than they do the person herself, although shame (sometimes in the denied form of shamelessness) is always a potential. Under serious stress, these immature defences come into full play and sometimes fail. The person's functioning reaches the "borderline" of psychosis (and thus the word "borderline" may primarily imply a level of severity of the personality disturbance) insofar as, preoccupied with survival within a two-person system, all considerations of what Lacan (1977; Muller, 1993) would call the Third disappear: the Third signifying the order of task, role, law, language, and society; in short, all that situates the two-person system in something meaningfully larger.

It is to the issue of the twosome that I would now like to return. My analysis of the "borderline", that is, of the dilemma *in* the clinician leading him to name a condition *in* the patient, a condition un-named in that way by the patient herself, focuses on the interaction between two people, rather than on the patient alone. To paraphrase Winnicott (1957), I am suggesting that there is no such thing as a "borderline" patient, only a couple interacting in a paradigmatically borderline way. Vaillant (1992) calls this couple "an enmeshed clinical dyad" (p. 120–121). To continue with Winnicott, this interaction bears striking similarity to the dynamic development of the false self (1960), particularly insofar as the spontaneous gesture from an evolving subject—that movement or feeling coming naturally from the patient and recognised as her own and as meaningful—is lost; in its place, there is substituted a need-driven gesture from the other, in the treatment situation the clinician's diagnostic action (and its theoretical underpinnings), around which the subject organises for defensive purposes.

As if

Here, in the link between "borderline" and the false self, we connect with Deutsch's (1942) brilliant, original formulation of the "as if" personality, and with Hilde Bruch's (1978) work on the development of anorexia nervosa, itself not an uncommon symptom in those labelled "borderline". Deutsch's definitional statement is illuminating:

> My only reason for using so unoriginal a label for the type of person I wish to present is that every attempt to understand the way of feeling and manner of life of this type forces on the observer the inescapable impression that the individual's whole relationship to life has something about it which is lacking in genuineness and yet outwardly runs along 'as if' it were complete. (p. 302)

In this one sentence, Deutsch anticipates the argument I am putting forward; that is, she pays conscious attention to the naming or labelling process, she sees it as the result of something *forced* inescapably on the clinician, and she highlights something utterly inauthentic in something that looks complete. Erikson (1956) might describe this seeming contradiction as the failed effort to use multiple, partial, and transient identifications to solve the crisis of identity.

It seems to me that our practice with "borderline" psychopathology must address this issue of the false and the true. So much from such a patient, and elicited by such a patient, can feel utterly inauthentic, a dealing with smoke and missing the fire; yet these patients also bring a true force that must be reckoned with. Indeed, this force or this intensity seems to be the bottom line of the "borderline", at least as I read diagnostic practice in psychiatry today. I believe that the falsity in the "borderline" represents that lack of spontaneous gesture, of play in the system that would be signatory of a secure, if ailing, personality; and it also represents a defensive adaptation to the system of care in which that person finds herself.

Here one finds enormous potential for collusion, the perhaps most crude if frequent example of which takes place in psychiatric hospitals. In these systems, increasingly impinged upon by externally imposed values—values of "cost containment", of "risk management", of "problem-oriented treatment plans", etc. (important values, perhaps, *if* integrated with treatment values)—a patient who speaks or acts "as if" she is suicidal meets, all too infrequently, an "as if" response: a response, analogous to the patient's pathology, based on external identifications rather than on the true identity of the hospital's treatment programme; a response that looks "as if" it is complete, except that it leaves out a genuine grappling with the communication within the patient's behaviour and both parties' responsibility for it. This patient may indeed be engaged in a serious manipulation of the system, while acting out hidden needs or wishes (e.g., to be seen, or touched, or vengeful, or chosen over others), but too often this kind of system has already defined itself as there to be manipulated, as therefore not worthy of the patient's respecting its function as a potential genuine container, and even as itself engaging in manipulation of the patient to get off some imagined hook of accountability.

André Green (1977) has written that "the borderline is the problem patient of our time" and that "the mythical prototype" is "no longer

Oedipus, but Hamlet" (p. 15). But the "to be or not to be" question raised at times so casually by patients in the systems described above and responded to so collusively represents a terrible miscarriage of communication and a chronic depletion of the language and human resources with which to meet the true problem. I will not elaborate here the treatment philosophy with which I am most familiar, concretised in an open and voluntary treatment setting, that grounds our efforts to meet this problem therapeutically; nor would I want to suggest that this particular programme is immune to these dynamics. Some years ago, as the programme was working its way toward a major leadership transition, the patients took to assembling—as a group project turned to by various people throughout the day and evening—huge jigsaw puzzles. And, as it was more recently adapting itself to various external exigencies facing psychiatry currently, the patients became concerned about, as one feature of their effort to organise their community life, the dangers of passive smoke. There are times when the distinction between manifest and latent seems to obscure the equally important distinction between manifest and blatant! The patients' wondering about how the parts fit together into a single, coherent picture and their worrying about the unseen effects of things everyone was quietly, regularly breathing in seem like essential communications in their basic self-preservative effort to correct any warp developing in the holding environment they so need. The only question is: can these communications be heard and honestly received? To the extent that treatment personnel are "supposed to know" (Muller, 1992), this necessary receptive capacity, and the vitalising dialogue it initiates, can be seriously compromised.

Use and abuse

For treatment personnel or for the individual practitioner, a patient's acting out around the powerful word "suicidal" is again their being placed, with urgency, on a border: between need and demand, often between management and interpretation. For the patient, it is many things: perhaps a response to the threat of being lost, but perhaps also, as Ghent (1992) points out, a response to the threat of being found in the treatment. The defensive function of false self adaptation (Winnicott, 1960) is to hide the true self, that core of personality seriously vulnerable to "primitive agonies" if ever it is allowed another "regression to dependency". All of these are Winnicott's terms. As Ghent suggests, we might see the demand or neediness of the patient, a barrage of affectivity so potentially disorienting to the therapist, as confounding and hiding the real need, a need threatened with potential exposure, as much to the patient herself as to her therapist. The therapeutic task is the sustaining of this paradox: the validation of need without regressive gratification of neediness; the holding, rather than splitting, of different emotional parts or points of view. For Ghent, "borderline" acting out is the result of real environmental failure and results in a tendency to ab-use the object rather than use it in the important sense outlined by Winnicott (1969) in one of his major and final theoretical statements.

In this paper, Winnicott describes the developmental movement from what he calls object relating, that early phase of one becoming two when the other is only perceived on the basis of projections and has only self-object or subjective status, to object-usage, the phase of two people, recognised as separate and different, though related. This is the object objectively perceived, available potentially for use according to its own inherent properties. This major developmental move, one feature of what Winnicott calls "realization" (1945), occurs through the child's aggression and the other's survival of that aggression without retaliation. In the child's act of destroying the fantasy-other, that which survives must be a real other, and inter-subjective living becomes a possibility. For Winnicott, the function of aggression in the finding of reality, and the belief that only the true self can feel real, are old themes. His "use of the object" concept sums up for him the major differentiation and integration achievements of the weaning process: the me from the not-me, fantasy from reality, the mother of care as one with the mother of hunger, and libidinal ruthlessness integrating with reparative capacities.

For the patient presenting us with the "borderline" problem, we can often see within this false self defensive enactment an enormously compromised appreciation of reality coordinate with major difficulties with aggression. As Knight (1953) wrote of "borderline states", "The break with reality, which is an ego alteration, must be thought of not as a sudden and unexpected snapping, as of a twig, but as the gradual bending as well ..." (p. 3). A recurrent clinical feature with some "borderline" patients is deeply aggressive behaviour wrapped in sentimentality, a chronic bending of reality, that once again invites, even plays upon, the clinician's collusion and choosing sides. But sentimentality so suffused with aggression both represents something and does something, and the representation can easily be lost in the doing, or vice versa. It conjures up an image of a good but lost object relationship, something evanescent, nostalgic, childishly purified of anything disruptive, fragile, and not fully real. But the clinician also *feels* the aggression and can choose to deny it, as the patient seems to, or to push it back into the patient and thus *become* the disruptive, destructive intruder into the sentimentalised internal relationship. This is the "borderline" place and pitfall. Both parts are true: there *is* a lost love relationship in this sentimentality, perhaps to a part of the self (Bollas, 1982) as well as to an other, and Winnicott's statement in his classic paper "Hate in the countertransference" (1947) also holds: that a person cannot tolerate "the full extent of his own hate in a senti-mental environment. He needs hate to hate" (p. 202).

André Green (1977) and Harold Searles (1986) have, in very differ-ent ways, highlighted the use of the countertransference with border-line patients. Green returns us to a concept of "borderline" inherent in Freud's definition of instinct:

> an 'instinct' appears to us as a *concept on the frontier* between the mental and the somatic, as the psychical representative of the stimuli originating from within the organism and reaching the mind, as a measure of the demand made upon the mind for work in consequence of its connection with the body. (Freud, 1915c, pp. 121–122, italicised by Green, 1977, p. 30)

For Freud, the work of the mind required optimal frustration. Green (1975) accents this condition differently; the work of the mind, or the capacity for thought, depends on the experience of tolerable absence, with its implication of potential presence. An object too much there or too utterly lost destroys the conditions for thinking.

Perhaps this underlies the "borderline" paradigm (see also Fonagy, 1991). That transformation from body to mind, that "border-line" which Freud called instinct, does not happen in a two-person psychology fraught with serious loss or intrusive affective presence. Instead of movement across a boundary, there is a split or barrier. Affectivity is simply evacuated, and, if there is a treatment situation, evacuated *into* the other, "forced upon us" (1942, p. 302) as Deutsch said. This other may or may not be able to do, and enlist the patient's assistance in doing, the work of transformation *within himself.* If he cannot, some variant of counter-projective processes must occur, the putting of the "borderline" back into the patient and holding it at arms length. If he can, there is an incremental sense of the reliability of the container and the tangibility of a content.

It is this failure of metabolisation in the primary other that Rosenfeld (1979) and many others see as central to this area of psychopathology. Winnicott writes: "In the extreme of a borderline case, everything boils down in the end to what I have tried to describe as the survival of the analyst" (Rodman, 1987, p. 181); by this, Winnicott meant surviving *as* an analyst, without retaliation and with technique and the analytic setting intact. Intact technique would mean, at least ideally, the analyst's ability to deal with his "borderline" or "frontier" problem: that is, to make that transformation from *his* body (given what the patient is bringing to it) to *his* mind that we call interpretation, delivered, if at all, with that gracefulness, possibly playfulness, so much a part of Winnicott's clinical care.

In a long-term follow-up study (Plakun, 1991), one set of results had to do with patients diagnosed as "borderline"; two variables, one historical, the other clinical, were predictors of good outcome: the absence of a parental history of divorce and the presence of self-destructive acting out during the course of treatment. If Erikson (1961) was accurate when he said that it is the task of the family, "in one of its exemplary forms", to help the child "gradually delineate where play ends and irreversible purpose begins" (p. 156), perhaps the converse is also true: families that do not survive create more severe "borderline" difficulties, including a constriction of the reversible processes of play, in confusion with something more irreversible and purposeful. And also, perhaps the treatment environment must be tested, used fully, and survive in a vital working way, in order for the patient to finally and securely achieve these differentiations, along with the "shrinking to life-size", in Harry Stack Sullivan's phrase (1940, p. 33), so joyfully experienced upon being survived. This is the task of establishing real and helpful boundaries, boundaries that are not barriers, but that establish both edges and intermediate zones for both interchange and contact.

No man's land

Winnicott (1971c) once wondered what would happen if the baby looked into his mother's eyes and did not see himself? What I suspect can happen is the simultaneous establishment of no-boundary and of enormous gap, the gap between an image held urgently by the mother and the child's felt potential in and of himself. The imposition of the former upon the latter is the boundary violation. Shapiro and colleague's (Shapiro, Zinner, Shjapiro, & Berkowitz, 1989) research on the contradictory, projectively-toned images of the child-at-risk held by each of her parents might lead to the same conclusion. Perhaps the "borderline" is the child's internalisation of the no-man's-land between his or her parents, or between image and inner experience, especially as parental figures receive and react to her developing personality and affectivity. This gap may also be the formative precursor of the fault lines in the treatment situation, which the patient must actively exploit rather than passively suffer. The actual meaning in the word "borderline" may most simply reflect the problems of people around boundaries. For some, the earliest efforts at contact and at separateness have encountered unbridgeable gaps, external then increasingly internal, brought in both hopeful and assaultive manners to the therapist, who feels, in the words of Francoise Davoine, "the paradox of frontiers": "that they are never more present than when they are broken by an invasion" (1989, p. 595).

The "splitting" so regularly described as basic to the "borderline" condition fits in here. It represents the failed integration, and then the exploited disintegration, of the unsuccessful depressive position. Two fully developed and fully perceived people do not emerge from this developmental landscape. Rather, two partial people do, each alternately deprived by and falsely enriched by projective processes, and each needing the other for conflictual equilibrium. Most importantly, hate is not saddened by love, nor is love matured by hate. Instead, the intensity of affects related to loss and to intrusion mitigates against such ordinary integrations and against the capacity for concern as well, which would be its natural outcome (Winnicott, 1963a). There is thus also superego pathology: a conscience that cannot accurately gauge the effect of behaviour on others and needs interpretation from the countertransference, and an ego ideal that knows it needs, but is otherwise without signifiers for, a real and truly meaningful grounding in something larger.

Hamlet, like Dr Stone, was haunted by dark suspicions. Like the false self, he was invited to live out a lie. Like trauma victims, which some research links to "borderline" functioning, his life, as we know it, begins after a death. He both feigns madness and actually carries the madness of overwhelming knowledge and feeling. While he places others in that quandary Deutsch describes—What is wrong with him?—he himself struggles with abandoning himself to a rage both vengeful and random, since all is already lost. He has no "other". Becoming an "other" for a patient so injured is not a task to be taken lightly. It is to meet both loss and rage, in the patient and in oneself. It requires a deeply and a well-grounded two-person perspective, and a steady effort to find the pulse of integrity within the shifting affective and defensive energies of the relationship. And, like the depressive position itself, that first paradigm of two-person related-ness, it challenges us to bring together empathic care with something in the direction of ruthlessness. Winnicott (Rodman, 1987) will have the last word:

> If the patient feels that it is worth doing, it is worth doing, in spite of the fact that every stage which could be called an advance brings the patient into closer contact with pain. In other words, the patient gives up defenses, and the pain is always there against which the defenses were organized. This kind of work, as I have pointed out in talking about the treatment of psychotic children, could be described as cruel. When it succeeds, of course, the cruelty and the suffering are forgotten (pp. 181–182).

CHAPTER THREE

Disturbances of self in the psychoanalytic setting

The analytic setting

In his paper, "Metapsychological and clinical aspects of regression within the psycho-analytical set-up" (1954a), Winnicott first discusses the concept of the analytic setting, along with his ideas about regression to dependence. The concept of the setting had been implicit in his work all along. Papers like "Primitive emotional development" (1945) and "Psychoses and child care" (1952) argue compellingly for a theory of the environment as, at the beginning, inseparable from the individual's developmental advance and failure. "There is no such thing as a baby", was Winnicott's (1957, p. 137) spontaneous and now famous claim; there is only the mother–baby couple, a unit by virtue of its biological and psychological inter-relatedness.

In the paper on regression, Winnicott makes the translation to the clinical situation explicit. He conceives of the clinical "environment" as something more than the therapist himself and certainly more than his technique. This "something more" is the analytic setting, the total personal and physical provision made by the analyst, that includes an ambience and concretely reliable arrangements; in another paper, Winnicott writes of the analytic setting as "the summation of the

details of management" (1955–1956, p. 297). Excerpts from his description of the analytic setting follow: the analyst "at a stated time daily
. . . puts himself at the service of the patient"; he is "reliably there, on
time, alive, breathing"; "for a limited period of time prearranged" he
"becomes preoccupied with the patient"; he expresses "love by the
positive interest taken, and hate in the strict start and finish and in
the matter of fees"; "the aim . . . (is) to get into touch with the process
of the patient"; "the analyst survives" (1954a, pp. 285–286).

Winnicott continues:

> This work [is] done in a room, not a passage, a room that is quiet and
> not liable to sudden unpredictable sounds, yet not dead quiet and not
> free from ordinary house noises. This room would be lit properly, but
> not by a light staring in the face, and not by a variable light. The room
> would certainly not be dark and it would be comfortably warm. The
> patient would be lying on a couch, that is to say, comfortable, if able
> to be comfortable . . .. (1954a, p. 285)

Winnicott was a theorist of the unnoticed obvious, in these last
remarks as well as in his rediscovery of security objects. In the regression paper, he makes the remarkable observation that, "Freud takes
for granted the early mothering situation and . . . *it turned up in his
provision of a setting for his work . . .*" (1954a, p. 284, Winnicott's italics).
Freud, that is, met his psychoneurotic patients with the good-enough
environment that they and he had known and thrived on in their
infancies. It could not have been otherwise. Freud could not have
offered something that was not already part of the fabric of his unconscious being, and his patients could not have naturally used a provision in which they had been seriously failed before. The mutual
difficulties and strangeness of psychoanalytic technique could be toler-
ated and negotiated via the background support of the analytic setting.

Put differently, given Winnicott's contention that "the setting of
analysis reproduces the early and earliest mothering techniques"
(1954a, p. 286), Freud and his patients could rely on their early experiences of the twosome in order to play out and address the com-
plications of the third or paternal element in psychic life. But with
those patients who have experienced early environmental failure—
failure within the mother–infant relationship—the setting materialises
as a problematic and sharply experiential factor. For it is these patients
who have a need for regression as essential to their healing process,

regression understood to mean an organised, risky, yet hope-filled "return to early dependence" (1954a, p. 286). Winnicott argues that the analytic setting "invites regression by reason of its reliability" (1954a, p. 286); thus part of the analytic task has to do with working with the patient's way of dealing with this invitation and its consequences.

In his 1975 essay dedicated to Winnicott's memory, André Green suggests that the serious psychological disturbances of our day function between dual terrors: of intrusion, persecution, a flooding of the self by the object, on the one hand, and of separation, decathexis, and a draining of the self into unrelatedness, on the other. The object is either pure impingement, filling the self with reactions and thus owning, even annihilating it, or pure loss, permanently inaccessible and emptying the self toward deadness. Bollas (1999) puts it this way: "Turmoil is the presence of the object . . . quiescence is abandonment . . ." (p. 131); he goes on to accent the traumatic attachment within and to states of overwhelming affectivity. Thus, the invitation of the analytic setting, an invitation into a dependable relationship, becomes a source of dread for such patients, as does its internal psychic homologue, the experience of a personal psychic potential that needs the other in order to actualise. At either extreme of these anxieties, the experience of absence, with its generative implication of potential, non-problematic presence, cannot be constituted as such.

Green views this problem of absence as crucial; he goes so far as to conclude that Winnicott's technique "gives the setting its appropriate place" because "it is the only one which gives the notion of absence its rightful place" (1975, p. 12). Where Freud sees the problem of wish, Winnicott, with severely disturbed patients, sees the problem of need, a continuing developmental need related to early environmental failure. Green replaces the problem of wish with the problem of the formation of thought, "for, as Freud was the first to see, it is in the absence of the object that the representation is formed, the source of all thought" (p. 8). To the extent that the experience of absence cannot be constituted, to that extent is thought itself crippled. If psychoanalysis is a "thinking cure" (Antonovsky, 1978) relating to the absent other of the transference, how are we to help with such profound disturbance?

Green evocatively describes the troubles within the psychotherapy of those patients who cannot take for granted the benign constancy of

the psychoanalytic setting. The setting is either one of absolute emptiness or of certain impingement. It is not a space of potential. Neither
is the internal space—the mind, if you will—able to be constituted as
a potential space, because for the ego to observe and for thinking to
take place, an absenting is necessary, a step back, a "cut" (in Lacan's
(1977) terms) in the immediacy of experience while retaining links to
it. Green describes the task of the analyst variously as that of "search-
ing for and preserving the minimum conditions for symbolization"
(1975, p. 12) and of "helping to form the positive cathexis of the empty
space" (p. 17).

The accomplishment of this task involves the analyst's capacity to
bear strain and to use his own mental and affective functioning differently than with neurotic patients. The more disturbed patient, unable
to relax into a less integrated state and give play to a psychic content,
falls back on action, on "drive . . . (as) an inchoate form of thought"
(1975, p. 9). According to Green, the analyst feels this as an action
against the setting and realises that he must "act through and within
the analytic setting as if to protect it from a threat" (p. 10). This effort
involves the transformation of the tension felt by the analyst via
"efforts of imagination" (p. 10). In other words, this is inductive work.
The patient's psychic content becomes an object for understanding,
indeed comes into being as a content per se, through the shaping it
enforces upon the analyst-as-container. What the analyst offers back
to the patient out of this process might be called potential sense; its
goal is to "ventilate" (p. 8) the analytic space, to offer something
conceivable as meaning without polarising the situation toward either
certainty or absurdity. In practice the analyst is required to live
through and use constructively exactly the same affective experiences
that afflict the patient: of overwhelming presence or stultifying
absence, both of which attack the analyst's capacity for thought.

Self-containment and self-possession

Both Winnicott and Green emphasise the disturbed patient's initial
incapacity to use the analytic setting as a potential space. As I see it,
this incapacity reflects both a defensive organisation and a failure of
self-development—a phobic self-containment, on the one hand, and a
radical failure of self-possession on the other. The former may take

shape clinically as a static, rigid, and emotionally stunted structure of self-explanation designed to avoid a particular terror—that of the truly "free" association, that might make one feel crazy or, as one patient said, "alone for an instant". This patient dreaded feeling in any way separate from the ego-coverage the analyst was providing, and in that gap or discontinuity, experiencing fleetingly something like a personal annihilation.

Around such a terror, a patient sometimes builds a structure of his own interpretations, the function of which is to suppress the existence of inner process and to foreclose a place for the other. These interpretations—about how the patient's trouble has come to be, or about the course of the treatment, or about any aspect of the patient's life—can on first hearing seem insightful and available for development. Over time, however, they come to seem more like a container than a content, something in which anything potentially new and therefore disconcerting in the patient's psychic life can be prematurely organised as though it were understood. Prefabricated and desensitised, they quickly come to feel more like a boundary between patient and therapist than a communication. In this sense, they function a bit like a delusional system, although their content does not include obviously disturbed reality testing. As with a delusional system, however, the "truth" of the patient's self-formulations is far less significant than the function of these static and ultimately protective constructs, and that function is primarily to contain a "self" felt at heart to be desperately weak, jeopardised, and permeable.

Such patients phobically and counterdependently contain themselves because, cut off from the spontaneous process of their inner life, they never feel as though they possess themselves. This radical failure of self-possession was captured beautifully by one patient who described his sense of himself as "like a sieve". He felt pressured within his therapy to "give my thoughts before I have them" and felt that the analyst's speculative comments were always premature and constituted a terrible threat; either they would be "toxic" to his "identity" or else "tattooed" onto it. From the patient's point of view, all relationships were asymmetric: a self meeting a non-self, with the latter struggling to avoid discovery, to acquire the inner stuff of the other, and to manage an affective life that threatened further erosion of self. One patient described a disorganising feeling of being "derailed", losing his sense of himself and his mental hold on events, upon recognising any feeling, especially any positive feeling, toward his therapist. In a dream, he described being on a two-man railroad handcar, on the track but motionless atop a very high bridge. In this two person situation, he felt absolutely terrified to move at all. To be "derailed" here would be to experience what Winnicott called a "primitive agony" (1962a), like "falling forever" or "going to pieces" (p. 58).

It is important to stress here these patients' vulnerability to seduction into a relationship in which they feel they will lose whatever tenuous sense of self they are working to contain. Particularly important is the centrifugality of affect and most importantly of envy. Envy may be felt by the patient in relation to the other's perceived selfhood or to the other's capacity to help or even to the other's "having" the subject in some way. One patient, for example, broke off her relationships with men as she began to feel loving toward them because of the tremendous envy she felt at their having her. In her subjective experience, she did not "have" them nor, more importantly, did she have or possess herself. Another patient fought off his analysts becoming important to him. He felt that any improvement he made would be for the analyst and not for himself; it would be "like winning the lottery and giving away the prize". He acted this out with long periods of absence from the sessions during which he communicated indirectly to the analyst his apparently real improvement, his sharply insightful ideas regarding their relationship, and his ongoing attachment, *from outside it*, to the analytic setting.

Transference reactions of any sort are sources of real disturbance for these patients, in part because they stimulate profound envy. They reflect the analyst's place in the patient's psychic life, an actual connection and therefore a power. The analyst is felt to "have" the patient, when the patient has neither the analyst nor himself. There is a peculiarly inverted self-esteem potential in this; this form of envy may imply the patient's cognitive awareness of desirable traits. Missing, however, is an indwelling or taken-for-granted sense of cohesion and impact as the person who circumscribes these and other traits. From this frame of reference, the negative therapeutic reaction takes on a new meaning; in Winnicott's descriptive terms, the patient, lacking a "kernel", pursues a hardening of the "shell". Put differently, the patient feels the scaffolding for a self-status, and therefore also a respite from envy, in the boundary formed by eliciting and then defending against the analyst's interpretive impingements.

At the beginning of a session, a patient said, "I notice that when I come here with nothing prepared to say, when I'm alone, I get very anxious". In this parapraxis, the patient was unconsciously equating his being without something prepared to say and his being alone. He did not seem to mean that he would feel alone in the analyst's presence—without some symbolic third thing or organisation to mediate between them. Rather, the patient was saying that if his mind were not structured for the session, subjectively he was alone. Neither the analyst nor the analytic setting actually existed. Put the other way around, he subjectively created the analyst out of nothing in the act of structuring himself to deal with him. From being the inaccessibly lost object, the analyst became the menacingly present object, to be fended off in and by the patient's mind rather than used for what he might be able to offer. Of course, to the degree that his presentation would be prepared, to that degree the truly analytic setting would not exist either because the possibility for free association would have been commensurately foreclosed.

In other words, for this patient a space of potential could not be constituted without serious anxiety. He had no leeway from his concerns about the analyst, or about what might occur spontaneously within him, to relax into the analytic setting. Play was not a feature of this person's relatedness, and in fact he reported no memories of non-competitive play in his growing up. His relatedness to the analyst was not symbiotic, with its connotation of intermix and mutuality; rather, it had a more surface-to-surface quality. The analyst's existence was subjectively created by, and ongoingly fed by, the patient's needs for him, and his immediate feeling of "self" was formed and secured at the "shell"—at the boundary between himself and the analyst—through ritualised, non-evolving contacts, that nevertheless had to be maintained. Echoing Winnicott's description of the false self (1960), this patient could feel himself and "have" a "self" only insofar as he was reactive to the other.

Beginning

In working with this kind of psychological trouble, the analyst must attend carefully from the beginning to the task of facilitating the development of a truly psychoanalytic setting, but in a way that also attends to the patient's vulnerabilities. This may be a lengthy task with many partial solutions, which in some ways is preliminary to the analysis proper and yet in other ways addresses the patient's central disturbance as it manifests itself with the analyst. A brief clinical illustration of one particular exchange toward the development of an analytic setting follows.

A patient began his psychotherapy following several years of short-term hospitalisations and chemical, physical, and psychological treatment attempts. He had broken down upon entering college and had been unable to return to his studies in any sustained way since. He had also become so despondent about his future that he had cut his wrists on one occasion. His life had evolved into a series of progressive and regressive movements that had led him to feel an increasing sense of frustration and meaninglessness alongside his already debilitating isolation and anxiety.

In the first two or three sessions, the patient's presentation was striking. He managed to convey several facts: he hated his father; his first doctor had left him abruptly; he therefore mistrusted, even hated, doctors; his father had been demanding of him; he now would accept no demands whatsoever. But more important was his way of being with me. From the opening moment of the treatment, he seemed "at" me. His verbal presentation was aggressive, belittling, and lecturing. He would talk in a driven way without pause for reflection or feeling, and without any hint of invitation for me to respond or to offer something. What he had to say was quite coherent; in a certain way, it was too coherent in that it was seamless and offered absolutely no room for any other vantage point, either from himself or from me. In that sense, the patient presented with the dogmatism of a fanatic although he also managed to convey the desperation underneath that.

The desperation and anxiety were most palpably evident in the various facial tics that periodically erupted into his discourse. I consciously tried to adapt to what felt like a barrage from the patient by being less naturally active than I might ordinarily have been and by hearing him out fully. I also found myself thinking a great deal about what might be called therapeutic minimalism; this patient seemed so aggressively determined to be in charge, and so certain that I would rigidly impose my psychiatric "morality" on him in a way that could only be iatrogenic, that my first task seemed to be simply my own survival and viability in role. It was clear that this patient's life had brought him to the point where he believed that only one person could exist in a relationship; the alternatives were to dominate or be dominated and consequently, to him, annihilated.

This world view or view of relationships was being immediately lived out with me in a highly charged, life-or-death way. The patient was dominating toward me to an extreme that began to feel like the annihilation of my existence, seemingly because he felt certain that *in any other place* I would annihilate his precarious sense of self. At this beginning point, there may indeed have been a serious risk of destruction for him, insofar as this patient may well have lost hope following another failed though well-intentioned treatment attempt that missed his incapacity to be in an analytic setting. And yet I also felt it imperative to protect some minimal space for that setting and for a genuine analytic therapy to develop.

At the end of the first week of sessions, an important interchange occurred. The patient told me about what he felt was a "life-saving" event in his life. He had once gone to group therapy, and, in the course of the group, he had interjected into the discussion that he was the "sickest" person in the group. This action subsequently came to seem to the patient to represent many things at once: a plea for more help; a proclamation of his superiority; a statement of how different and isolated he felt from others; a recognition that he knew terrible things about himself that they did not know, and so on. At the time he found himself taken totally by surprise when another man in the group said, "No, you're not". With more vehemence, the patient repeated his assertion that he was "the sickest", and with equal firmness, the other man again countered him.

At that point, the patient felt the "life-saving" feeling: he felt calm, relieved, real, and human. He felt that he was in fact only a person among persons, and that he had been previously captivated by a distorted, grotesque, and addictive image of himself from which finally he had been freed. The patient refused to look in a mirror after this experience and quit the part-time job that seemed associated with the old image. Instead, he felt a longing to be with the group around the clock and to stay away from others. He wanted the group's care, and he wanted to rest. This actual experience lasted only a few days, but its impact as a model for cure imprinted itself on the patient. He sought in his current treatment the rest he needed, and he would eventually seek from me the word-key that had released him before.

This story was communicated to me by the patient in the same offensive and defensive manner that had characterised his presentation throughout the first three sessions. His tone seemed to be saying, "I know everything about my problem and about its cure; you know nothing except insofar as I instruct you", as well as, "you will need to attack this account and take it from me; I will attack you first". Toward the end of the session, in a way not consciously related to the material of the hour, the patient said that he wanted only one scheduled session per week, despite the fact that all patients in this particular intensive treatment centre know of before admission—and in fact decide by being admitted to engage in—the four times weekly analytic psychotherapy that is the primary mode of treatment.

Several things about this moment struck me. First, that the patient seemed to be expressing a need, as opposed to a demand, insofar as he seemed to be communicating his genuine terror of the analytic setting. Second, that his statement included some hint of a request to me, some recognition that for this to be a treatment, I had to be party to the contract in some minimal but real way. Third, that interpretation, confronting resistance, or temporising in an effort to develop further what lay behind his request were absolutely out of the question as interventions. Fourth, that out of this moment might come a beginning alliance toward eventually constituting an analytic setting, or just as easily various misalliances, that would eventually cripple the analysis. Most particularly, I felt that my insisting on our meeting four times weekly, or worse, my presenting myself as in any way knowing in advance that psychotherapy would or should be valuable to the patient, would be not only inappropriate, but also confirmatory of this patient's highly charged and rigidly held views of the psychiatric machinery and establishment. This would provoke either serious acting out or, less likely in this case, a false compliance with the treatment. On the other hand, it was equally clear that to agree to a once weekly schedule *in this setting* would be to sign a contract as to his being "the sickest". In doing so, I would foreclose the place of potentially saving otherness, which he had managed to communicate, in a way rather movingly, as so necessary for him. And I would also have confirmed for myself a role as mirror to the patient, that he had already said was the trap to his identity and that, I felt sure, would erode mine as well.

I told him that I would schedule four sessions per week with him, and I gave him the appointment times. I told him that I would be there at those times and that it would be up to him whether he came or not. He could come or not come as he wished. I added that from what he had said so far, I could imagine he might find therapy useful to him eventually, and that when he chose not to come to his sessions, I would consider the possibility that something between us was bothering him. The patient easily accepted this. He came to one session per week, usually prior to a weekend. Sometimes he came twice weekly and, on a few occasions, he missed two or three weeks of sessions at a time. During these times, I occasionally received lengthy notes from him, and when he would come to a session, despite the length of the intervening period, he recalled clearly and with feeling what had transpired between us during our last meeting. In fact, I never felt out of communication with him, and indeed felt the absences were serving important functions—for example, his testing the fantasy that I needed him or his sparing me a rage that he thought I might not survive. After the first six months of treatment, the patient attended all of his sessions without fail.

This vignette illustrates both the difficulties certain patients have entering the analytic setting and the therapist's task of helping to constitute that setting. I felt with this patient the requirement to foster the coexistence—within the limits of his identity and mine—of both a "yes" and a "no": a "yes" insofar as his need could be recognised and a "no" insofar as the setting itself, which included my potentially useful otherness to him, must exist intact, in a going-on-being way, in order to be available to him. To return to Green's (1975) terms, my effort was to ventilate the contractual space between us, to allow openings for both our existences, for their connectedness, and for the possibility of the development of the analytic process. I also offered him implicitly my capacity to feel and to tolerate his absence and to use it to think about him. This patient, as Green describes, seemed stuck in the experiential alternatives of impingement or isolation, and he seemed forced to use his mind to know rather than to think. Absence, its attendant affects, and its possibilities toward the development of thought seemed something that I as therapist needed to hold and represent before the patient could do so himself.

The capacity to dream

Parallel to and commensurate with a patient's capacity to deliver himself into the analytic setting is the patient's capacity to constitute his dreams as a setting for psychological development. Masud Khan (1972a) has written of this aspect of dreaming as the dream space, an inner space of safety and privilege within which at its best the subject can play out different configurations to pressing, perhaps older and unarticulated matters. This is a situation of health. In certain forms of psychological illness, we see the incapacity to constitute, to use, and to communicate the dream space (Ogden, 2005a,b). What follows is very condensed illustration of clinical work in this area.

For a long time in his therapy, the patient, whose clinical history included psychotic liabilities, said nothing of his dreaming. Eventually he let me know that he had had a dream, followed by a short statement of its content, given as though he felt compelled to deposit it with me. He actively recoiled from or belittled even the most tentative effort I might make toward elaboration of the dream or working with it in any way. This kind of response was not infrequent to my interventions, but his evasive reaction to dreams seemed particularly intense. He categorically dismissed them as meaningless and unintelligible; even worse, his granting us the right to consider them would threaten him with a seduction into a relationship on my terms. He would find himself being defined by me, perhaps wishing to be defined by me and totally lost to himself. Eventually, it also became clear that dreams, almost as a category, terrified him inasmuch as he equated the feeling of dreaming with psychosis. His foreclosing the dream space, and of the space within the analysis for dreams to have potential meaning, was thus parallel to the sealing over of a psychosis. It was, as described above, a form of phobic self-containment that reflected his lack of self-possession and his fear of its further erosion into being possessed by me.

The few dreams the patient did report during the lengthy phase described here were recurrent and stereotyped. In one, he was on the ground watching a plane take off into flight; he would make the plane crash by wishing that it would. In another, he would be engaged in sexual foreplay with a woman; inevitably he would wake up frustrated just before entering her. It is not my intention here to elaborate the various meanings that these dreams might have had or subsequently came to be seen as having. Taken separately, they seem to condense primary conflicts in his relationships with his father, who travelled a great deal, and his mother, respectively. Taken together, they can be seen to formulate the triangulation of those relationships. My focus here, however, is on his incapacity, and my being forbidden, to work on them in the therapy. At a certain level of abstraction, the content of these dreams can be seen simply as settings—for movement, for exhilaration, for something new, for being carried away, for great excitement, or perhaps for loss or castration—which he could neither enter nor relinquish.

Translated to the analytic setting, the first dream can be imagined to represent his thriving on the power to keep anything between us from taking off as well as his staying grounded, in the dual sense of reality-oriented and emotionally depleted, in doing so. From this same angle, the second dream similarly seems to comment on his desire and fear about entering the relationship with me and perhaps allowing me to conceive of something for him and by him inside myself. The patient's emotional position in the dream is the same as that to the dream and to his dream report: he stays safely outside of something that is meant for him. He places me, too, in a similar relation to the dream as a setting, chronically aware of my status as an outsider to something meant at some level as a communication to me. It is this sense of the patient's being outside his own inner process, unable to allow it play or development internally in the dream space or externally in the analytic setting, which needs to be recognised and understood as a fact within the analysis. The analyst's function is a form of resistance analysis, having to do with elaborating in words the patient's concern about the fate of the self if it moves beyond containment in its own rigidified frame of knowledge and hands itself over to the live process of the analysis.

Obviously this occurs in a bit by bit fashion, but it is possible to highlight the gradual development of the patient's capacity to use the analytic setting by noticing the patient's increased capacity to dream and to use his dreams. In a session later in his treatment, this particular patient spoke of feeling frightened to expose to me or to anyone else the spontaneous and playful parts of his personality. He also spoke of wishing that he could feel his father's help to him, for example, the fact that his father was paying for his treatment; he had the idea that he might be able to give up his rage at his father if he could feel his father's love. He spoke then, with a gingerliness that betrayed an intense anxiety, of an inchoate fear of "losing myself" and of his various ways of holding on. At other points, this patient also spoke of the fear of falling helplessly through space, without a hold on anything and without end.

Over time, the anality of his psychological organisation had become clear and somewhat available for work: his wish to evacuate on to me his rage, that he experienced as a thing, a mess inside him that otherwise might simply explode; or his conflict around speaking to me, experiencing his words as products, coerced or seduced by me, or withheld by him for purposes of autonomy and revenge. Early memories of bathroom experiences in relation to both his parents had been recovered and shared with considerable emotion. Finally, he seemed to enact unconsciously a transference aspect of these early experiences during a phase of absent-mindedly shredding and littering bits of Kleenex as he talked, apparently expecting without telling himself so, that I would, either in humiliation or love, clean up after him.

During the session in which he spoke of losing himself, again something about the anal organisation of his psychology came into the material, and I said to him that he feared being spontaneous with me because that would feel like losing himself in me. If he were to relax his hold on himself, he might get caught up with me into feeling something, and he feared that his sense of himself would simply disappear and not return to him spontaneously afterward. To my surprise, the patient expressed rare, unambivalent agreement with my statement, and he said that he thought that his phase of constipation as a child had something to do with his effort "to have a self". I said to him that children sometimes feel that to let go of what is inside them and actually have a bowel movement means to lose literally a part of oneself.

That night the patient had an unusual dream, that he reported as thrilling during the next session. In the dream, I was carrying him in my arms, and we were flying over a deep blue wintry landscape. He was frightened but also exhilarated, even joyous. He did not feel totally safe with my carrying him; he feared that he might fall, but he felt secure enough to enjoy the experience and to notice the scene below. In a second dream that same night, his father, looking tired and depressed, was sitting at the kitchen table and said something to the patient about his (the father's) being unhappy; only the patient was in the room with him. He associated the first dream to rides he had taken in Disneyland, one called a Peter Pan Ride, that gave the illusion of great speed and great height. He also associated to the paradoxically very warm memory of shovelling snow at night with a boyhood friend, a memory that gave him the good feeling of being part of a solid home after all. To the second dream, he said that he wished his father had been able to show him other, more human sides of himself during his growing up, and he then reflected on his early experiences of his father with a greater range of feeling.

My primary response was quietly congratulatory; I said to him that I understood that these dreams might indeed be cause for happiness because, for one thing, he had been able in one of them to let go of himself and to let me carry him, and that rather than experiencing a loss of himself, he had instead had a new experience and new access to older experiences. He understood everything I said. This dream, and his way of elaborating it, shows startling progress compared to his earlier incapacity. He dreams now in a way that is much less frozen. He tells me the dream and associates to it in a way that clearly opens it to me. He brings me into the dream. His dream clearly picks up the thread of the previous session, in that he seems to have experienced my understanding something as already holding him. The dream unfolds new aspects of both himself and his father. It even allows the two experiences so dreadfully stunted in his two recurrent stereotyped dreams: the experience of close physical contact and of flight, of process taking off.

There are, of course, many alternative readings of these dreams: for example, their possible depiction of an idealising transference in either its defensive or primitive narcissistic forms. But it seems to me that these dreams, in the context of this patient's difficulties, primarily offer evidence for the analytic setting as a newly constituted holding environment, including elements of safe dependency, illusion, and active interest in both seeing and experiencing. Winnicott speaks in one place of "go(ing) back with the patient . . . and displac(ing) the original environmental failure situation" (1954a, p. 287). Whatever vexing questions such a notion might raise for clinical psychoanalysis—and they are many—Winnicott is saying that something different must happen in the present experience between analyst and patient than happened in the past and continues to happen through the patient's own self-contained enactments of life. This patient's dream, in its content and in its fully being brought into the work, signified that the analytic process had indeed been entered and that a holding by the human aspects of the analytic setting was being tested. Perhaps only by representing and experiencing the analyst's capacity to hold him could he then bear the weight of looking at his childhood in less brittle fashion, such that it could come to include his loves and strengths as well as his father's human weaknesses. This dream marked for this patient a qualitative and sustained shift in his capacity to use his dreams and to use the analytic setting to crystallise important, previously dissociated experiences.

Hard and soft objects

The patients discussed in this chapter present with an incapacity to accommodate easily to, and use, the analytic setting. As described in Chapter One, the analytic setting can be described through the complementary concepts of frame and medium (Balint, 1968; Bleger, 1966; Khan, 1960; Langs, 1976; Milner, 1952; Winnicott, 1954a). The frame refers generally to the boundedness and structure of the analytic setting: to roles, methods, and "arrangements". The frame establishes rhythm, privacy, and constancy to the work. It presupposes the analyst's knowledge, and therefore reflects her professional authority and identity. The concept of medium, by contrast, has to do with that which is ambiguous, pliable, and not pre-formed. The setting as a medium—considering the range of ordinary meanings of that word—implies materials or a milieu available for the patient's creative use. A medium exists to externalise something, to spawn something, to form something, to transmit something, or to reflect something. The analytic setting as medium connotes the experiential or process level of the treatment. The transference and the counter-transference broadly defined are aspects of the analyst's availability for this function of medium.

With the patients discussed here the action of the treatment for a long time is along its frame. There is a surface-to-surface quality, in the sense that arrangements, methods, roles, even the physical environment of the office, all of which include something of the analyst's authority, often lead the patient toward reactions of a countering or differentiating sort. It is tempting here to borrow Tustin's (1981) distinction between hard and soft objects, and to say that these patients make their first and lengthy adaptation to the analytic setting as a hard object; that is, to its tangible, immobile, even inanimate aspects, whether these be the furniture, or the clock, or the schedule of sessions, or the technical ways the analyst works. Occasionally, some engagement occurs between patient and analyst, that serves the function of a hard object; it establishes both parties' separateness and reality as well as both parties', especially the analyst's, survival capacity. In these ways, the patient's "self" remains safely contained and yet contiguous with another person. All of this occupies the foreground of the treatment. Masud Khan (1969) commented about certain patients that: "they needed my presence in the analytic situation so they could disregard and negate me, and in their lives so they could be related to themselves" (p. 84).

In the background is the patient's incapacity to use the analytic setting and the analyst as a medium. The patient dreads the "spontaneous gesture", as Winnicott (1960) puts it, and dreads the loss of any rudimentary self-development if that gesture is handed over to the analyst. In Tustin's (1981) terms, the patient fears the analyst as soft object or confusional object and fears perhaps becoming a confusional object for the analyst; that is, the patient fears an object relationship in which the "self" is absorbed and lost in the other or, if returned, has an uncanny not-me quality, a quality of having been changed in some discontinuous way such that the new "self" is not assuredly the original "self". The analyst as medium is easily felt to be too animated already by his constructs about the patient, too much on the move with his own life and needs, and also too easily destroyed by the patient's active use. The clinical illustrations earlier had to do with, first, the establishment of a viable frame to the treatment and, second, the changeover, as evidenced in the patient's dream life, from being held by the frame to being held by the medium, a move utterly critical to the patient's growth.

The transitional self

Masud Khan (1969) writes of the possible background to some patients' troubles that, "the 'self of the child functions as a 'transitional object' between the child's ego and the mother. It is treated as special, idealized and at one remove psychically from both parties" (p. 86). His line of thought seems to organise considerable historical and transferential data, including: the parental need to create for the child a role that comforts and completes the parent; the phases of vacancy in the child's experience when no transitional function was needed by the parent; the experience of the parent as mirror and of oneself as mirroring the parent; the parental inclination to localise stimulation along a particular physical or psychological surface of the child; the child's increasing pleasure and facility in handling an image of self felt as distinct from something inner; and the parental anxiety in response to the child's spontaneous presentations, especially if these are instinct related.

Such children are very highly valued within the confines of the primary relationship and develop a precocious and heightened sense of their worth and their capacity to re-elicit evidence of it, little of which carries over easily or automatically outside that relationship. They also sense that the aspects of "self" upon which regard is so easily bestowed are not fully coincident with their total person, that what they are valued for is not-fully-me or not-really-me, but rather the partial self that the parent needs to see. Hence, the child inter-nalises a dread of inner life because of its disruptive potential to the special relationship with the primary other—a potential for the loss of the object, but also for injury to the nascent self if the object cannot remain psychologically present to meet and reflect it. For purposes of security, therefore, the child attaches herself to, supports and borrows against a construct and image of self, felt to exist between herself and the other, as though it were a pact. Further, the child views her natural unfolding development—the nutriments for a genuine sense of self— as threatening her passively with the loss of a special relationship, and she learns quickly to dissociate aspects of her inner life in order to actively maintain that relationship.

Thus the legitimised self, the self felt to exist as valued between mother and child, is addictively conjured up as a kind of "fix", in the dual sense of an emotional charge and a reparative reorientation. Doing is accentuated over being. As one patient described it, "my trouble began before I did", meaning that by the time in his life when he could begin to conceive of a "self", a sense of I, he was already well into the habit and activity of comparing himself to others, of defining himself through external measurement, and of trading on impressions of himself. He both lived out the early mirroring relationship and felt trapped by it.

All of these issues are replayed in the transference as the patient initially fears the unmasking of self-weakness or the total loss of self-possession in the analytic setting, and then as the patient strives to actualise and ultimately to move past early object relationships of such intensity and promise. The analytic setting, if it can become a holding environment for such patients, does what the patient's group did for him: it provides a space of rest, of being rather than doing; it provides reliable care; and it provides a loosening from the consuming image, the image associated with the transitional object-self, such that the patient can begin to feel that he is a real person among other real persons after all. This is the end, or goal, of our work, sometimes negotiated in the very beginning of the treatment.

CHAPTER FOUR

The hope in hopelessness

I t's not fair that my therapist can't be my mother". What a striking and yet not unusual "chief complaint" this is—at least for some patients! After all, how could one person be another person? It is as though the patient aspires to—even demands—a life only in the trans- ference, a life that would erase the distinction between reality and fantasy. When therapists hear this kind of complaint, they sometimes feel uneasy about the "borderline" (see Chapter Two) zone in which they are being placed, a zone that seems to have no borders, and old theoretical concerns about corrective emotional experience begin to feel like vexingly real clinical problems.

Borderline psychopathology—which, in its anger, aloneness, and identificatory fluidity this patient's complaint can be seen as repre- senting—might be thought of as an admixture of three trends: a depressive trend (it is indeed pain about loss that often brings these patients into treatment); a hysterical trend (it is often the symptomatic or self-mutilated body—or its ascetic anorexic opposite—that is presented in treatment); and a delinquent trend. By the latter I am referring to Winnicott's concept of the anti-social tendency (1956a). In this conceptualisation, the patient has actually experienced an early deprivation, "a loss of something good that has been positive in the child's experience up to a certain date and that has been withdrawn" (p. 309). The child dimly perceives—because of having matured to the capacity for differentiation—the source of the deprivation as "out there." Her impulse, felt with righteousness, even integrity, and eventually in the adult patient, with a profound passion for the impossible, is to "get it back".

Many such patients present with a deep sense of grievance and an absolute commitment to reparations. The transference is not a space of deep play, not the imaginary in some faint relation to the symbolic (Lacan, 1977); rather, it is the imaginary-made-real, an arena for deadly, concrete enactment in which the patient will no longer be tantalised by the out-of-reach other. Growth and learning are felt as giving in to further loss. The patient rejects the ordinary goals of treatment, feeling them in the transference to be the therapist's agenda and refusing to be seduced or corrupted into once again participating in one's own deprivation. Instead, atonement—and as Brenman-Gibson (personal communication) parses that word, at-one-ment—are the patient's goals.

The hope for atonement, in both its senses, is a primary force in organising this form of psychopathology and both a primary motivation for, and a primary resistance to, its treatment. It is, for example, what so often leads to endless sequences of medications or complex and contradictory medication regimens, in the patient's ongoing quest not only for relief, but as reparation for the help that has so far not come. This determined hope also eventuates in multiple treaters. Given the degree of rage the patient feels, the transference force may indeed need to be distributed among members of a clinical team, but just as frequently, this clinical situation functions to offer a transference hope that the next treater will make good on the promise the previous treater disappointed or frustrated.

Upon hearing of one such treatment, I found myself thinking that "her only hope is her hopelessness". In this chapter, I will examine pathological hope based on a defensive grievance organisation and explore the intrapsychic obstacles to the patient's experiencing and accepting loss as loss and the past as past. I will consider the hypothesis that the patient's belief in the transference, that is, her conviction that her therapist *could* be her mother, is a primary obstacle to the mourning process and that this derives from the patient's experience of unconsciously living life as a transference object for a troubled parent. In other words, the patient believes her therapist could actually be somebody else because she has lived her own life, at some unconscious level, as somebody else herself.

Alarm

When this eldest child was a toddler, a sibling was born who became gravely ill, as did, soon thereafter, her father. Both lived, the father in and out of chronic illness for many years. These events inexorably defined the culture of the family as organised around illness. The patient felt this as a Sword of Damocles that never fell, in part because of her own omnipotent reaction formations. She became the good, strong, self-sufficient child, the one who did not need anything, thereby protecting her sibling and the rest of her family. She felt, and relatives actually said, that she needed to stay healthy, so that her family could manage the strain it was going through. But the patient also became a timid child who preferred solitary play rather than play with other children; indeed, she felt that her mother's wanting her to play with other children really represented her mother's need for her daughter to be taken care of elsewhere, so that she could take care of people at home. This conflict with her mother, like others, could not be dealt with directly; instead, disagreements only seemed to make a bad situation worse. Feeling more the care-taker than the one cared for, she recalled how much she longed for the reprieve of sleep and hated the alarm clock that signalled the demand that she return to responsible functioning.

In his classic paper on "Sleep, narcissistic neurosis and the analytic situation", Bertram Lewin (1954) discusses the alarm clock. He outlines the oral triad, that is, the coincident experience in infancy of eating, being eaten (in the sense of merging into one's mother during the feeding experience), and sleeping at the breast. This first sleep is the natural outcome of the blissfulness and holding of the good feed— the baby's dependency truly satisfied. From this angle—which Lewin links to sleep disturbances, to various forms of psychopathology, and to the analytic situation—awakening takes on a weaning connotation and becomes associated with primitive superego functioning: the superego as the hated awakener who takes the breast away or who will not allow the blissful surrender in the first place; the superego experienced as a voice, snapping the child into anxious wakefulness. Lewin links the auditoriness of the awakening superego with the alarm clock.

What happens to a child when the transition from sleep to wakefulness is consistently unmediated by a parent's ministrations—the touch, the calling, the help? For this patient, the outcome seems to have been a constellation of cumulative resentment, precocious but resigned functioning, and chronic insecurity. And then, much earlier than her peers, she entered puberty, leading her to feel that her childhood was now irretrievably taken from her by her own body. She experienced her mother's announcing her first period as mortifying in itself, but her additional comment that her father would die if he heard about it was both mystifying and maddening. Does growing up kill people? Does sexuality? Or does it only kill the child's embattled hope for the childhood she has already lost to other people's illnesses? And if the inevitability of growing up is going to kill people, maybe those ill people should go ahead and die, and get this threat hanging over her head over with.

This young woman, who grew so much bigger than others in her class, developed a restrictive eating disorder through which she also discovered amenorrhea. She thereby attempted to hold onto the childhood she was losing, to protect all of those who might be harmed by her growing up, and to shield herself from the mortifying comments of both her peers and her family. And when she could not stop her classmates cutting remarks, she took to cutting herself. The pathological transformation here is from a sign in the social field—whatever her period meant in her family, whatever her growth meant to her classmates, and whatever both meant to her—to symptomatic enactment on the body. The dialogue turned inward and became concrete.

This young woman's adolescence and early adulthood were marked by multiple short-term hospitalisations, which she ended before they could be of real help to her, and multiple educational forays, which she interrupted just before any real achievement. She seemed perpetually in-between, never allowing herself a true holding or a true advance. When she finally found a psychotherapist she could work with, the longing and demand that this capable female therapist actually *be* her mother opened up with a vengeance. Things took a more critical turn following the patient's suicide attempt, the plan for which she kept from her therapist. Consciously motivated by her hatred of her body, the attempt also occurred after her maternal uncle's death, an event devastating to the patient's mother because, given the circumstances, she felt some responsibility for it. Instead of taking care of her sick brother, the patient's mother was taking care of her own minor illness; she was both grief-struck and overcome with guilt when her brother died. The event signalled again that illness may authorise attention, but separation kills.

Delinquency

Winnicott considered delinquency to be a sign of hope, at least delinquency in its original form, when the delinquent act of the child was meant to call to the attention of a potentially responsive parent that the child was feeling hurt or deprived. The purpose of delinquency was to "compel the environment to be important" through "compel(ling) someone to attend to management" (1956a, p. 309). Winnicott described two broad categories of delinquency: stealing, which he related to maternal deprivation, and aggression, which he related to paternal deprivation. But delinquency can also harden into a repetitive pattern through various forms of secondary gain, including not only the immediate material gain from the delinquent act, but the sense of mastery, the release of aggression, the omnipotence of getting away with it, and, perhaps especially, the predictability of the responses of others. One definition of chronicity (Will, 1964) is that a stereotyped presentation meets a stereotyped response. The delinquent act becomes a chronic pattern through the reassuringly predictable, identity-structuring, and gratifyingly distressed responses of other people.

Cutting and anorexia might be considered to be distinctly female forms of delinquency, and secondary gain is clearly derived from these behaviours. In the psychic economy, they regulate painful affect states. They express aggression in disguised form even as they invite care-taking responses. They also express the wish to be seen and tended to, and simultaneously punish that wish. They generate feelings of omnipotence and triumph in the self—the ability to endure pain on one's own—as they also export painful feelings of helplessness into others.

But, in that more original sense, what might these delinquencies attempt to "steal back?" Perhaps, for someone like this patient, her delinquency attempts to steal back her body as her own—the body that grew so quickly it stole her childhood from her, or the body that was accused of hurting others, or the body that others felt so free to criticise. And perhaps it also steals back the early mother whom the child feels to be an extension of her own body—the mother before separateness, before divergent agendas would have been conceivable. And perhaps it steals back to that era when the original place of care belonged by rights and unselfconsciously to the child herself rather than to other members of her family. The eventual therapist who feels called upon to ignore the fantasy–reality distinction is registering anxiously, in the countertranference, the patient's hoped-for return to an undifferentiated moment, the moment when need and gratification, wish and fulfilment were inseparable and there was no perceived "out there" to rupture that necessary illusion.

This is the hope embedded in the borderline patient's delinquent act. It is a hope experienced tenaciously and unswervingly. It knows what it hopes for, and it will not again be betrayed by the person's own capacities. By that I mean that to the degree the patient is able to accomplish things—to take care of herself; later, to make progress in her treatment—to that degree the patient feels that she is loved for what she can do, rather than for who she is. She feels a deep competition with her abilities (Cooperman, personal communication), and she absolutely will not let them—and her being seduced into using them— deprive her again. This may be why such patients interrupt their movement toward graduations with hospitalisations. Graduation is felt to finally close off the right to be taken care of. It represents a true self betrayal behind a false self achievement (Winnicott, 1960).

But there is a corollary question as to why patients like this sometimes cannot use hospitalisations—for the patient being discussed, why as soon as she entered a treatment programme she thought about getting out of it. Perhaps the answer here is the same as to the earlier question about graduations; that is, she experienced a treatment programme as attempting to take something away from her rather than make up for her deprivation. The negative therapeutic reaction, always a possibility for patients with this constellation of pathology, would therefore represent the refusal to surrender the hope for actual reparations through collusion with the progress of the treatment.

There is another possibility though. Perhaps the patient could not actually use her treatments because, at some level, the place of care was not a legitimate one for her. While fiercely and righteously steal-ing it back, at the same time she may have felt that she was truly steal-ing it from others—most immediately the desperately needy sibling part of her could have just as well done without. She felt deeply that the recovery of others depended on her staying well, that she had to function because others could not. A patient in these circumstances is plagued with the feeling of illegitimacy. While others' illnesses are real, hers are self-created. Her father loses weight from illness; the patient starves herself. Transfusions are needed for a sibling's illness; the patient bleeds from her own action. She does it to herself, and she knows it. She is *willing* herself into the role of patient, and the fact that she does so because she has been willed out of the role of child, and into the role of care-taker, by others, does nothing to legit-imise her sense of herself. In that care-taker role, she cannot have needs, she must have strengths, and she may not separate, lest those in her care suffer.

This recognition of will, like the recognition that there was a true deprivation coming from a sufficiently differentiated "out there," speaks to the developmental level at which the traumatic loss took place. In this case, it occurred during her toddlerhood when her mastery over her body and her ability to mobilise a pleasurably wilful "No" were allowing more autonomous functioning. As with her early adolescent experience, she must have, during this earlier phase, linked achievement with loss: what she could do for herself others need not do for her. Given that the loss was associated with illness and the near-death of others, the aggressive feelings experienced in relation to it must have been highly conflictual, leading to hypervigilence and precocious wilfulness about containing them. Prelinger (2004) des-cribes hate as a "condition of active but paralyzed aggression" (p. 34), and one can so easily imagine the early origin of states of hatred and self-hatred in someone like this patient.

Prelinger goes on to say that "Hate cannot be 'abreacted'," but that it has "an agenda" (p. 34). In this patient's case, the agenda became that her therapist "be my mother", and it felt completely unfair that she could not or would not. In Prelinger's words, the "intent" behind hate "is held onto by patience and fierce persistence" (p. 34). It rep-resents a kind of hope, and the patient's frequent expressions in treat-ment of hopelessness and depression had to do with this hope's not being realised . . . yet. Thus it was not a true depression because it was not truly about loss. Rather it was about deprivation, grievance, and frustrated but tenaciously ongoing hope.

A cut

Well into a stormy but productive treatment, the patient's long delayed and conflictually experienced final graduation led to a phase of acting out culminating in her cutting herself. On a visit to the clinic in which her therapist practiced, she went to a small kitchen area and rubbed salt in her wound. With an attitude of *la belle indifference*, she initially ignored the significance of this action. Her therapist, who— after phases of the treatment that had included the various transference meanings of her demand that he "certify" her as truly ill—confronted her with her use of his materials and his space to harm herself. He addressed this behaviour as abusive toward him—abusiveness being another feature of the patient's home life after the father recovered from his illness—and stated his intention not to simply live out the abused–abusing roles of her parents. He pushed hard for what she wanted from him as her therapist as well as for what had happened between them that led to this attack. She responded seriously and said that she wanted help with her hatred.

In the next session, the patient found herself sobbing; she *wanted* her mother, and for the first time in all her years of treatment, she let loose with the full simple expression of that feeling. This feeling related directly to her having lost her mother to anxiety and depression after the younger, very ill child was born. These were not the sobs of grievance, but of abject loss; not of an urgently demanded future, but of an irretrievable but desperately longed for past. When the patient returned again, she was frightened. She had seen her face in the mirror and realised she was alone. Her hope to find a new mother, which had become transferentially entwined with a number of people in her life, including her therapist, was now untangled; people were simply themselves, and her longing for and loss of her mother were now felt to be distinct from the actual people in her life, existing on its own as a kind of emotional *Das Ding*.

In this affective context, she felt profoundly that she did not want to live and feared that she might actually commit suicide. She felt faced with the ending of "false hopes", and this person, who had so often come across as dangerous but not serious, precariously alive but actually invulnerable, felt for the first time in a genuine way that she could not take her survival for granted. Neither she, nor her therapist, nor anyone else knew in advance how this emotional cataclysm would turn out. This was a moment of maximal risk and maximal dependence in her treatment. It was certainly an ending point—potentially even a permanent one—but also a potential starting point insofar as the hope for a realisable future could arise only if the hopelessness about the unrealisable past was experienced and survived. To her shock, this brilliant young woman told her therapist that "I realised my problem was that I didn't accept that I was learning here, but—I don't know—that I was telling you and you would teach me".

In his classic paper on "Hate in the countertransference" (1947), Winnicott wrote that "it seems to me doubtful whether a human child as he develops is capable of tolerating the full extent of his own hate in a sentimental environment. He needs hate to hate" (p. 202). As he did later on, when he talked about love and hate being "honestly expressed" by the analyst, "love by the positive interest taken, and hate in the strict start and finish and in the matter of fees" (1954a, p. 285), Winnicott was considering hate—the hate structured into the task and role relationships of psychoanalysis—to be a therapeutic provision, an especially necessary one for patients who want help with their hatred. This patient's family environment, for its own complicated and tragic reasons, had come to be suffused with hate-filled abuse and hate-inspiring neglect, managed by a smothering sentimentality and compulsive care-taking, the latter murderous in their own way toward any serious grappling with honest feeling. The patient's cutting enacted hatefulness about (and marked the fact of) separateness between her therapist and herself. Her therapist's separating himself from the simple living out of a transference object role triggered what came to seem like an essential experience of hopelessness and a first recognition about learning.

"Maybe it's so"

"Hope and losing hope are two ways of thinking about the reality of times to come" (Mehler & Argentieri, 1989, p. 295). So begins a paper by two Roman psychoanalysts, Jacqueline Amati Mehler and Simona Argentieri, published in the *International Journal of Psychoanalysis* in

1989. The authors speak of "particular clinical situations in which . . . the statement of loss of hope . . . assumes a specific meaning of resistance, and imposes on the analyst not only the difficult task of understanding and interpreting it but also a strenuous and delicate technical problem" (p. 295). Each author had independently encountered a certain kind of stalemate in the work with one of her patients, a stalemate occurring after the analysis was quite far along and had actually been very productive. The analysis had become "blocked by . . . monotonous communications such as; 'I just can't make it' " (p. 295). Another was "ruled by a perpetual lamentation, 'I'm so miserable . . . I'm always worse . . . it's all useless' " (p. 296).

This was "the leitmotiv at the beginning of every session, in which improvement and gains attained through the analytic work were systematically ignored or cancelled by the usual complaints" (p. 296). Both analyses had dealt extensively with transference and counter-transference issues, including aggressive motives and defeating processes. Then, during one session in response to the patient's statement that "I'm afraid there is nothing else to do", one analyst responded spontaneously with the statement "Maybe it's so" (p. 296). The patient reacted to this statement "as if she had been struck" (p. 296). She was silent; then the tone of complaint changed. She experienced her analyst's words as "harsh, but also extremely real, as if for the first time she had actually realized that there was a genuine possibility that analysis could come to an end without her having made adequate use of it" (p. 296).

The second analyst came to a similar moment and made a similar comment in the face of the patient's repetitive declarations of uselessness. From the analyst's point of view, her patient's,

> intent was to show that, no matter what was done, it was just not the thing she needed. This was, in fact, inevitable and true to some extent, because (the patient) wanted nothing so badly as for her mother to be still alive and with her, as she wanted her to be . . . (S)he tried to corner the analyst into becoming the impossible substitute for the lost object and for all that she was unwilling to recognize as irreparably gone or spoiled forever . . . Refusing thus to forsake the illusion of obtaining the impossible, she also managed to release aggression, depriving herself and tantalizing the unsuccessful analyst, or accusing others of neglect and deprivation. The high price she paid for this was the feeling of not participating in life . . .. (p. 299)

According to this analyst, this "realization that analysis could no longer be maintained in a dead-end, atemporal, immutable dimension became a turning point" (p. 300) of this patient's treatment. The authors continue:

> What is common (in these two cases) is the technical problem . . . whereby the patient's condition is not transformable by transference interpretations, although paradoxically the problem lies precisely there . . . (i)n the fact that certain patients either try to impose or succeed in imposing on the analyst a stereotyped role in accordance with a fixed, immutable internal figure that . . . comes closer to actual and factual reality . . . The analysis and the analyst are invested with an unrealistic task, which consists in preserving the illusion that what is past or lost forever can still be provided and restored. The perpetuation of this demand, accompanied by resentment about the lack of its fulfillment, is the extreme defense against the threat of separation . . . The upshot, though, is a constant pattern . . . confirming each time . . . both that there is no hope at all ('I just can't make it') and the hope that trying again may fulfill the illusion . . . (T)here is an eternal present in which loss is furiously felt, but the 'drama', which *has already irreparably happened* is not recognized or realized as such. (p. 300)

Confronted with this "cult of an illusion" within which "insight into the transference implications still does not provoke decision-making" (p. 301), these analysts found themselves with the need to act so as to establish their own separateness and the reality of their task. "(B)oth statements (the analysts' statements), once verbalized, placed the analyst as a real, whole person who would no longer allow her patients to make her play an omnipotent or impotent role" (p. 301). The authors add: "(I)t is most significant that the analyst should suddenly have introduced the temporal dimension—the passing of the years and the end of things—whereas it is in this regard that the resistance appeared to aim at exactly the opposite result: to enchain life and the analysis in an eternal and interminable dimension even at the price of pain and failure" (p. 296).

The authors recognise that "the analyst statements were an active and sudden rupture of the transference and therefore inevitably traumatic, inevitably introducing separateness between patient and analyst" (p. 303). They thus felt quite concerned about their being misinterpreted as recommending a technical device to be used, perhaps even strategically, in any situation of therapeutic stasis. This dramatic moment, should it occur, must evolve from a sufficiency of analytic understanding, transference work, and therapeutic relatedness. But, as with the patient discussed in this chapter, such a critical moment may indeed develop and may be essential to the patient's further progress.

The word "realisation" used by Mehler and Argentieri to describe that progress was also used early on by Winnicott (1945) to describe what he later thought of as the capacity to use an object (1969). He was describing the child's transition from relating to the object as a subjective phenomenon to relating to the object as objective, that is, as having its own usable existence independent of the child's projections. This came about, thought Winnicott, through the child's destructiveness and the object's survival in role. This is the phenomenon being described by Mehler and Argentieri, and in the treatment described in this chapter. The patient's insistence on the transference as the whole truth and a permanent state of being is a kind of necessary destructiveness in the service of finding reality. The analyst survives as analyst by the eventual reintroduction and recognition of the separateness implicit in task and role, holding in the process the distinction between generative transference illusion and what feels closer to delusion. The analyst's actions mark the transference as a subjective and partial truth, not a state of being but a space for learning. In Farber's (1966) terms, this crisis could be seen as one of "therapeutic despair" (p. 155), first in the analyst, then in the patient; a crisis that moves the transference from a pathological linking process (Volkan, 1981) to one of true mourning.

Being my mother

How is it that certain patients can press upon the therapist so tenaciously and relentlessly the requirement of becoming the maternal transference object? The answer to this question probably ranges from the patient's need to avoid at all costs the unbearableness of the original loss to the ways in which the process of analytic understanding awakens and incites further the hope for gratification within a maternally-toned matrix. I want to suggest one more possibility: the patient's ferocious conviction that the therapist could "be my mother" may derive from experiences of having herself been related to as a transference object throughout her life. She has grown up both being "herself" (however one might think of this more true version of the self) and being someone else. This "someone else" aspect certainly relates to unconscious role assignment in the family. The patient clearly felt assigned the role of care-taker in her family—actually a role rather like the Sword of Damocles itself; if she fell, everyone fell. This kind of emotional context becomes unbearable for a child; she comes to want the sword to fall, to get the disaster over with, and to feel it must fall because of the weight of suppressed aggression suffusing her autonomy and underlying her care-taking.

But family roles derive from deeper sources. The patient had come to feel that she had to mother her mother while the latter mothered others, including her own intermittently needy and ailing husband. She had to be her mother's mother, not only in the care-taking tasks she undertook on her behalf, but in listening while her mother confided in her about the strains of her life. In other words, this role reversal may well have reflected her mother's transference to her—as though to the mother she herself needed. There came a moment in her growing up when the patient angrily refused her mother's request to do an errand for her ailing father; her mother did it herself but told the father that the patient had done it. "Someone else" was being presented to the ill father, a "someone else" intermingling images of good daughter, but also the good mother who takes care of both the stressed mother and the ailing father. Playing out a maternal transference role for her mother may have been part of the fabric of the patient's growing up and part of her deprivation. Hence, both the conviction that the therapist *could* play out the desired transference role and the motivation to insist on it may derive from having been the object of this belief and this force from a parent.

I am speculating here about the transference of the transference process itself, rather than only the transference of particular contents —a transference process related to early maternal authority within which unconscious communications and handlings shape both the message and the reality that "you are who I say you are". If this is true, we can understand further the trauma associated with facing the potentially liberating hopelessness of whatever is marked off as "beyond transference" with the analyst. For the patient, there is no certainty about any "beyond". So much of her identity is bound up with, not only seeking, but being a transference object, the patient doubts her actual survival or coherence as a person outside the original dyad. It is beyond the scope of this chapter to discuss this third position and the critical role of the father in either substantiating or foreclosing this alternative (Muller, 1996). Suffice it to say that the weakened reality sense of these patients, such that a moment of "realisation" becomes so crucial, extends to their sense of precarious existence with any degree of separateness apart from maternal projections, and therefore outside of transference. I am reminded here of Freida Fromm-Reichmann's correction of Freud: it is not that the psychotic is untreatable psychoanalytically because he cannot form a transference; it is that treatment will be difficult because he can form nothing else (1959).

This train of thought leads directly to the importance of analysing the countertransference. The patients I have been describing often have such strengths and such appeal that, during those phases of work when pathological hope is less ascendant, they easily arouse the therapist's hope for a good outcome. Indeed, studies have shown (Hauser, 2006) that the ability to elicit another person's interest is central to what makes for resilience, and these patients tend to have that capacity. The transference arena for them is full of vitality; in some very basic way, it is where they have lived. With this particular patient, her therapist realised that he had come to feel not only warmly toward her but also, in a sustained and unexamined way, *hopeful* that she would get better and have a full life. Indeed, given her managing school requirements and a long distance commute to see him, he had become quite flexible with scheduling appointments and receiving payments.

It came to seem to him, in the midst of the crisis described earlier, that not only her hope was implicated in the crisis, but perhaps his as well, and that the cut the patient needed to make might have been to that countertransference. This sobering realisation of possible enactment, of who the patient might have become to the therapist rather than only vice versa, deepens the work considerably, and, in this case, was a step toward both therapist and patient coming to terms with the limits of the treatment arrangements they were attempting, and working toward more realistic ones. More basically, a phase like this may come to include affects having to do with the mutual acceptance of the fact that patient and therapist cannot be everything to each other, and why that illusion might have been desirable. With that can come a more genuine discovery of others as both resources and people. As I have been arguing in this chapter, deeply cherished, but illusory hope gives way to authentic hope only through a therapeutic process in which both parties must grapple with very real and painful hopelessness.

CHAPTER FIVE

Something opened up

Cutting

Self-mutilation is frequently a symptom within the borderline spectrum of psychopathology. But this phenomenon might more usefully be abstracted from what is, after all, a problematic personality diagnosis (see Chapter Two) and considered as an admixture of depressive, hysterical, and delinquent trends (see Chapter Four): depressive insofar as this tearing at the flesh may occur during moods of agitated hopelessness and severe self-criticism, hysterical insofar as it is the body, often in an unconscious erotised state, that speaks, and delinquent insofar as it, in Winnicott's words, "compels the environment to be important" and "to attend to management" (1956a, p. 309).

In this chapter, I will discuss work with a patient who cut herself periodically, focusing in particular on her preconscious fantasies of grandiose destructiveness and the role of aggression in the treatment relationship. This patient was not a daily cutter, nor did she require major suturing; nevertheless, her cutting horrified her family and frightened the patient as well, because she saw it as both "crazy" and yet as an action necessary to prevent her from killing herself. Her therapy took place in a small, open, residential treatment centre in which a patient's freedom to live daily life as fully as possible carries with it the responsibility to manage oneself and to use the collective resources of those around to assist with this. The work was relatively short-term, lasting about three months. It temporarily interrupted ongoing outpatient psychotherapy, and served various purposes, including containing, experiencing, and understanding the patient's rage while protecting her outpatient life from it. The treatment produced for the patient genuinely surprising insights leading to a shifting understanding of the locus of her difficulties. It also re-engaged a process of aborted mourning and led the patient toward risky efforts at reparation.

"Something opened up"

"A year ago, something closed and something else opened up, and I can't close it again; and the person who could isn't here to." That person was the patient's father, whose death the year before had precipitated the emotional tectonics she described. This mid-thirty's lawyer became intractably depressed and self-destructive, challenged further, on the one hand, by problems with subordinates at work, which called for a firm response, and, on the other, by her boss's illnesses and absences. Given this problematic work situation, the patient felt confined to a silent, angry stoicism through which she endeavoured to "hold it together" at all costs. As it turned out, this situation replicated her own unhappy adolescence when the combination of a mother's illness and younger siblings' acting out had led the patient toward an angry perfectionism. This effort seemed unconsciously designed, though not destined, to be noticed by her father, whom she had adored all of her life and whose career as a top lawyer she had tried to emulate. This outgoing, intellectual man impressed many who knew him and occupied a larger-than-life place in the feelings and fantasies of his first child and only daughter.

Upon her depressive breakdown, the patient began an intensive analytic psychotherapy as an outpatient with a man considerably older than herself. She experienced the treatment as enormously helpful to her understanding of her difficulties and yet as simultaneously terrifying because of the intensity of feeling this sensitive man and reliable setting opened up. She began to engage in acts of self-cutting and to struggle with suicidal impulses. Short-term hospitalisation, medication, and other forms of intervention neither turned nor slowed this momentum toward destructiveness. The patient was then referred for residential treatment; her stay was quite brief by psychotherapeutic standards, and yet relatively long for a person so highly involved in her professional life.

As it turned out, the patient's coming to a residential treatment setting enacted at a transference level an effort to find an omnipotent container for fantastically larger-than-life feelings of love and rage toward her father. It was a protective act toward her family, friends, and colleagues, but it also came to be seen as containing a number of bitter and multiply determined notes, like "it's my turn now" and "it's not working with me, so let's see what you can do without me". These latter feelings related specifically to her mother's illness and hospitalisation in the patient's early adolescence and to her own vengeful leaving of her family for a boyfriend in later adolescence. Quasi-hospitalisation in a residential treatment setting began as both a parameter for her treatment and also a transference enactment.

Immediately, the patient used an administrative role I was also in to leap into the role of good citizen and perfect daughter. This gave her a headache. It also did not give me in the transference the help and pride she hoped it would, and so, with interpretive help, she allowed herself to begin to seriously face her depression, including the anger within it, that she dreaded. She worked hard to avoid experiencing sadness or anger because she felt terrified that these feelings would cascade endlessly in a completely out-of-control free-fall. She also felt certain that I would abandon her if she showed me her rage or jealousy. She magically kept me with her through her guardedness, her constriction, and her guilty reparations. This closed fantasy system was self-fulfilling, a form of false self functioning (Winnicott, 1960) that actually worked in getting people's sympathetic attention and caring, if also thin and suffocating, companionship.

The patient could, however, focus this relatively brief therapy by conveying with a sense of gravity what she needed to accomplish with me: to talk with me about certain things she considered bad and to work out a different way of being in her work life and family. These two objectives anchored the psychotherapy trajectory in the patient's desires and became a touchstone for where we were in the treatment.

Her comment that "if you were more of a bastard, I could talk to you more freely" was offered as guidance for how to get there. As Winnicott commented: a person "needs hate to hate" (1947, p. 202).

Desecration

Indeed, immediately after conveying that she needed to speak with me about things she had done that she considered bad, she became extremely conflicted about speaking at all. The next day she came to her hour having cut herself in the woodworking area of the treatment programme's activities department. She said that she was afraid of coming to the session because she had done this bad thing. After the theme of badness, and her ways of managing me in relation to it, had been explored, I was mildly confrontational with her, and said: "You don't have to prove to me that you're bad. Though I don't think of myself as here to judge you, it's also not my place to dispute your declaring yourself to be a bad person. For me, the question is: do you want to understand whatever it is you are calling bad so that you can consider what you might want to do about it?"

We quickly got to her cutting as a way of getting me to agree with her view of herself as bad and of provoking me to punish her so that she would not have to talk. Eventually, I said to her that she might also be communicating something to me in the act itself and in its context: "Cutting yourself in the activities department desecrates what people here consider to be a sacred space, and cutting can also be seen as desecrating your body. Maybe you're trying to tell me about desecration in a way I can feel".

Initially, the patient defensively reached for a management response: should she move to that part of the programme with more nursing coverage? I suggested that she wanted the loving care of nurses to overcome and outweigh the badness she felt inside herself, rather than to talk with me about that feeling of badness; I told her I did not think there was a programme for what she wanted. She was silent. I had the impression that both of us were recognising choices: she could choose not to speak to me, but neither was I required to suffocate her with staff responses more appropriate to a crisis hospital setting. Then in a tone of great seriousness, she told me about an early romantic entanglement with an older man who had "opened up the world" to her. For all of its joys, she felt deeply guilty. This began a phase of disclosures and understandings about her sexual life and her relationships with men. She soon felt proud of herself for speaking about this and much more grounded in our relationship's capacity to survive (Winnicott, 1969) and indeed grow from aggressive exchange (Khan, 1972b).

"I want him back"

Things changed at this still early point of her psychotherapy. Her deep and ongoing lament about her father—his power over her, her longing for his love, her hurt feelings, her bitterness about how things should have been, and her declarations of rage at him—shifted into the background as the first truly live anger she expressed in the hours occurred in relation to her mother's "delicate sensibility". She let herself feel more about her mother, including about the quieter trauma of her early life, when her mother withdrew into low-key but chronic substance abuse as she tried to deal with young children and an ambitious husband. This shift in the site of her rage stunned the patient and she found herself wanting to stop cutting herself.

On an anniversary day associated with her father, the patient let go with full tears about his death and a passionate cry of "I want him back". After this, she immersed herself again in her feelings about her mother. She recovered positive memories, she worked in the transference on her fear of claiming me because other patients needed me, she took the terrifying step of writing to her mother to ask if they could talk frankly about their relationship, and she risked being overtly angry with me for my being a few minutes late to a session. She got to this anger through a transference displacement. At first, she was angry at a nurse who did not have time for her. Near the end of the session, she said she was suicidal. I said that saving that statement until the end was an angry thing to do to me. On quick reflection, she thought she was enacting her feeling that if I did not want to deal with her trouble, which was what my being late meant to her, she would not bring it to me. She realised then that this was her early family experience: her mother too burdened by demanding children to be emotionally available, as I might have been late because of emergencies with other patients. At this point, the patient got hold of her suicidal feeling as an angry effort to punish me and an angry claim on my lost attention.

Soon thereafter she suddenly realised that since that session about wanting her father back, she was no longer angry with him. Instead, she simply missed him. But she also felt that she had him with her in a different way, as an internal presence and support. Indeed, for the first time since his death, she could actually look at pictures of him.

"I'm so sorry"

Soon after this, the patient visited her mother for the agreed-upon purpose of talking about their relationship and the contribution of early family life to her difficulties. The patient asked me to join this session. She spoke to her mother about how angry she was at her for not being there for her as a child. She went into some detail about this and spoke with feeling. Her mother replied, "You're right; I wasn't really there; I'm so sorry". In retrospect, her mother felt allowed to absent herself from family involvement through the "privileged position" she found herself in by virtue of her husband's protectiveness toward her. "I didn't understand it and I didn't want it to change. I had no power growing up; this powerful person gave me such wonderful power."

My patient's mother then revealed to her daughter an early romantic trauma in her own life. She felt devastated by it until her husband-to-be came along and emotionally rescued her. It played a major role in her withdrawing from the artistic career her talents and interest had guided her toward, a loss that her daughter could understand from her own experience. The grief and shame about these events, along with the demands of young children, had pushed her toward her minimally available way of mothering.

Indeed, my patient's mother realised in our conversation the extent of her grief at losing her active relationship to art and how inevitably the task of mothering had prevented her from entering the creative space that formerly had been so sustaining to her. Creativity had been for her "the most meaningful experience of my life". She realised at that moment in the session that it had also brought "a special joy" to her sad and withdrawn father; "he didn't talk about it, but we could meet there".

The patient's mother then reported that when her daughter was in her late teens, the entire family had had a family consultation at a child guidance clinic, for the purpose of dealing with the younger siblings' acting out. A major part of the patient's resentment was that, during her adolescence, family life revolved around their behavioural problems. For the first time, her mother told her that the primary advice the parents had received during this consultation was to pay attention to their daughter's difficulties. They were shocked, given the patient's apparently excellent functioning and their wish to rely on that; they did not follow up with future consultation. This information shocked the patient, who declared "I *was* in trouble but I didn't want to talk to a therapist; I wanted to talk to *you*." And so, many years and considerable pain later, both people were now talking to each other about, among other things, the meaning of fathers to both of them.

The patient followed up this important family meeting with a second one, this time with the siblings she resented and envied. She gave herself the right to be angry and to acknowledge limits in both her family and work lives. She stopped cutting herself. She worked through a termination phase that included revisiting feelings related to her father's death, after which she returned to her outpatient psychotherapy with a far better experiential grasp of her life and difficulties. Her therapist, through consultation with us during her treatment, seemed clearer about the central role of aggression in the patient's difficulties, both in her depression and in her efforts to get well.

Closing and opening

What had closed and what had opened up for this patient upon her father's death? The first answer to the latter part of this question is: her passionate body. She cut open her body. Losing the reality of her father's presence and the ongoing opportunity for the idealised love and recognition she had for so long desired, she had found herself flooded with narcissistic longing for his admiration and rage about its frustration. These feelings burned for release and found it through her cutting. But this cathartic (and displacing) function of cutting was not the whole story; this simultaneously gratifying and punishing marking of her body also signified the deeply conflicted Oedipal dimension of the patient's relationship to her father. She brought two "openings" together in the confrontational session I reported: the opening of her body in the activities department, an action that she used to provoke me toward closing our communication, and the opening up, following my recognition of her "desecrating" her body, of her love life, specifically of her involvement with the older man who "opened up the world" to her, with thrilling but devastating consequences.

The patient presented her "badness", her larger-than-life guilt, as her central problem. By enacting it, especially by cutting herself in the activities department, she offered one of those "borderline" moments (Chapter Two) to her therapist. Her tone of agonised self-criticism pushed for a sympathetic response, in Winnicott's words, a "sentimental environment" (1947, p. 202). And yet there was hate and betrayal in her action. In this particular context, her cutting attacked and potentially spoiled the creative work environment other patients need for their growth. In other words, at a transference level, it assaulted an aspect of family life; in fact, it specifically enacted her unconscious childhood role as the destroyer of her mother's creative life. If I as her therapist had not held and worked with this aggressive meaning, I risked living out with the patient a quiet and superficially caring collusion, in fact either a frightened withdrawal from her aggression or an Oedipal pairing that could only promote more guilt. Indeed, privileging Oedipal guilt, embedded in the agony she brought to her session, over the needs and rights of others is itself a form of Oedipal victory.

In the patient's cutting, we see straightforwardly acting-out as resistance (the action as a way of diverting speech) and as enactment with the therapist of that which needs to be spoken (namely, the forbidden use of her body). Following my effort to meet and work with what the patient felt was her grandiose destructiveness, she told me of her romantic entanglement with the older man. She felt that to have been a true betrayal, leading to genuine damage in her life for which she felt real guilt. Having spoken it, she opened up the possibility of deeper learning, and she grounded her acting out in a dimension of truth, in which I was no longer the secret partner but rather witness and potential interpreter.

Pairs and the Third

My patient's conscious frustration had to do with pairings that excluded her: her parents' with her troubled siblings, her father's with the ill mother of her adolescence, and the attractive, fragile mother of her childhood. What the patient found after her confession of a guilty pairing with an older man (and my refusal of a similar pairing) was the ruptured pairing between herself as a very young child and her withdrawn and damaged mother. She could experience this with fully felt anger that made sense to her (Winnicott, 1955–1956), having realised that I would not protect us from anger nor would we necessarily be destroyed by it.

Indeed, she recognised how she had interpreted the entire spectrum of aggressive feeling as beyond her mother's capacity to withstand, and that her mother's painful absence had left both a need for a present parent and a vacancy for her Oedipal strivings. It was to her great credit that she then directly engaged her mother and her great good fortune that her mother was now willing and able to engage in return. Through this affective re-engagement, my patient re-discovered her mother as both a resource and a person. In the process, she learned of her mother's secret, painful, and joyful pairings: in an unmerited "privileged" position with her husband (which had to do with his own history of loss), in an early catastrophic romance, and, most importantly, in those forgotten but precious meetings with her father through art.

In psychotherapy, the therapist both joins a new pair and holds the place of the Third (Muller, 1996). Transference affect is the therapeutic dynamism of this new pair; transference analysis is the structural intervention that directly or indirectly recognises the other fundamentally important pairs in a person's life. It is holding to this recognition, sustained in the face of transference–countertransference affectivity, that constitutes Thirdness. The treatment programme, including its parts and other patients, functioned as a Third for me, helping me hold in mind for interpretive work my other significant pairs as well as the patient's.

An X on a map

The patient's relationship to her affective life was premised upon the unconscious fantasy of grandiose destructiveness, of there being no limits to her feelings but drastic limits to the capacity of others to survive them. The early template for this fantasy may well have been what Winnicott calls a "primitive agony" (1962a), specifically the patient's recurrent night terrors as a very young child from which she could not be awakened. This childhood sleep disturbance occurred right after the birth of her sibling, whose difficulties were manifest quite early. This fantasy of unbounded power, and also of endless anguish, was lodged in, and in a sense contained by, her cutting: the "see what I can stand but you can't" and "nothing can stop me" messages within it, as well as the way in which terrifying haemorrhage can actually be bandaged. The core of her treatment had to do with the emergence of this fantasy in its various forms in the transference, and our analysing and living through it experientially, which led to a more realistic appraisal of herself and those around her.

Clearly, however, though specific experiences of overwhelming affect may lay the groundwork for fantasies and fears of grandiose destructiveness, the ongoing vulnerability of the patient's mother during her early childhood—her liability not to survive the patient's aggression, Oedipal or otherwise—must have been a central factor. Perhaps this explains that interesting moment when, in the context of discovering her rage at her mother—within an Oedipal transference relationship that allowed it and wanted to understand it—the patient found herself *wanting* to stop her cutting. It is as though cutting were no longer needed as either a silencing action or a secret libidinal one; via her experience of rage at her mother—the first anger in the sessions that felt spontaneous and alive—she also became *interested* in her again. Her arrested grief process may not have been because she could not let go of her father, but rather because she could not have him without guilt. That is, she could not take him in as a comfortable presence until she had begun to address the rage toward her mother that had fuelled her Oedipal claim. As it turned out this arrested grief toward her father was built upon an earlier grief at the patient's loss of her mother, a loss related to a powerful grief in the mother's own life.

Winnicott wrote:

When there is an antisocial tendency, *there has been a true deprivation . . .* a loss of something good that has been positive in the child's experience up to a certain date, and that has been withdrawn; the withdrawal has extended over a period of time longer than that over which the child can keep the memory of the experience alive. (1956a, p. 309)

Given the three trends within cutting that I addressed at the beginning of this paper, might we consider this patient's cut as a marker, like an X on a map, of that deprivation moment, that had been lost to memory. As hysterical, it silently signifies an Oedipal claim, but as depressive, it recognises that Oedipal victories not only bring about serious losses, they compensate for them. This patient's psychotherapy, brief as it was, included two especially powerful moments in which *she*, rather than *something*, opened up: the *cri de coeur* of "I want him back", which released the grieving process, and, in that intimate conversation with her mother, the poignant "I wanted to talk to *you*." These two statements mark with words a trajectory from Oedipal passion to pre-Oedipal love and loss. Having been made, they rendered the secret code of cutting its own form of loss and far less necessary.

The minds of clinicians

Serious resource limitations have become an ongoing fact of life for many patients and mental health professionals. Most of us who have practiced psychotherapy with severely disturbed patients in relation to an institutional context have been greatly affected by these external forces. We have been challenged to re-consider our working assumptions so that what is essential to treatment is not lost in an effort to adapt to the patient's circumstances, including financial ones. As Lewis (1991) suggests, if the institution's mission does not survive, it makes no difference if the institution survives. How many mental health institutions today have retained their names but actually long since lost or completely changed their identities? Lewis (quoting Kramer, 1990) adds a chilling admonition: these days "the battle" is for "the minds of clinicians" (p. 9).

For those of us who have made up our minds about the critical value of in-depth psychoanalytically-oriented psychotherapy for very troubled people, we may also want to consider changing our minds as to the role of shorter-term but intensive treatment interventions, especially as part of longer-term outpatient therapy. Patients, in whatever setting, often feel the need for more treatment, but just as often "needs" defined in an open-ended sense reflect something about the patient's subjective sense of suffering and a defensive, unarticulated, countertransference-inviting agenda about how cure is to be accomplished, primarily through making up for in treatment what has been lost in life (see Chapter Four). Attending to reality in a more full sense—that is, to the seriousness of the patient's trouble *and* to the resources to deal with it—is also a treatment need. This may lead to a re-calibration that takes seriously the progress intensive treatment in an institutional context can bring about in a relatively short time, as well as to a developing awareness that resource limitation, especially in the context of the emotional limitations of patients' families, is a transference problem as well (Shapiro, 1997).

The treatment described in this chapter was in its own way a larger-than-life intervention, in terms of the career it interrupted and the resources brought to bear on the trouble—in a sense a grand intervention to meet a grandiose fantasy. The patient's story could actually be heard as one of resource limitations leading to efforts at larger-than-life solutions. A withdrawn and damaged mother both incites in her oldest daughter and leaves unattended powerful Oedipal strivings for a powerful father. A boss's ailments provoke longings for, and memories of, powerful men. A father's death precipitates a life crisis brought to a male therapist with whom the patient terrifying discovers the full intensity of her feeling. An outpatient setting, within a family and work context, fails to contain that intensity, and a new treatment setting is both imagined and found—imagined because that setting becomes in fantasy the larger-than-life container for that larger-than-life intensity. In a sense, it is the heir to the Oedipal situation, meant to contain the "badness" of replacing a limited resource with a more powerful one *and* to enact that passionate intensity in a new pair.

The time-limited (by virtue of finances) nature of this patient's treatment may have to some degree contributed to its success. Time-limitation contained rescue fantasies, invited aggression, and pushed toward testing the survival capacities of the therapy. Winnicott (1954a) describes the end of the hour and "the matter of fees" (p. 285) as representing the analyst's hate, which he considers a symbolic provision; so too time-limitation structures into the treatment the hatefulness of ending and to some degree frees the patient from false self burdens.

While much was indeed lived through in this patient's treatment, and important people newly discovered, her difficulties were not fully worked through in three months. Indeed, despite many real changes in the patient's grasp of herself and in her capacities for love and work, there was the risk that this good result might remain encapsulated in its own narcissistic bubble, a kind of "affair space", if not integrated in an experiential way into her subsequent outpatient treatment. It is possible that this patient might need future hospitalisation as a major resource allocation toward the distribution, containment, and interpretation of intense transference, but it is also true that hospitalisation can represent for her a form of flight in response to the dangerous anger that wells up in her when the other person seems insufficiently present. Facing this necessary work both seems and is risky in an outpatient setting. More can be worked through there than therapists sometimes imagine, especially with consultative help (see Chapter Nine), and much depends on the therapist's ability to form an alliance in which aggression can be met and worked with interpretively. Sometimes though, this is not possible, and institutional treatment settings are needed to allow the patient an opportunity for deeper experiential engagement and to allow both parties a chance for reflection on what could not be "opened up", contained, and brought into language in the outpatient work.

CHAPTER SIX

From bodies to words

Bodies

In his discussion of psychosomatic symptoms, Adam Phillips (1996) writes,

> It is the psychoanalytic wish that words can lure bodies back to words . . . It is always worth wondering . . . what picture we have of what words can do to someone's body, of how they work inside him. And conversely, what bodily symptoms . . . can do to our own words and bodies. (p. 36)

Nina Coltart (1986) makes a similar point:

> We could say that a psychosomatic symptom represents that which is determined to remain unconscious, or unknowable, but which at the same time has actually made itself conscious in a very heavy disguise; it is speakable about only in a dense and enigmatic code . . . How do we build a bridge which *really holds* over the secret area of the body-mind divide? Can the unthinkable become thinkable? (p. 198)

The clinical situation to be described in this chapter approaches these questions through the concepts of transitional phenomena and enactment. The patient's presenting symptoms focused around serious substance abuse and depression. His substance abuse began as a way of dealing with migraine headaches, among other bodily symptoms of extreme tension, which itself was related to severe anxiety in his vocational and social life. I hope to illustrate a number of clinical points in this discussion, including: 1) the way in which the constellation of feelings around the patient's drug use replicated in a very specific way, and yet also displaced and disguised, a constellation of feelings around childhood sexual abuse, experiences for which the patient had for many years been amnesic; 2) what came to seem like a corrupt relation between his drug cravings and his psychosomatic symptoms; and 3) most importantly, the way in which the act of substance abuse assumed powerful transference meaning situating the drug's function of affect regulation within a matrix of early object relationships and fantasies.

Drugs and sex

The patient, an appealing but inhibited young man, came to therapy following his third inpatient hospitalisation for substance abuse treatment. His promising career had collapsed because of his addiction to opiate medication, drugs that had actually become his secret solution to the intense anxiety, desperation to please, and frantic over-investment he experienced in his work life. While this level of driven devotion had earned him promotions and the regard of his boss, it was unsustainable, and this basic fact registered as extreme distress in the patient's body. Simultaneously, his first serious love relationship was also collapsing under the strain of his effort to please his partner, his jealous certainty that he could not, and his intense conflict about his own sexual pleasure.

The patient arrived for treatment very depressed, mildly disorganised, full of insecurity and self-criticism, and suffering a number of bodily symptoms of extreme tension: neck and jaw stiffness, backache, stomach upset, and recurrent migraine headaches. For his headaches, that the patient reported and his family observed to be unbearably painful, the internist to whom I refer patients like this—an experienced doctor who is generally very conservative—continued the patient's prescription of potentially addictive pain-killing medication—to be used in limited doses for short periods of time after other remedies for his migraines had been tried. The patient formed a good therapeutic alliance, and, over time, began to recognise that the unbearable anxiety that had led to his addiction had two important contexts as its background: the death of his mother several years before and periodic sexual abuse by a camp counsellor during his latency years. The patient reported, quite believably, that he had repressed the memory of these summer sexual events throughout his rather withdrawn adolescence, but that his beginning to date in college had brought them back with disorganising clarity.

Over time, as this not-particularly-psychologically-minded but hard-working patient put his experiences of addiction and of sexuality into words, and especially as he noticed his associations moving from one to the other recurrently, it began to seem to both of us that a powerful unconscious relationship existed between them. Indeed, it increasingly looked as if the intrapsychic scenario around drug abuse functioned both to hide, but also to represent in disguised form, the specific constellation of repressed feelings and memories relating to sexual abuse. Slowly the patient developed the ability to articulate these feelings, first in relation to drugs and then cautiously in relation to the childhood sexual scenario. He described feelings of emptiness and of being left out, which led to a need for something to make him feel better. The possibility of having this need met by a drug—or by the camp counsellor's attention—brought excitement, craving, and a sense of compulsion. It also brought fear, since he recognised that something forbidden was happening. Both situations also made him feel special and pleasurably powerful. He felt the power to get something he wanted, to have a secret, and to get away with something. Afterward, he felt ashamed, isolated, damaged, and in need of punishment. As though to cement this deepening connection between drug abuse and sexuality, the patient reported that he had taken to using drugs to numb current sexual excitement with his girlfriend because he felt paralysed with her and could not relax into allowing himself sexual pleasure as an adult.

This powerfully convincing phase of therapeutic work, which brought considerable relief to the patient's chronic anxiety and bodily tension, came fully alive in relation to his headaches and his use of prescribed but potentially addictive medication to treat them. As the feelings described above became increasingly conscious to the patient, he came to understand that a corrupt relationship existed between his headaches and his drug cravings. In essence, he realised that he no longer needed medication for his headaches; he needed headaches for the medication. His headaches were the outcome of the burgeoning tension of his craving for pain-relieving medication. Whenever his cravings started, he made efforts to deny and suppress them, while also simultaneously calculating the risks and rationalising the pleasures associated with getting what he wanted. Eventually, a headache would actually develop, which both truly "needed", but also paid off the guilt for, his getting the forbidden substance.

Insight and enactment

Erikson titled one of his collections of essays *Insight and Responsibility* (1964). The patient had come to realise with conviction that he was continuing his addiction (and his psychosomatic symptoms) with medication prescribed by my colleague. What was his responsibility now to his treatment and to the prescriber? And, given that I had referred him to this physician, what was mine? The patient's insight did not lead him to spontaneously initiate a reduction of pain-killing medication; instead he played out the status quo with ever more clarity about what he was doing. In the transference–countertransference situation, I began to feel like the illicit partner in the forbidden childhood scenario, yet I felt it important not to react from a superego position to the collusive aspects of this situation. The patient had made a critical discovery in the midst of our enacting the trouble (enacting it by my providing the forbidden substance through my colleague in the first place, and then by my silence toward him). I felt I had to tolerate this collusion for the time being, so that *from inside the transference situation*, we might find the words to describe the dilemma and its potential meanings. If the psychotherapy could function as a holding environment for this situation, the patient might find a way to take the lead in getting us out of it.

Working through this dilemma began with our recognising the "panic" the patient felt at the thought that his medications would be "taken away" if he spoke honestly to the prescriber. This feeling did not come across as an exaggeration; it was as though some basic life-sustaining connection would be severed or a life-support plug pulled.

I put this highly charged metaphor back to the patient, with the half-formed fantasy in my mind that he clung to his medications the way a panicky young child clings to a security blanket. To my surprise, this psychologically rather unsophisticated patient associated to giving up breast-feeding as an infant. He did indeed discover transitional objects at that time to which he became powerfully, if mournfully, attached. Most of all, he recalled an ongoing unsatisfied craving for his mother during his early childhood, and how uncomprehending his mother seemed to have been about his need for her. Over time, we learned that this youngest child and only son was, among other things, looking to his mother for protection from the ongoing resentment and envy of his physically aggressive older sister. His mother, however, who had lost her own mother early in her life, was oriented more toward pleasing her daughter than setting limits for her. Given the father's prolonged absences because of his career, the patient submerged his anger in a defensive and unworkable identification with his mother, which left him quite vulnerable to the attention of the camp counsellor and later to the demands of his boss.

Suddenly, the early childhood sexuality for which he felt so guilty seemed now to have a complex context to it, including painful experiences of problematic weaning, oral longing, and defensive pleasing of the other. With this new perspective, the patient began to feel the beginnings of empathy for himself. He recalled one particularly disturbing but also paradigmatic scene of early childhood in which his mother simply could not understand why her son was so upset nor could he explain it. This scene captured the "taken away" feeling in the sense that the patient could not reach his mother communicatively, and she lost patience with him and turned her attention elsewhere.

As this understanding took shape, I brought the patient back to our present dilemma, and I suggested to him that rather than telling the prescriber he no longer needed his medication in the amount available, he might take it upon himself to use as little as possible, eventually stopping it altogether. In this way, medication would not be taken away; rather he would be letting it go. This shift of the locus of authority placed the medications into—or more accurately, recognised the medications as already in—a transitional space (Winnicott, 1951) over which the child-in-the-patient feels a sense of rights. In framing this possibility, I was recognising the patient's unconscious needs for both oral nurturance and survivable weaning. The patient took my recommendation fully, used considerably less of an already relatively small amount of medication, and had fewer headaches in the process. He felt much more in charge of himself and more deeply engaged in his therapy.

Survival

There was, however, a crucial next phase to this problem. After a number of months of very little use of his pain-killing medication, the patient made no move in the direction of formally discontinuing the prescription. Instead, he occasionally used it as an anti-anxiety agent, rather than as a treatment for migraines. Once more, I soon had the gathering feeling of being his illicit partner and also the idealised, but in some ways corrupt, father who paid for his absences by allowing his son to do whatever he wanted. Interpretation of this transference–countertransference dynamic, however, did not really take hold until, in Winnicott's (1969) language about a child's coming to be able to "use the object", I moved to place myself outside the patient's projections and inside my connection to my prescribing colleague. In a different language, the patient's transitional relationship to his medication seemed to have drifted contentedly into a low-key omnipotence in relation to it and to me, and I found myself feeling an approaching limit inside myself.

Eventually, I made a focused intervention with the patient. I reviewed with him very specifically what he and I had come to learn about the meaning of these medications both in his history and in the transference, and what their consequences were now for his self-esteem and psychosomatic inclination. I reviewed his experience over some months of doing almost completely without the medications. I noted his own recognition of the importance of moving to a forthright relationship with the prescriber and of taking the risk to trust him to provide what the patient needed should he suffer a recurrence of symptoms in the future. And yet, he had not taken the necessary next step, and I pressed him to examine why. The patient experienced this as a serious confrontation and found himself responding with immediacy and conviction. Why had he avoided the next step? Because then I would experience him without drugs (and without the refuge of their self-managed availability); I would see his "ugly side", especially the side that would want more from me than I could give, and I would not be able to stand it.

In a sense, this was the patient's serious confrontation of me in return, and it opened up the deeper transference feelings toward his mother whom he felt could not stand his childhood needs and to a family culture he saw as buying off ugly needs with pacifying gifts, while keeping up appearances in the process. In the transference fantasy, my allowing these medications had been my pacifying gift all along, one that neither of us would be able to do without. Through this critical exchange, aggression, and the potential that both of us might survive it (Winnicott, 1969), had entered the transference relationship experientially. The patient could now take the risk of leaving us unprotected by fully terminating his prescription, which he did.

Occasional incidents of drug use (the patient was very skilled at acquiring the drugs he needed) occurred thereafter, usually on trips home. Each such incident led to microanalysis and deeper insight. I attempted to maintain a stance of benign neutrality about the state of our alliance around his acquiring further drugs: I neither believed him nor disbelieved him about his being drug-free, a stance that seemed to free him to lead his own effort toward growth. Later in his treatment, he admitted periodic dishonesty with me during this post-prescription phase, each instance of which had to do once again with imagined protection of himself and me. At one point, he thought that I might take his few brief, self-managed relapses as a sign that he needed a drug treatment programme, and "if you had sent me away, I would have felt like killing you", a statement I experienced as containing completely uncensored anger and something in the direction of the rock-bottom dependency within the transference from which people really grow.

Bridges

As noted earlier, Coltart (1986, p. 198) wonders about a "bridge" that "really holds" over "the body-mind divide," the idea of a "divide" describing a split between soma and psyche. Is there an analogue here to Winnicott's (1960, p. 148) description of the gap between the true and false self? The former is primarily bodily experience, "no more than . . . the details of the experience of aliveness", ordinary, and indeed at the beginning, autonomic. Conversely, the "false self" represents a hypertrophied and dissociative form of psychic adaptation, sometimes localised in the mind. Coltart's "bridge" also suggests the concept of instinct, which Freud (1915c, p. 122) tells us exists "on the frontier" between body and mind, as well as the concept of transitional space (Winnicott, 1951), which itself is a form of psychic bridge-building, the restorative experience of enough similarity within difference, or proximity within separateness, such that the self as agent can bridge the gap to the other.

Both concepts seem relevant to the work with this patient. My initial stance regarding his medications might be viewed as instinctual enactment in "that secret area," as Coltart (1986, p. 198) puts it, of body-mind divide. I had allowed my colleague to prescribe addicting medication from the beginning, and then did not initiate discontinuing it once its meaning had become clear and the use of it unnecessary. Had it not been for our longstanding and trusting working relationship, the physician and I could easily have seemed, or actually become, like the patient's parents, absent to each other and absent as a holding pair for the patient. For me, it was essential that I keep both my colleague and the patient in mind as I found my bearings within the enactment. In this space, what the patient and I discovered was the transitional function of the medications. For him, the medications were not only about restoring security through the illusion of omnipotently having what he needed; they were also the proto-symbolic bridge across the early gap between the bodily distress of the needy child and the failures of comprehension (or, in Fonagy's (Fonagy, Gergely, Jurist, & Target , 2002) terms, mentalisation) within his mother. In the transference, they represented his defence against depending fully on me and against the rage he would have felt had I failed him in a similar way.

The patient used this phase of what might be called transitional enactment—that is, enactment in the service of bridging a critical gap between self and other—to wean himself from the medications, but even more to rediscover the lost child within what he had taken to be only the bad child. My recommendation to him about his taking it upon himself to reduce and discontinue his medications functioned technically as an interpretation of the transitional meaning of the medications and conveyed to him that I understood something he felt his mother had not. In the context of a now stronger therapeutic alliance, he could take more risks.

This phase of enactment, however, eventually had to come to a complete end if a genuine and durable level of dependency on me and on those who helped me was to be achieved. This latter move meant the patient's forfeiting the protections of transitional space, giving up his medications altogether, and risking a directness of aggression between us. As we worked through and lived through this successfully, the patient was able to take up a job, in which he worked hard but did not feel driven to please, and to his great amazement, he began a sexually fulfilling love relationship with a woman.

Actions and words

Analytic literature on substance abuse rightly highlights its *function* of affect regulation (Khantzian, 1999). What I hope to have illustrated in this focused clinical contribution is the *meaning* within the act itself: the way in which a constellation of feelings and unconscious fantasies in relation to the act of substance abuse played out a specific childhood scenario in the transference related to childhood sexual abuse. The anxiety, anger, and guilt related to his sexuality were lodged in the patient's body in the painful psychosomatic tension states that seriously interrupted his functioning. His letting go of his psychosomatic symptoms, his drugs, and in the transference his conflicted claim on his mother came about first through the establishment of a transitional space in which I was positioned as his secret, potentially collusive partner.

Within this "secret partner" relationship, as perhaps had also been true to some degree with the camp counsellor, I carried the condensation of two sets of transference elements. First, like his mother before weaning, I was to continue the supply of love, solace, and holding-in-mind that he felt he so abruptly lost. I was to be the silent, maternal partner of early life, who disappears into the child's illusion that he actually has rights over this bit of the external world, indeed that he has invented it in the first place. But, second, I eventually felt something quite powerful in the countertransference, and this feeling too needed to be integrated into the treatment, as both an understanding and an intervention. Indeed, I felt the patient's longing to move beyond the imprisoning dyad with his mother and to contact the too frequently absent father, someone who might step into the frustrated estrangement between mother and son, and mobilise and survive the potentially progressive aggression in that earlier relationship. The sexuality with the camp counsellor, for all its seriously damaging effects, represented, from this angle, a push forward in psychosexual development, an effort to find a man who could help him move beyond the maternal relationship. The complex collusion around substance abuse—my both joining it and then limiting it—served the same purpose.

This phase of enactment within the psychotherapy was eventually terminated less by interpretation than by my decision, based on my assessment of his developing insight and strengths, to confront this form of relating as a newly evolved resistance. His action met mine. These moments require careful "handling", which is Winnicott's (1954a) word for that early child care process in which the primary care-taker introduces and re-introduces the baby to her body through the communicative quality of physical ministrations. There may be a corollary in analysis in which, perhaps especially with psychosomatic patients, our words, our thinking, and our voice "handle" the patient's psyche (Sacksteder, 1989), bridge the "divide" between physicality and mindfulness, and facilitate the process of bringing "bodies back to words".

On the other hand, "handling" is first of all a maternal function, and, as I have noted, my interpretive words with this patient did not truly effect the enactment until I changed my location, so to speak, and moved in the direction represented by my prescribing colleague. Perhaps, transitional space, for all its generative potential, had with this patient settled into a defensive, simply dyadic space, the un-integratable space of secret gratification and omnipotent illusion. The move I needed to make was toward Thirdness (Muller, 1996): concretely, toward the third party of the internist; transferentially, toward the third party of the father; and symbolically, toward the social order in which I had my role and my patient might eventually find his. Winnicott's insight into the use of the object (1969) can also be read as describing this crucial opening onto Thirdness. What he most uniquely adds to the understanding of Thirdness is that it is discovered in early development through destructiveness and survival.

This destructiveness, quiet though it may have been with this patient, registered in the countertransference and needed to become the basis for non-retaliatory analytic responsiveness from a place outside transitional space. The patient's transitional enactment with me needed to be met, after some time, with a return action from me— a mobilising of the growing feeling in *my* body—in order for words to assume and carry psychic weight. The "bridge" in this clinical situation between soma and psyche was in effect a two-step process, beginning with the establishment of a transitional space—and an enactment within it—and ending with the discovery of workable otherness.

CHAPTER SEVEN

Illusion and desire

It is a fact, though a paradoxical one, that psychoanalysts now tend to consider illusion as a psychic category and to refer to it in a specific way. Today the term would find its place in a dictionary of psycho-analysis . . . and Winnicott is undoubtedly responsible for this. But remember, too, the ambiguous function of illusion in Lacan: the ego as a place of *misunderstanding*, the object as a bait for desire. (Pontalis, 1981, p. 77)

I n this statement, Pontalis links some of the fundamental insights of Winnicott and Lacan. The object as "bait for desire" invites a consideration of the Imaginary Order (Lacan, 1977), a narcissistic degeneration of desire into a demand for a mirroring other whose own desire excites a sense of self—how true or how false being open to question—into coherence. Lacan's Imaginary underlines the impor-tance of recognition and of mis-recognition in psychic development.

Contrast Pontalis' statement with a comment by the great historian of Chinese science, Joseph Needham (1969, p. 176): "Only the wholly other can inspire the deepest love and the profoundest desire to learn". In this statement, desire has shifted from a mirroring other to a separate other, from the safety of sameness to the awesomeness of difference. Developmentally, the arena of difference was conceptu-alised by Winnicott as involving a transition from the object as subjec-tive to the object as objective, a transition crucially determined by the subject's destructiveness and the object's survival. A similar transition can be considered in Lacan's theory: if a desire to learn presupposes the recognition and acceptance of lack or insufficiency in oneself, then we have entered the Symbolic Order.

These concepts are inextricably a part of our daily clinical work. The desire to have or to fulfil *vs.* the desire to learn is a fulcrum on which the clinical weight of the moment is always balanced. In this chapter, I will present a detailed case report from a French analyst of a patient who could be seen as having lived out a mirroring illusion in his relationship with his mother and then in the transference (Peraldi, 2010). At a certain point in the analysis, a point unconsciously pre-determined by the patient, an exchange occurred between patient and analyst that totally shifted the atmosphere of the analysis and the patient's way of being. It is also a moment that illustrates the phenom-enon of sudden change in analysis, as evidenced by a major shift in the patient's psychic position, especially in his relationship to desire.

Three years

A single man came to analysis for several reasons: a writing in-hibition, fear of authority, a feeling of being trapped in a loving but oppressive relationship with his domineering mother, and most im-mediately, his failing his final music conservatory examination. In the initial consultation, the analyst was struck with the patient's way of carrying himself and his style of speaking: he made no gestures what-soever and spoke only in an elegant rhetorical fashion. At the end of the interview, the patient said that he thought three years of analysis would suffice and that he had made financial arrangements for that. The analyst knew that the patient knew that the length of analysis could not be decided in advance. Without commenting on this, he accepted him into treatment.

The patient had initially been a literature student and had hoped for a literary career. His writing inhibition and his mother's pushing him toward the conservatory interrupted this ambition. The patient knew nothing of his father's family. He did know that when his maternal grandmother died, his mother and her sister took care of their father and their much younger brother, who himself died a few years later. The patient was named for this uncle. The mother's father had been a butcher and had become senile after his wife's death. The patient recalled nothing of his life before the age of four. He remembered having no relationship with his father whom he saw as silent and disinterested, but he adored his mother and aunt. He recalled his mother's entertaining him with elaborate fairy tales and stories. He would sit in her lap every evening until he was thirteen years old. If he was anxious, he would cry for the chair, and his mother would hold him, rock him, and tell him stories.

The first three years of his treatment were filled with a fascinating display of memories and childhood images, like the fictional world built up between mother and son. The patient also nurtured an imaginary connection to the analyst through admiring references to a literary friend of the analyst. The analyst reported that he remained relatively inactive and very often silent during these three years, actively refraining from the enthralling power of the patient's narrative and from colluding in a mutual enthrallment. The patient interpreted this silence in two ways. First, it was the silence of his father, representing indifference or contempt, that the patient must strive to overcome. Second, he interpreted this silence as the position he himself occupied as a child, dazzled and overwhelmed by his mother's stories, just as he hoped to dazzle and enthral the analyst. During these first three years, no conflict occurred within the analysis.

Illusion

Luepnitz (2009) and Kirshner (2011) have written evocatively of working in the space between Winnicott and Lacan, and it is this clinical space that I would like to explore. From a Winnicottian point of view, this long phase of enactment by the patient and silence by the analyst might be seen as a phase of illusion. In the transference, the patient excitedly surrounds the analyst, who is experienced as a subjective object, something of the patient's own creation. In this space, speech is slippery. The analyst felt that interpretive speech on his part could easily become ensnared in the patient's longing to be the object of the analyst's story telling. In Lacan's view, the patient is not necessarily seeking insight; the desire of human beings is to *be* the desire of the other, their total completion, their mirror. Hence, the Lacanian emphasis on the snare or the lure that hooks the other's desire. Winnicott (1951), though, might argue that this phase of semi-omnipotence and re-living in the present is necessary as the foundation for something else. Transitional object relating is indeed magic, but it's also a magical reversal of time and loss. Thus, though it may serve defensive functions, it may also be essential to the patient's regaining a sense of power and relatedness.

For Winnicott, the outcome of satisfactory transitional object experience—the magical experience of "I need, I have" supplied by an as-yet un-discovered partner—is the child's robust confidence that he can find or make what he needs in a truly cathected world. The analyst's silence, in the face of the patient's enactment, could be seen as allowing for that sufficiency of the experience of illusion—that no-questions-asked space about the illusion of mother–son togetherness—necessary to manage anxiety preliminary to facing it, and preliminary as well to the differentiated experience of personal desire. It is clinically interesting that the illusion is sustained. The patient never pushes things toward delusion, or toward requiring confirmation, or disconfirmation from the analyst, and the analyst never feels called upon to either collude with or to transgress the patient's relatedness.

Graduation

As the three-year mark approached, the patient was indeed feeling considerably better. But the analyst had early on noted to himself "warning signs": the patient's failure to pass the examination, which this Lacanian analyst thought of as Winnicottian (1956a) anti-social behaviour; the patient's periodic heavy silences; an early dream in which the patient's mother had gone insane and he had said to himself "This time is it; we can't stop it". Finally, there was a dream just before the first session: the patient was happily in a car with a friendly unknown man who was driving from the back seat. A yellow car cut them off. Later he witnessed a conflict between international powers. Someone gave him documents that would protect him. He only pretended to accept them because he knew he would get out without having to take part in the conflict.

The analyst's act of holding these warning signs in mind across long stretches of time and experience is precisely what Winnicott meant by a holding environment. The analyst holds the markers of that which the patient has not yet integrated, indeed that he has defensively dis-integrated. What might these particular markers mean? The analyst considered the failure of the exam to be a manifestation of the anti-social tendency, which has to do with the child's impulsive grasping for that which has been deprived to him, and which by rights is his. So, at this moment of potential graduation from the conservatory, this young man steals back his freedom and unconsciously refuses closure within the false self relationship with his mother, whose demand it was that he became a musician in the first place.

The patient's heavy silences and the dream of losing his mother to psychotic depression speak to a side of the material that has yet to come into the work, a void not filled by the patient's and his mother's manic storytelling. They hint at a specific early environmental failure: maternal depression with which the patient himself may be identified. Finally, the dream with, one assumes, the analyst driving from behind the couch. The pleasantness is cut across, and the happy young man becomes a witness. There are documents that can ultimately protect, but the patient only pretends to accept them, believing he will get through without having to take part in the conflict. Is this the patient's prediction of the scenario of his treatment? Living out a false self or imaginary dynamic, he will appear to accept something, but he will actually hold himself apart from the process. He will get through untouched. He will at all costs avoid bearing witness. From a Lacanian perspective, he is not ready to inscribe himself in the Symbolic Order (Muller, personal communication).

Thus, the patient approaches another equally false graduation: his three-year limit, his way of getting out before getting in. Winnicott might see this arbitrary time frame as an extreme of self-holding, a temporal skin so to speak, a boundary that prevents real contact but that also allows whatever sort of contact there has been. In Lacanian terms, the Imaginary offers refuge from the Real, the Real for this patient being perhaps his impulse to call for the couch and to be swallowed permanently in his identification with the analyst–mother, whose need for him is measured by the depth of her depression.

Change

At the end of the three years, the patient had a dream. He and the analyst were looking at a fantastic show with two actresses on stage, one playing Marie Antoinette, the other her sister. At the same time, the patient *was* Marie Antoinette, walking to her death in a beautiful costume. The executioner could be seen in a shadowy corner of the stage. The analyst asked, "What is underneath that beautiful costume?" After a silence, the patient replied "a sickly body" using a peculiar though accurate word for "sickly". What an odd question at first glance! It comes from the Lacanian idea that the mirror image—the basis for the imaginary deceptions of the ego—is first grasped as a cover—a costume even—offering an illusory wholeness to the child who as yet can only feel inadequacy or fragmentation in the area of body control.

Soon after this exchange, the patient said, "I've come for three years, which is what I had planned on. I feel better; I'll finish at the end of the month". The analyst replied: "Yes, you have finished something, but you had decided to put an end to your analysis before you had even begun. Now that you have reached the end, perhaps *you* can really begin your analysis." The patient was struck by these words and for a number of sessions was very quiet, after which he decided to continue.

Following this, there was a complete change in the atmosphere of the analysis. Gestures occurred, and the patient's speech developed rhythm, exclamation, and detour. Play seemed to have entered the system. Moreover, the analyst's silence was felt now as totally supportive. Instead of continuing to speak about his mother or to re-enact his relationship to her, the patient began with great difficulty to discover his early relationship with his father. He slowly recalled his father as an active man, before the patient was four, who taught his little boy how to do things with his hands and who had quietly approved of his son's achievements. Coinciding with these memories of his relationship to his father around handicraft, the patient's writing inhibition lifted Once rediscovered, this relationship to his father served as a protection as he began to explore a more dangerous aspect of his experience of his mother.

Two becoming three

What a remarkable set of events! From a Lacanian point of view, there seems to have been a shift from one order of experience, the

Imaginary, to another, the Symbolic, pivoting around the exchange at the three-year mark. Indeed it seems as though the analyst has called the patient to this different order from what Lacan would think of as "the place of the third", a place outside the mother–son symbiosis. In Winnicottian (1969) terms, the patient has moved from relating to the other as part of the self to using the other for what he might actually have to offer. This fundamental developmental shift, opening the self to what an art historian (Hughes, 1981) calls "the shock of the new", has to do with placing the other outside the patient's projective processes and is accomplished, says Winnicott, through destruction and the other's survival of that destruction.

Might we think of the patient's decision to terminate after three years as that act of destruction? Taken against the analyst as a fantasy object, this act and the analyst's response, indicating his survival with technique intact, placed the analyst outside the patient's self-object realm and offered him the exhilarating experience of reality, a reality in which someone with expertise was holding his three years so far and inviting him to let go of the self-holding. Thus, the patient came to feel the deep support of the analytic setting. This is the regression to genuine dependency Winnicott (1954a, 1960) considered essential to successful treatment of serious disturbance. For a long time, the patient held himself to guarantee his survival in a setting that, Winnicott argues, necessarily duplicates the early maternal failure. But the work must eventually bring the patient to risk allowing true dependence on this new setting and person, experienced now as real and reliable.

"Now that you have reached the end, perhaps you can really begin your analysis." These words brought about sudden change in the patient and in the total atmosphere and material of the analysis. They were spoken with authority and recognition. In Lacan's terms, they inflicted a "cut", a symbolic castration, in the fantasy of imaginary wholeness or completion. As his Marie Antoinette dream depicted, the patient and analyst were indeed watching him walk toward another termination, but underneath the extravagant identification with a woman, the body was still sick and the "cut" he was walking toward would sever him from his mind. The analyst's "cut" used speech to recognise lack: unfinishedness at a moment of imaginary finishing. His words fit well with Winnicott's remarks at the end of his paper on the True and False Self:

A principle might be enunciated, that in the False Self area of analytic practice, we find we make more headway by recognition of the patient's non-existence than by a long-continued working with the patient on the basis of ego-defense mechanisms . . . (T)his (latter) un-rewarding work is only *cut* short profitably when the analyst can point to and specify an absence of some essential feature: 'you have no mouth', 'you have not started to exist yet' . . . (T)his recognition of important fact, made clear at the right moment, paves the way for communication with the True Self . . . (The) False Self . . . deceives the analyst if the latter fails to notice that, regarded as a whole function-ing person, the False Self . . . lacks something, and that something is the essential central element of creative originality. (1960, p. 152, my italics)

Perhaps you can begin

The shift in the patient's psychic position is, I would argue, from living as the desire *of* the other to an original moment, the beginning discovery of desire *for* an other, in relation to which learning must occur and actual help can be offered. What the patient then finds is that third figure in his family, his father, whom he, perhaps not coin-cidentally, lost after three years. Both Winnicott and Lacan believe that children find ways of recording the early life situations in which they have been seriously failed. "Three years" may have been such a signifier, as though the patient had been saying to the absent father–analyst from the start "I will lose you after I'm three". The word for "sickly" was also a critically important signifier.

This word in French contained two parts. One related to the word "malignancy" and opened up the devastation of breast cancer through four generations on his mother's side. The second part had to do with anger and with the word "rat". The patient recalled that his father had killed a rat in the family restaurant when he was a boy. He then made inquiries about his mother's father, who had been a butcher, like the executioner in the dream. He learned that before becoming senile this grandfather had become criminally insane, not only butchering shop animals against accepted standards, but also butchering house pets. His daughters had him committed to a mental institution when he became physically threatening toward them.

The patient felt that these horrific secrets had been hidden from him his entire life behind his mother's manic chatter. At the core of their relationship, however, was her deep depression, from which he had had to protect her. In Winnicott's terms (1948), he had been her magically reparative object, the one who not only would make her happy, but whom she would successfully comfort and animate, as she had not been able to save her brother—the patient's namesake—or her father. But in this process, anything aggressive in her son, anything too individuating or too representative of the horror she had experienced with her father, had to be defensively disintegrated, thus leading to the symptoms that brought the patient into treatment. These last parts of the analysis were painful, sobering, liberating, and deeply maturational for this patient.

Après coup

It is a Lacanian truism that Oedipus never went through the Oedipus complex. Oedipus never encountered within himself the experience of the desires, and their forbiddenness, that have become—via psychoanalysis—synonymous with his name. Rather, he was actually named for the mark left on him by his troubled father in the course of the latter's terrified and murderous abandoning him to fate. Oedipus blindly lived out this fate only to learn *after the fact* its meaning. His impulsively blinding himself was a mad effort to stop seeing what he had already done. It was only later, at Colonus, that Oedipus, now like Tiresias, could see in his blindness and realise so deeply that he did not know what he was doing and never *wanted* to do it. Oedipus did not enact Oedipal desires. He was not a subject of his own desires; rather he was the subject of—or more accurately, to—desires at the parental level. He represented something unbearable for them, that ultimately found concrete expression, though not signification—until it was too late—in his name.

The same could be said of the patient whose treatment I have been discussing. His name, too, made him a signifier of his mother's traumatic and denied history (Fromm, 2012). In a sense, the analytic situation represents the possibility of interpreting the patient-as-signifier such that the work of truly bearing witness can be undertaken. The movement is from illusion, the imaginary of deep transference relatedness, to some sense of reality, finiteness, and contact with the more "wholly" other. Perhaps we should include the homophonic meaning of that adjective here: the "holy" other that one sees more clearly now as human and who can be both loved and learned about. This comes about through the quietly held "otherness" of the analyst and, at some point, the patient's unconscious invitation to engage that otherness at its deepest levels.

"Perhaps now you can begin." Pontalis, with whom I began this chapter, titled his autobiography *Love of Beginnings* (1993). The beginning for this patient represented his birth, not without birth trauma, as a desiring subject. Winnicott calls it a "starting point" (1963b, p. 192), and it is one way to describe the end of our work.

CHAPTER EIGHT

Unconscious creative activity and the restoration of reverie

Activity

"Concepts can never be presented to me merely; they must be knitted into the structure of my being, and this can only be done through my own activity" (Follett, 1930, quoted in Milner, 1957, p. xi). So begins, epigrammatically, Marion Milner's intensely personal study, *On Not Being Able to Paint* (1957). This moving articulate reverie lays out for us the human subject in the process of finding her subjectivity, a process of both excitement and peril. As a psychoanalytic text, it is without precedent and without duplication since. As Michael Podro (1990) writes, "What has been largely absent (within psychoanalytic considerations of painting) is an insight into how the activity of painting itself was a matter of urgency and of satisfaction: how painting was itself valuable to us" (p. 401).

It is precisely this "urgency" that catches a dimension of creative activity akin to the clinical, and indeed, so attuned, one easily finds clinical examples of activity, in some distinction to interpretation, as critically important vehicles for the mastery and integration of unconscious feeling and for, in Kohut's terms (1977), the restoration of self. This largely unconscious process may offer another angle on what it means to work through. But the emphasis in the Follett quote on "my own activity" may obscure the degree to which creative activity always takes place in some relational context, within which such activity might also be quite vulnerable. In this chapter, I hope to illustrate the creative use of activity to deal with developmental challenges, but also how dependent that creativity can be on a primary relationship in the person's life.

In an earlier paper (Fromm, 1989b), I noted a passing observation made by Masud Khan (1963). Describing his adolescent patient's effort to recover from a serious breakdown, Khan commented on "the strange way this youth found his way back to mobility and aliveness through skating" (p. 179). I gave two further examples of this process of the investment of energy in an activity corollary to working toward the restoration of psychic health. The first involved an unplanned child, born to older parents, both fully involved in their work lives, whose other children were already in their teens. In early childhood, this youngest fell from a dock into the water and was rescued by a sibling. He suffered from asthma attacks, especially at night, within which intense feelings of dependency on his mother, panic about separation, and struggles for control were expressed and enacted. Though he lived very near the sea and the beach was a favourite local playground, he remained frightened of the water, to the extent that he mastered swimming at a considerably later time than his buddies.

Once he did, however, swimming assumed a central place in the restructuring of a weakened sense of self. Through swimming, he turned passively experienced trauma into active mastery. Swimming became a vehicle for the integration of competence, self-sufficiency, masculinity, the ability to separate and return, and very importantly, the ability to face the feared constriction of breath and to accomplish a regularity of breathing. In his later years, following a marital crisis he felt to be life-threatening, so anxiety-arousing he at times could not breathe, he managed the aftermath by spontaneously returning to swimming. Again, this activity stabilised him and renewed him as a strong person, capable of self-sufficiency and of agency in the face of threat. During his therapy, swimming took on an additional function; it became a primary occasion for reverie, as though through involving his body in rhythmic mastering and calming activity, he had created a physical setting in which to be in touch with himself.

My second example became the central subject of the paper mentioned above. It described a young man who spontaneously discovered the activity of photography at the time of his mother's death. This young man's story suggested strongly the developmental connection between the activity of photography and his first transitional object, a blanket cathected powerfully in early childhood in a context of maternal illness. This clinical example persuaded me that what Erikson calls "the silent doings of ego synthesis" (1956, p. 57) might be extended to include the silent work of transitional activity. This work, like this young man's photography, temporarily relieves the subject of the unbearable strain of reality acceptance by allowing him the sense of his creative capacity to invest the world anew and to make and hold aspects of it. For the young photographer, his creative ability to stop time mitigated his serious potential for catastrophic reaction to the loss of his mother and the dangerous possibility that he might turn permanently away from the reality of such a depleted world.

This example and others invite our attention to organic activities of self-healing. I am quite sure that there are many important functions for an activities programme within a treatment centre, but perhaps this is one of them (J. Erikson, 1976)—not so much as an activities "therapy", which risks disruption through interpretation, but through the provision of space and support for personally found and personally meaningful activity. At stake here is the whole question of sublimation as an unconscious healing process. As a treatment value, the importance of which may be directly proportionate to the degree of disturbance of the patient, its jeopardy in this era of very short-term and rigidly structured treatment programmes is of great consequence.

On not being able to paint

Another way of speaking about this "gyroscopic function"" (Sandler & Sandler, 1986) and as well about the "silent doings of ego synthesis" (Erikson, 1956, p. 57) would be in those terms relatively unique to Marion Milner, Winnicott and others in the "middle school" of British psychoanalysis. These terms accent the human subject's ongoing task of relating inner and outer experience. It was Winnicott's (1951) genius to bring together a paediatric and psychoanalytic attention on the unnoticed but obvious experience of early childhood around security objects. He quickly realised that these "objects", like the teddy bear, occupied a psychic position for the child between inner experience and outer experience; they were thus "transitional", less important as objects in themselves, than as the vehicles for necessary psychic and physical activity. This activity intermingled the benignly omnipotent early sense of self with the realities of separateness and differentiation. As such, it prefigured and precipitated the birth of fully symbolic activity.

Elsewhere (Fromm, 1989a), I have noted some of the theoretical links between Winnicott's work and Erikson's, two brilliant paediatrically-oriented psychoanalysts working simultaneously on different sides of the Atlantic. Echoing Erikson's more elaborated explication of the mutuality in the developing life cycle, Winnicott argues that the human individual is never free from the strain of relating inner and outer experience. It can be argued that it was Marion Milner's genius to have illustrated what he meant before he said it, and to have shown us that such integration is not only the carrying out of an essential function, but, at least for some, the source of creativity as well.

In *On Not Being Able to Paint* (1957), one of several autobiographical books, Milner studies creativity from the vantage point of herself as a "Sunday painter" making her own efforts to learn to draw and paint. Milner discovers, in first-hand ways that come through with the authenticity and freshness of a person speaking to herself, some of the parallels between the painter and the analytic patient. As Anna Freud writes in the "Introduction" to Milner's book:

> Both ventures, the analytic as well as the creative one, seem to demand similar external and internal conditions. There is the same need for "circumstances in which it is safe to be absent-minded" . . . there is the same unwillingness to transgress beyond the reassuring limits of the secondary process and "to accept chaos as a temporary stage". There is the same fear of the "plunge into no-differentiation" and the disbelief in the "spontaneous ordering forces" which emerge, once the plunge is taken. There is, above all, the same terror of the unknown. (Milner, 1957, p. xiii)

Milner captures the oppressiveness and the reassurances of conscious logic and preconceived ideas when it comes to creativity. She describes the defensive interference with, and the reach to closure of, the creative process when the uncertainty could not be borne further. Note again that all of this describes what is at stake emotionally in the *activity* of painting, rather than, as is often the case in psychoanalytic discussions of this subject, in what a particular painting might mean, either as a set of images or as a psycho-historical event. There is a correspondence here with the work of Anton Kris (1982) and Christopher Bollas (2002) who speak of the establishment of the process of free association, not as a prerequisite for psychoanalytic therapy, but as its basic therapeutic action and outcome.

Milner's table of contents captures the simplicity and the truly personal nature of the encounter between the inner and outer worlds: "What the eye likes", "Being separate and being together", "The plunge into color", "The necessity of illusion" (p. vii). In one of her later chapters, she discusses personally invested activity as the "medium" for the relating of inner and outer life, and so introduces what to my mind is a psychoanalytic term of equal importance to that of the "frame" (see Chapter One). In the following lengthy passage, she outlines this concept, including its developmental and treatment significance, and, almost in passing, suggests a diagnostic schema of some interest to analysts working with pre-Oedipal psychological conditions:

> The problem of the relation between the painter and his world . . . became basically a problem of one's own need and the needs of the "other", a problem of reciprocity between "you" and "me"; with "you" and "me" meaning originally mother and child. But if this was the earth from which the foundations for true dialogue relations with the outside world should spring, did they always get established there? . . . It looked as if for many people they only became established partially, that there were always certain areas of psychic country in which they failed; and what was established instead, as always when dialogue relationship fails, was dictatorship, the dominance of one side or the other. It seemed that in those areas in which one had lost hope of making any real contact with the outside world one of three things could happen. First one could try to deny the external demand and become an active, dictatorial egoist, actively denying the need of the other, trying to make one's own wishes alone determine what happened. Secondly one could become a passive egoist, retreating from public reality altogether and taking refuge in a world of unexpressed

dreams, becoming remote and inaccessible. Thirdly, one could allow the outside world to become dictator, one could fit in to external reality and its demands, but fit in all too well; the placating of external reality could become one's main preoccupation; doing what other people wanted could become the centre of life; one could become seduced by objectivity into complete betrayal of one's own side of the matter . . ..

This idea of being seduced by objectivity raised again the whole question of the actual ways in which one's relation to the outside world develops, from the moment of birth onwards. It suggested that such a dictatorship of the external could be set up in infancy, even with the best of intentions on the part of the adults, simply by inability to give time for the wish to enter into relationship to come from the child's end; thus the establishing of reciprocity could fail simply because the child's time rhythms of need and wish are different from the adult's. Or not only could it fail from wrong timing, it could fail through inability to establish communication, since the child's small gestures of relationship are so easily overlooked or misunderstood. Of course this failure of relationship is inevitable at times, it is part of the agonizing side of being a child; but here came in the particular aspect of the free drawing method that apparently made it partly able to compensate for that failure, able to act as a bridge between the public and the private worlds. For by it one could find an "other", a public reality, that was very pliant and undemanding; pencil and chalk and paper provided a simplified situation in which the other gave of itself easily and immediately to take the form of the dream, it did not stridently insist on its own public nature . . . So by means of this there could perhaps come about the correcting of the bias of a too docilely accepted public vision and a denied private one. And apparently it could come about just because there was this experience of togetherness with one's medium lived through together. Because of this one could reclaim some of the lost land of one's experience, find in the medium, in its pliability yet irreducible otherness, the "other" that had inevitably had to fail one at times in one's first efforts at realizing togetherness. Granted that it was a very primitive togetherness, one that allowed the other only a very small amount of identity of its own, yet it did seem able to serve as the essential basis for a more mature form in which both other and self have an equal claim to the recognition of needs and individuality; just as psycho-analysis does through the analyst acting as a pliant medium, giving back the patient's own thought to him, in a clarified form, rather than intruding his own needs and ideas. (pp. 116–118).

Milner (1969) describes in detail the treatment of one of her more seriously disturbed patients and the importance of this patient's painting in her recovery. The patient speaks of her illness as a "breakdown into reality" (p. 10). She thus captures one side of the catastrophe potentially suffered by the developing self too early disillusioned about its capacity to relate to the outer world; this area of illusion is either forced toward delusion, says Winnicott (1951), or toward a collapse of the self into a depleted relation to reality. In contrast is the essential, if silent, partnership between child and primary care-taker, whose easy adaptation to the child's needs provides an ordinary experience of omnipotence, the experience of "I want, I have", which becomes the grounding for a confident, creative relationship to the world. It is this relational background to the breakdown and restoration of creativity that I will now try to illustrate through parallel reports of a patient's psychotherapy and her work with her art teacher.

Breakdown and engagement

The patient is someone for whom this idea of a breakdown into reality made sense. Her breakdown in life, which occurred shortly after she left home to attend college, felt to her like the final movement in a gradual loss of the formerly sustaining illusion that she was emotionally connected to others. In college, she fell into a deep aloneness without the psychic ability to conjure up any feeling of inner life or relatedness. In this state, she could never allow herself to relax or even to sleep fully; instead she felt compelled to frantically grasp for people.

Talking about the chaotic and clinging relationships in her life during her effort to live alone, the patient became reflective: "Even some of the bad experiences with people were still experiences, like paint thrown on the blank, empty canvas of my life before and since". She once thought of herself as a puppet that had a life as long as someone was pulling the strings. Early in her therapy, she saw herself as without a puppet master, collapsed on a dark stage, helpless, alone, but free and beginning to discover an inner life, at first only through the experience of self-inflicted pain.

One of the patient's first statements in therapy was: "I always felt that I have been totally uninteresting. I'd never be the topic at the dinner table or at school. I don't have anything of a self that interests people, that strongly grabs people. I have no energy to do that. I'm a dead and deadening person. I don't make waves". This statement fit with an early impression I had of her: that, given her attributes and experiences so far in life, she could be seen as quite an interesting person, but that she had totally lost interest in herself. Her statement contrasts strongly, however, with the series of tidal wave dreams that almost immediately followed, dreams that conveyed her inner conviction that she could not manage what was indeed intensely alive within her by herself.

The patient felt that her teachers had never listened to her and recalled how her peers had teased her as "spacey". I came to feel that part of her difficulty might be thought of as a disturbance in the capacity for reverie. Early on, the therapeutic action of the work seemed to have to do with moments of silence or lull in the hour, moments when her demand for me to fill that space betrayed her conviction of total lack within herself. It was a good sign when she eventually became surprised, even delighted, to find that "something comes next". The therapeutic task had to do with the transformation of the patient's "spaciness" into free association (Bollas, 2002), and the way that the therapeutic relationship legitimised this process as not only productive (which was a highly charged value for her), but also a vital function. She had been an amateur though accomplished singer, but had become terrified of forgetting her lines. Her conviction that her mind would not work automatically to remember her lines related to this disturbance of reverie, and reflected also what she took to be her family's belief that she would not work naturally to become an educated person. Within this way of seeing things, however, I felt it important to hold for myself the distinction between nurturing and relying on an organic integrative drive and the more problematic idea that the patient's growth could be taken for granted, that she and it would go on by itself.

This understanding of my patient brought me back to a passage in the "Appendix" of Milner's book *On Not Being Able to Paint* (1957):

> The expressive word "reverie" has been . . . largely dropped from the language of psycho-pathology, and the overworked word phantasy made to carry such a heavy burden of meaning. "Reverie" does emphasize the aspect of absent-mindedness, and therefore . . . the

necessity for a certain quality of protectiveness in the environment. For there are obviously many circumstances in which it is not safe to be absent-minded; it needs a setting, both physical and mental . . . a physical setting in which we are free, for the time being, from the need for immediate practical expedient action and . . . a mental setting, an attitude, both in the people around and in oneself, a tolerance of something which may at moments look very like madness. . ..

Just as sleep dreaming is necessary (said Freud) to preserve sleep, so both conscious and unconscious daydreaming is necessary to preserve creative being awake. Clinical psycho-analytic experience suggests that many of the impediments to going forward into living are the result of a failure of the child's environment to provide the necessary setting for such absent-mindedness. For it seems likely that, in this phase of not distinguishing the "me" and the "not-me" we are particularly vulnerable to the happenings in the inner life of those nearest to us emotionally. (pp. 163–164)

This patient "always knew" she could not take care of herself in college. She had felt sheltered, spoiled, nagged, and defined by her parents' idealised images of her as well as their demonised images of her sister. On the other hand, she felt that she had never been trusted, taught or, in a certain sense, left alone to find herself. She knew "for sure" that when the puppetry was over, she would collapse, as indeed she did. She did not know that this edge of her life, this flat-earth moment of leaving home for college, may well have been such an edge because it had been, in quite different ways, for both of her parents. She had come to a critical moment of identity formation, the late adolescent version of "distinguishing the 'me' and the 'not me' ", and she was indeed "particularly vulnerable to the happenings in the inner life of those nearest to [her]" (Milner, 1957, p. 164).

The patient was certain that she could not meet this developmental challenge. She knew that she would be utterly alone and utterly resourceless, despite a fine intelligence, talents, a pleasant-enough personality, and her family's material resources. She also sensed that her family's difficulties with ordinary dependency and loss might lead them to attack, as she herself did, those feelings in her. Thus she experienced this moment of separation not only as falling into space, but as leading to rage and narcissistic disappointment should she try to return. This absence of play in the intrapsychic and familial systems, this absence of in-between space and room for experiment and rapprochement, seemed to guarantee for this patient enormous anxiety and almost certain failure at the task of separation.

An interesting feature of both parents' earlier life development was the way in which their own areas of necessary illusion had suffered assault. In early adulthood, the patient's father felt terribly traumatised by seeing "too much too soon" as a young military recruit. On the other side, the patient's mother felt crushed by her own mother's cruel life lessons, one of which used her daughter's doll as vehicle of the instruction. This harsh and possibly envious action seemed to echo a generation later in the patient's nihilism and her experience of external life as crushing her internal life. As a kind of generational transmission (Fromm, 2012), her mother's longing to resuscitate the lost potential of the mother–daughter relationship may well have expressed itself in her description of the patient as a baby: "Like a doll; people were shocked that she moved".

On Not Being Able to Paint opens for us a window onto anxiety-driven resistances to engagement in a creative relation to the world. In this patient's treatment, this seemed like the first and in some ways the most basic problem. It seemed to me that my task was to offer "a setting for absent-mindedness" (Milner, 1957, p. 164), an opportunity for a silence that might become generative. But to do that, I would have to be fully present with her, and this turned out to be, at least at the beginning, the most difficult part of the work. The patient created in me the experience of her, in her own extreme terms, as "dead and deadening", as superficial and disconnected, and as trying to cover that inner sense of emptiness with half-hearted demands that I feed her. At one point a friend had harshly accused her of "sucking my blood", needing too much, but my experience of her, in spite of her demands, was that she did not suck at all; as she said, "I don't grab". This way of being seemed like the current version within the analytic setting of an actual and sudden early childhood illness that the patient had suffered, in which listlessness and lack of appetite were serious symptoms.

This is almost certainly what led me to welcome those occasions when tension developed in the hours or when direct questions occurred. I found myself taking those rare opportunities to become declarative with her, to show her my own separate thinking and emotional life, with the hope that they might actually become resources to her. For example, after a desultory and sullenly dependent session, a session in which she complained that she felt "on a string" with other people and yet also complained that she did not feel like she was on a string with me, she burst out with, "What are we doing? What's progress?" I said to her that the notion of progress might be complicated by her own and others' expectations of her, but that I would think of progress for her as bringing her head, heart, and gut together and letting herself be herself, apart from what others might have in mind for her. At moments like this, she seemed to call me into presence for her, after which she was slightly more able to relax into the session. Soon after this, she said, "I can't believe I've tried so hard to please people, to be the perfect child . . . I feel now that I'm hiding in the dark, not doing things for other people but not knowing yet what I want for myself".

Early painting

The treatment setting made available a number of programmes, including an activities programme to which, early on, her skills and interests brought her. It offered a wide array of creative possibilities and was staffed by artists and craftsmen who offered the patient the true experience of apprenticeship within the role of student or worker, rather than a role organised around treating an illness. The patient found her way to the art teacher, an older man, himself a successful artist, devoted to the process of painting as a daring breaking through to what is authentic in a person and therefore inevitably beautiful. The quotes below are from his notes (Garel, personal communication).

As it turned out, he too was encountering with this patient the problem of engagement, and, like me, experienced himself as held resolutely outside while being offered a small glimpse of a true inner life. She began with her teacher by talking of her past painting experience and asking him for acrylic paints. But in response to the teacher's question about what size canvas she wanted, she produced:

> a little, twisted piece of driftwood, about two inches long and a quarter inch in diameter. Still puzzled, I watched her take out a very fine brush with tiny bristles, her own that she had brought with her, and in a quite short time, working intently and steadily, she transformed the little wood into an exquisite object, improvising a complex, detailed design as she was painting.

It was to become a piece of jewellery.

Realising that he was working with a talented person, the teacher asked the patient about her jewellery, but she shrugged off his question with a disinterested, "I don't know". When she returned to class, she painted two abstractions, which seemed to her teacher sensitive but also busy and decorative. He offered her his responses. "When I talked to her about the dynamics of space, I could feel my words bouncing off her as she looked at me stonily. It appears that this is a girl who does not like criticism or suggestions and so I decided to just let her go her own talented way".

Later, she painted a simple, silhouetted nude girl, a work that her teacher thought was exceptional, but,

> she seemed to ignore my praise, so I more firmly decided that it might be best, at the moment, to just let her express her own independence in any direction . . . I let her choose her own pattern of work. It seems that my relation to her is one of leaving all decisions up to her and just being around. Apparently she accepts me if I don't interfere with her very limited tolerance of outside direction.

These comments precisely paralleled my experience and position in the early part of this patient's psychotherapy.

Over time, the patient actually asked her teacher for help. In attempting to draw a person, she could not understand how to give the figure a certain body posture. She sought his instruction, but once she got it, she made no further attempt at working on the painting. Instead, she took all of her art materials back to her room. She asked her teacher if this arrangement suited him, and he agreed on the condition that she show him everything she did there, including what she considered to be her failures, so that they could discuss them. This approach puzzled her, though she agreed to it. For a while, she brought him very little new work, instead showing him the painting assignments she had produced in art classes earlier in her life. Her teacher recognised their technical merit, but added: "I don't teach this way. I expected her to develop and change, but this would be an experiment and distillation from her own needs".

In the month prior to a break in her therapy because of my summer vacation, the patient did not experiment with or go deeper with her painting. Instead she mobilised her taste and craftsmanship in the extensive production of tiny ceramic beads, which she would string together into necklaces, and then of many unusual and personally designed note cards. She painted both, the former with dabs of colour in abstract design and the latter with pastel hues of watercolour that faded into each other forming a subdued and elegant background design.

Rupture and reciprocity

As one might expect, the summer break in therapy seriously disrupted this patient's tentative efforts to integrate her inner and outer life, and she fell back into sullen detachment and the driven, shallow craving of attention characteristic of earlier times. In parallel fashion, she did not paint at all during my several weeks' absence. When I returned, we began a critical phase of her treatment. This phase began with her wish to see a different therapist, but her then proceeding in her sessions as though she were working with me. After a while, she again brought up her wish to discontinue her work with me and to see someone else. We made little progress in understanding or even elaborating her reasons for this wish, and I found it important to make clear to her my position, which was that it did not make sense to me to work with her if she did not want to work with me. I added that I hoped she would learn what she could in the process of coming to a decision.

Throughout this, it seemed impossible to get to her feelings about my having been away or about our work together at all; we could only see clearly that she was frightened of her anger toward me. On the day that she had scheduled her meeting with a consulting therapist, she found herself recalling a dream from earlier in the summer. Interestingly, I too had found myself thinking about this dream. In the dream, the staff and patients of the treatment centre were welcoming a new medical director. Some of the staff were naked, and the patient was embarrassed to notice that neither I nor the medical director had penises. To distract everyone from this shameful exposure, she took off her shirt and displayed her large breasts.

In the sessions during this phase of consultation, I more steadily worked toward interpreting the transference. This greater focus on what might be happening in the room between us led to a more confrontational mood in the patient. Eventually, she asked me when we had begun therapy; I told her the date. She said that she did not want to think about how bad she felt then and how isolated she was. I recognised in this her acknowledgement that treatment had helped her feel a bit better, and I added that therapy is difficult because it involves thinking about these painful feelings. She belligerently said that she got nothing from therapy. Though she had still not talked explicitly about the trouble she was having with me, she made it clear that she had decided to change therapists and that she was now just going through the motions and doing her duty with me. It was also clear that she felt that the consulting therapist was simply doing his duty with her and that we were all going to try to get her, in one way or another, to continue seeing me.

I confronted her about this. I told her that she did not believe me when I said that I did not want to work with her unless she wanted to work with me. I added that she was angry with *me* because *she* was just waiting, as though I could open up what her trouble was for her. She quickly switched the subject to a friend who "might be playing with my mind". I asked her if she saw the connection between that statement and her feelings with me now. She erupted. "Both have to do with men; I hate them and I hate you." She added, "I feel a love potential but that's risky". I said to her that it is hard for her to look at her decision about her therapy and to open that up with me because she worries that I will play with her head. For the first time she consciously considered, with a mixture of enjoyment and anxiety, the possible relationship between her feelings toward me and toward other men in her life.

She then faced me and said, "Where do you think I am in treatment?" I said to her that I thought she had made a good start at scratching the surface, not realising that I was capturing in my language her habit of savagely picking at her skin, just as she picks at, in a more figurative sense, her shortcomings. She then asked me if I saw any progress at all, and I told her specifically the progress I thought I saw, both outside of her therapy by the reports of others as well as herself, but also inside her therapy. She then asked me what I saw as the important issues for her in her therapy. I told her that therapy was an unfolding and so I could not really predict what might become crucial for her, but that I could see clearly something about her relationships with men, particularly a feeling of so much anger that she was afraid it could not be dealt with. I added that I thought that had to be worked out directly with somebody.

Obviously, these exchanges are a bit unusual in psychoanalytic therapy. My responses were not primarily interpretive, because I did not feel authorised by the patient to do so. In particular, I did not interpret the impotence she was convinced of or intending to create in me. Instead, I felt that my patient had re-claimed her status as client and needed to be met at the frame of her treatment, at the place of a potential contract, where she could feel clearly the limits and the potential of our work together. It was important, I thought, to survive as her therapist (Winnicott, 1969) in the face of her massive passive-aggression, and to register my presence as a person who could think about her across the gap of the summer break and through the waves of her pent-up anger. I felt that the possibility of a restored capacity for creative reverie in my patient depended on the security that might come from her feeling these boundaries as well as her true choice about joining or not.

After this, the patient said to me, "Why haven't we talked this way until now? We've piddled away this time". I acknowledged her complaint that I had let her be wasteful; I added that it simply may not have been safe to talk this way until now, having in the back of my mind that all of this had to await my leaving for vacation and my return. She left this session saying, "I've noticed that my feelings seem more real lately. When I cried with my friend yesterday, they were not my usual tears of self-pity, but tears of actual closeness with her".

In the next session, she reported feeling manipulated by me. Why was I telling her these things now? Was I trying to hold onto her? I said to her that I told her these things now because she asked, and this was the first time that she had done so. I added that until now she may have been taking care of me, protecting me from her need to get to this anger. I reminded her that the main thing she was doing in the dream was taking care of me in my inadequacy. She said that the preceding day she had felt "a wave of something". In saying this, she noted the word "wave" because waves were always in her dreams. There was a tone of pleasure and recognition at the metaphor we had created together. "A wave of fear and of being dependent on some-body I don't trust; I didn't like it at all and then I became afraid that under the surface there might be awful things." One particularly disturbing sexual thought from her past had come back to her instantly the day before when I had said to her that she had scratched the surface. It seemed clear that, though she did not feel at all sure about the meaning of this thought: she had been stuck with her own frightened and encapsulated interpretation of it for many years.

We then spoke about the dream that had occurred to both of us during the consultative process. Eventually, I told her what I thought the dream might mean in the context of our current work: that if I do not have a penis, I am no threat to her, but I also cannot help her because I have no potency. She found herself then considering again her idea that she had grown up with people whose self-esteem injuries had led them to insist that she reflect their goodness and their potency. She could not believe that I would not want that myself, and so this work must be manipulative. Nor could she yet formulate that she might want this kind of narcissistic gratification from me and that her collapse during my absence might relate to that un-met longing.

When she came back the next day, she said, "I *have* been protecting you. It's like in that dream." She took a further step in realising that in the dream she was covering me by exposing herself. She could see parallels in other relationships, particularly with men, and she could see her identification with her mother as a protector. She felt her father needed protection, needed to know that he was loved. She said, "I'd hate it too if someone didn't want me. Maybe I project that here". She was referring to making me feel unwanted, but she could also begin to consider that perhaps she had felt unwanted by me when I went away.

The patient appreciated her new tentative ability to be angry with me, but then worried she could become "vicious". She hoped I could manage her anger, then added, "And don't let me babble". I said, "Fair enough, but now we know that your babbling has been your way of protecting me", a form of verbal self-exposure unconsciously covering her fantasy of my impotence. She said, "So therapy is about this relationship and what goes on here". I said that it was, and she said with sudden affection, "That's a new perspective; I'll have to think about that".

Later painting

During this extended post-vacation phase of her psychotherapy, her art teacher also struggled with re-engagement. Again, the following quotes are from his notes. She showed him:

a drawing of hands, almost in prayer, actually more pleading than in prayer, with a chalice and lit candles. This took up most of the paper, but in the four corners were beautifully done small vignettes, some with couples and bare, spiky trees, all depressed scenes. I praised the drawing, but added that this showed a deep expression that her lovely decorative jewellery does not deal with. She wanted to know what I meant by that. I explained that jewellery design shows nothing of her problems, which must be a big part of her life now. She stated angrily, 'I have no problems!' . . . and then said quietly with a frown, 'Maybe I do'.

With the approaching student exhibition and with her teacher's recognition of her feelings coming through in her painting, the patient got back to work, always in her room, but steadily and regularly showing her work to her teacher.

> She listens carefully to my criticisms and though she says very little, only asking me to repeat things that she does not understand, she will then act in her room in a way that is a direct result of our talks. My suggestions are never related to changes that should be made on the picture she shows me, but rather to general concepts of what I think art should be and demands that her talent can handle to give her work more depth.
>
> She then brought in a very pleasant abstraction, nice and tasteful. I praised her for it, but I also spoke about the need for conflict in a picture, conflict that was resolved rather than avoided. Though I only talked in abstract terms, her next picture had pictorial expression as well as abstract conflict. Instead of just being shapes with opposing forces, there was a strong depiction of flames and smoke. The picture following that was even more specific . . . constantly more expressive involvement.

The patient was very interested in displaying her paintings in the student exhibition. To her teacher's surprise, she continued intense work after the show had begun.

> Everything she has done since (the exhibition) is just in pencil and is not as elaborately finished in colour: mainly expressive for herself and to show me, not concerned about impressing people. She has told me that she feels much better since she began to express her feelings in drawings and sometimes she writes on the back of these pictures: "depressed", "feeling lousy", a whole litany of such words. Though these pictures come out of depression, they are all very vigorous, definite and bold, drawn by applying great pressure, actually angry force in depicting complicated scenes . . ..
>
> Besides these, she also does some drawing in a journal . . . I was surprised that these drawings were quite mild, really casual doodles, just

small drawings that were interspersed between voluminous writing, something she would do while thinking of what else to say. I presume that her emotion was put into the writing, the drawings being unimportant expressions . . ..

One day at lunch the patient asked her teacher to look at a sculpture she had made.

> Intrigued, I went to her room, and saw a huge three-dimensional spider. It had a diameter of about nine feet, made up of bits of junk and rags into a convincing form with an interesting fierce head. What then was most impressive was that she went to one corner and began manipulating long strings attached like reins to the hind legs and made the creature move ominously. It was humorous yet threatening. I enjoyed it and congratulated her.
>
> A few days later I came into the art room and saw a beautiful acrylic abstraction with wild colour and experimental textures, free painting that was unlike any student I was familiar with. I thought it might be hers though she had not done any painting here before. It showed the special talent and skill she had shown in other work. Sure enough it was hers, and when she came, she showed me how she got the unusual textures by using a steel comb we use to clean dry paintbrushes. It was the first time she had ever done an acrylic painting and she had immediately *played* with the new medium.

This blossoming capacity for play, as well as the energetic revealing of herself in her painting (now done in the public space of the art room) and in her sculpture, followed immediately upon her decision to continue her psychotherapeutic work with me. We entered a phase of much deeper contact with her feelings and greater self-awareness. She had a long phone conversation with her father and found herself with many very positive childhood memories of their relationship. For the first time, she cried hard in her session as she felt her long-buried love for him and her feelings of loss in that relationship. These memories were powerful and specific. She got herself into something of a wild argument with two female friends over an apparent betrayal involving a young man, but she came out of this saying, "I was happy about it. For the first time, I made noise with my feelings. I never felt so involved with so many people, so cared about".

With the agreement of her psychopharmacologist, she decided to discontinue her antidepressant medication and declared to me, "This is the place where I'm going to work things out". She seemed pleased, relieved, and much stronger, as though her medication had represented her own and perhaps her family's fear of depression and their need to force a functioning they were sure could not happen from inner resources or relational work. Now, the patient *wanted* to look inside, despite thoughts that had seriously scared her, all of which found their way into her paintings. With this new-found wish to dig, she largely dropped her habit of picking at her skin, and the nagging question "What's wrong with me?" became a more bold "What's happening with me?"

The restoration of reverie

What I hope to have illustrated in this lengthy clinical report is, to return to Milner's language, the establishment of reciprocity in a psychotherapeutic encounter. The pattern of simply "fitting in", of "placating . . . external reality" (Milner, 1957, p. 116) seemed to be the patient's unconscious way of being with me, and also seemed to be what she expected me to do with her. All of this had parallels in her painting and in her relationship to her art teacher. The idea of driftwood captured an important piece of her self-image. She had felt cut adrift by her parents (as she soon would by me during my vacation) and headed for the inevitable failure on her own that a programmed upbringing, at least as she felt it, implied. To claim her life and transform it, she needed to be let go of, to see where those dream waves might take her, and then to learn the inevitability and the value of failure. Her art teacher insisted on her showing him *all* her work, including failed efforts, so that learning might occur. In her psychotherapy, the work with my potential failure, as a consequence of my really failing her in my absence, was equally important. As Masud Khan (1972b) writes of a similar patient:

> I help her because I fail her and am not shamed by her accusations but accept her anger as right and just. And what is even more important for her is that I accept my failures and am not devalued in my eyes by them. Nothing could be more damaging to her growth and discovery of herself than an *ideal fit* in the clinical alliance. (p. 277)

This patient did indeed seem to have broken down into reality during my absence, unable to sustain what she was capable of creatively during that time, with telling exceptions: she kept stringing things together (her beads) and she created in her lovely note cards the idea of communication across a distance. On my return, she presented as lifeless, until I could find a way to integrate my own and her affect into the hours, to throw those paints onto a blank canvas. Contrary to her fantasy, this allowed her to feel that the treatment relationship was durable enough to re-engage with. It was during this work that couples and conflict came into her painting, that she actually listened to her teacher, that aggressive energy was put into the action of draw-ing, and that words became interspersed with her pictures. Her teacher wrote that she doodled in her journal "while thinking of what else to say". In other words, we see here a restored capacity for reverie, and drawing as transitional activity. Her spider sculpture re-works the puppet metaphor, now from a new position of affect, perspective, and agency, even as it also captures anxieties about devouring and being devoured in the transference. Along with her daring return to painting, it illustrates her re-discovered capacity for vigorous play, a capacity mirrored as well in the confrontational, deep-play exchanges between patient and therapist.

Not long after the events described above, the patient had a poignant dream in which she was holding in her hands two tiny, fragile, but beautifully speckled eggs. In the dream, she felt terribly frightened that any movement on her part might lead one egg to crush the other. Whether these eggs represented her parents, her embattled sibling relationship, her longing to be held by her mother, or her frag-ile but precious connection to me, this dream captures an action of loving care-taking and consequent paralysis. This intrapsychic situa-tion, in which the subject, to use Winnicott's phrase, is a "caretaker self" (1960, p. 142), forecloses the integration of a real affective life, especially the mobilisation of aggression in encountering the world. Thus, the patient's recovery from the psychic disaster of my leaving her seemed to require a phase of transgressing each other, and our mutual survival (Winnicott, 1969), toward an outcome of making sense of the transference relationship. This work re-established the treatment in a "third" position (Muller, 1996), in which the vicissi-tudes of early relationships, and their coming to life in the transfer-ence, could be held by the therapy rather than by the patient. To get there, the patient had to find and use the analytic relationship as a medium, to fully experience its pliancy, durability, and richness, and to discover the potential creativity in actions she assumed to be purely destructive.

In his paper on Marion Milner's idea of "answering activity", Michael Parsons (1990) reconsiders Ferenczi's (1928) concept of the elasticity of psychoanalytic technique. He describes it as "the analyst's allowing himself to yield, to be moved by the patient: not so that the patient shall necessarily come to agree with him, but to allow some new position, unknown so far to either patient or analyst, to be discovered" (p. 420). This seems an apt way to describe the work with this patient. Parsons finds in Marion Milner's work a language for psychoanalytic creativity and a conviction about its centrality to genuine processes of growth and mutuality. He concludes by saying:

> Technique is about how to do something. If creativity is something that happens between analyst and patient, in which they both participate, its theoretical basis will be of a different sort. A theory of psychoanalytic creativity will not be a theory about the best way of doing something, but about how to make something possible between people. (p. 423)

CHAPTER NINE

Taking the transference

This chapter reports on and explores the process of consulting to the psychotherapy of a very troubled man. I hope to illustrate the difficulty, importance and meaning of what Symington calls "tak(ing) the transference" (1986, p. 321). The patient's female therapist requested the consultation, and her words about it were telling. They reflected, I suspect, the gap between her inner experience and her actions with her patient. She described the treatment situation as "nearly intolerable" for her, but with her patient, she "propose(d) (an) idea", the idea of asking for a consultation. The affect and the action do not match. If psychotherapy consultation works, it works first of all for the person requesting it, and it works toward both the therapist's greater ability to contain experience formerly considered intolerable as well as her greater ability to get it into the work.

The patient's initial rejection of his therapist's proposal for consultation, as well as his regular attendance at sessions, suggested to me that the evolving transference–countertransference relationship might well be in a direction necessary to the patient's growth, therefore progressive, even if deadly and deeply inarticulate. I think here of Nina Coltart's (1986) brilliant reflections on Yeats's poem: "And what rough beast, its hour come round at last, / Slouches toward Bethlehem to be born?" (p. 186) "Some people have seen this as pessimistic", she says, adding in a tone so collected and wilfully independent as to seem almost regal, "you will gather that I have seen it differently" (p. 186). She continues:

> However much we gain confidence, refine our technique, decide more creatively when and how and what to interpret, each hour with each patient is also in its way an act of faith: faith in ourselves, in the process, and faith in the secret, unknown, unthinkable things in our patients which, in the space which is the analysis, are slouching towards the time when their hour comes round at last. (p. 187)

This patient's silence and self-described "shitiness" constituted a new depth of assault on his therapist. After reluctantly agreeing to the psychotherapy consultation, he then missed his sessions for a week, returning to tell his therapist how cold and mean she was, and how useless therapy was since he would be psychotic for the rest of his life.

My two meetings with the patient were low-key and relatively uneventful. He knew me from my role in the therapeutic community programme of this residential treatment centre and from an important interaction very early in his stay. At about 8 a.m., while I was doing paperwork in my office, someone knocked on my closed door. This is a rare event given the fact that patients in this setting quickly learn to make appointments and even more quickly learn that knocking on a closed door may constitute a serious interruption. But I said: "Come in", and there stood this very large, quite mad-looking man, whom I recognised as one of the newer patients. My first reaction was fear; I felt cornered with someone unpredictable, and for a moment, I was speechless.

I asked him who he was, and he told me. I asked him if he knew who I was, and he did. I invited him to come in and sit down. He did and seemed to relax a bit. I asked why he had come to see me. He told me that he was afraid, and I immediately realised that my fear must have related to his. He told me that he had been walking down the street in front of my office, had heard church bells, and thought that he should become a priest, even though he eventually wanted to marry. He thought he should tell this to someone, and so he found me.

I told him that I was glad he had told me, that he sounded like a person who was in conflict about his life, and that therapy might be a good place to sort that out. I added that it must be frightening to be in a new place with so many new people. He said that it was. I told him that I had some work to do, so I could not talk with him any longer, but that I hoped things would work out well for him. He thanked me and left. It was this interaction that led him to occasionally call me "Father Fromm" in therapeutic community meetings— apparently a condensation of his spiritual and familial aspirations, as well as a transference paradigm for what was to come.

Anger and tears

So, five months later, we met again in my role as psychotherapy consultant. He told me that he was angry with his therapist because she could not fix him, but it became quickly apparent that he felt his psychosis to have been a catastrophic experience, a set of losses so profound that no one could fix him. I fished around for what he might have learned from his psychosis. He understood this idea, but did not understand his psychosis at all. He had learned from it, however, that he remained angry with his father. He dated this to the time after his mother's death, when he "still needed raising, but my father didn't want to be bothered". This spoke to my immediate experience; I felt I needed something from the patient, so that I could begin to make sense of the trouble he was having with his therapist, but the patient seemed to be approaching the consultation with an attitude of not wanting to be bothered.

I worked to get at what he might want from this consultation, and eventually with some animation, he said he wanted his therapist to stop pushing him and to stop telling him what he thought. He said that with me as a mediator, she might listen. I found myself thinking that he must have felt left too alone with his mother during her illness, as indeed he had throughout his life. We ended this meeting with our agreeing that we would both bring this discussion to his therapist, he in his sessions and I in a meeting with her, and that he would call me if he wanted another appointment.

He did soon after. When we met, he told me that things had gone better in therapy; there had been more "dialoguing". He told me that he did not understand therapy. As it turned out, he actually did understand that therapy was about coming to know, tolerate, and express feelings. The new idea he took from me had to do with a person's tendency to relive important, unresolved aspects of his life in his relationship to the therapist. He did not recall much about our first meeting, except that he felt bombarded with questions by me, an impression quite in contrast to what I thought I was doing. He did not come out of that first session liking his therapist, as he had hoped. Rather, he was angry with her and did not understand why.

He then added an important, specific reaction: he felt that she saw him as a "crybaby" and he thought she felt repulsed by that. Again he thought of his mother's death. He remembered feeling terribly sad at that time, but he refused to show that to anyone, for fear of being shamed as a "crybaby". (A note about history: the patient was an only child of his parents' marriage, considerably younger than his half-siblings. He was very attached to his mother and easily embarrassed about his relationship with her.) At this point in this second consultation session, the point of maximal emotional contact, the patient said, rather defiantly, that he thought he had a lot to cry about, and I said indeed he did. He made it clear to me that he did not want to change to a different therapist. I simply encouraged him to put into words the thoughts and feelings he was having with his therapist, especially the "crybaby" feeling.

As I said, these sessions were in no way dramatically productive. I tried simply to bring the patient out, to hear his understanding of the problem, to make emotional contact, and to find his language. That he initiated a second session I took to be a good sign. Overall, I felt that the importance of these sessions was not in *what* happened, but in *that* they happened, that a third person was allowed to insert himself into an ailing treatment dyad and to find a way to frame and hold the treatment task.

Trusting the process

In my meetings with the therapist, we talked about the patient's non-attendance to sessions as representing a narcissistic injury in response to her request for a consultation, which he took to mean her refusal to be with him during a difficult time. She told me of his wish for a note certifying a permanent remission from psychosis; this seemed transparently related to painful temporary improvements in his mother's condition and to the patient's enraged disappointment and fearfulness about help and hope.

As we explored the transference–countertransference matrix, we began to think the patient might be living out with his therapist a profound paradox—the task, as Masud Khan (1972b) put it, being to sustain the paradox and prevent it from degenerating into irreconcilable conflict. That paradox seemed to have to do with a terminal situation that was not supposed to change at all. His therapist and I talked about various ways of sticking with the patient and of listening to his "technical" suggestions. Most importantly, this former emergency medical technician (EMT) and I talked about simply accepting her feelings and letting them be, simply holding and going into the countertransference, particularly the helplessness at being unable to save someone wasting away in front of you. From that starting point, some kind of understanding and some words might eventually come.

As I look back on it, my talk with this patient's therapist was about one of the most basic and powerful, if least written about and understood, aspects of psychotherapy. Neville Symington (1986), in his "Last lecture", a Credo to what for him is central to his life's work, puts it this way:

> Each new patient . . . challenges the analyst to further his emotional development. . . . It is for this reason that I have stressed that the most difficult matter for the analyst is to "take" a transference. The interpretation of it is relatively easy, but taking a transference has a special difficulty . . . for the transference is a distorted truth about the analyst . . . (p. 321)

> . . . The analyst cannot make an interpretation when he is too anxious about the topic . . . (p. 322)

> . . . What is he to do before he becomes conscious of [his difficulty]? [T]here is the patient and the analyst in the consulting room, but there is also a process. This is the third term in which trust is ultimately placed. The process of analysis is the master of both analyst and patient. (p. 324)

My consultation may well have helped the therapist trust the process; it may have given it communicative form and allowed her to let go a bit into it. Certainly a change occurred in the patient: a first dream, curiosity, playfulness, in the therapist's words, "use of the psychotherapy to examine his experience". She felt that I had "saved" the therapy. But on reflection, she realised that the material seemed very much the same; while he had indeed changed, the patient was not a "changed man". Rather, the therapist had changed. "In retrospect, it appears that the consultation served to shore up my discouragement and confusion about why my interpretations could not make this deadly transference–countertransference interaction abate".

I would underline the verb "make." As the therapist said to me, she found herself in the midst of the patient's transference assault, looking for the interpretation "that would make it all stop". In other words, her emotional burden was leading her to use interpretation not to understand the transference, but to refuse it. Hence her rather pressured way of interpreting indicated to the patient his therapist's jeopardised survival and therefore could not be used by him. In my experience, this is a common phenomenon for therapists, regardless of training level, when working with very troubled patients. Grinberg (1997) writes of "the analyst's possible fear and concealed rejection of the transference" (p. 4). Ogden (2005c) describes this as our understandable difficulty in "facing the music" (p. 21). But, as with any crisis, this situation holds both danger and opportunity.

Medium

In Chapter One, I described variants of psychotherapy impasse as reflecting what I have called pathological transitional relatedness. I focused in particular on two technical functions of the analyst: the establishment and maintenance of the frame and the offering of the analyst's emotional responsiveness and total mental functioning as a medium for metabolising and articulating the patient's heretofore unconscious experience. This concept of medium was developed by Marion Milner in various papers, including her autobiographical work *On Not Being Able to Paint* (1957) (see also Chapter Eight).

In this work, she wrote of the problem of reciprocity between one's own need and the need of the other. She described a developmental failure in which the child "had lost hope of making any real contact with the outside world" (p. 116) and the possibility that in creative activity might be found "an experience of togetherness with one's medium lived through together" (p. 118), an experience of "pliability yet irreducible otherness" (p. 118). Thus, "the 'other' that had inevitably had to fail one at times in one's first efforts to realize togetherness" (p. 118) might be rejoined from the position of a newly revived subject.

It is indeed this transformative, becoming-conscious, lived-through togetherness that was at stake between this patient and his therapist, given the burgeoning demand on her capacity as medium. This demand—to be with him as he dies, to accept helplessness, to feel guilt, despair and rage, to never leave, and to hold on to her strength in the face of assault—was thoroughly embedded in the patient's experience of himself and his mother at the time of her illness and death. Most of all, nothing was to change, then or now, since underneath his whistling-in-the-dark grandiosity, change meant only loss and guilt for his destructiveness.

This is the problem of serving as medium when that term carries its connotation of facilitating contact with the dead. The transference–countertransference relatedness with this patient felt like a death grip. To the extent that his therapist's interpretations were in fact a way of leaving the patient, a way that his ailment, like his mother's, was not survivable, the content they delivered could not be integrated. Even more, they enacted and repeated the patient's specific childhood experiences with his mother, the "let-me-out-of-here" effort, which never actually worked, and the "take-this-to-make-me-feel-better", which did not either. A therapist's being used for what she really has to offer can only happen, says Winnicott (1969), when the therapist has become placed outside the patient's projective field, placed there by the patient's destructiveness and the therapist's real survival with technique intact.

Grief

Is this essential move in the direction of object use what happened through the consultative process? The patient announced in his first therapy session that the problem would be grieving his mother's death. His first reaction to the therapist was to feel hurt that she "disowned" his feelings, as though rupturing a oneness he desperately wanted with her. He went on to lament that she was too this or too that, like an inconsolable child or a child whose skin sensitivity makes any physical contact with another person a source of irritation. He could not stand it that he affected his therapist's way of working, and then he took sadistic pleasure in the effects he could not help but have on her. In response to her interpretation of what both he and his father needed from doctors, he spoke angrily of what he was promised, what he is owed, and of course what he has been deprived of.

This *is* the work of grieving. His therapist interprets to "abate" a process, but ironically interpretation deepens the process if the interpretation is accurate, and escalates the process if it constitutes a transference refusal. One or the other seems to have been the case at this juncture of this patient's treatment. In his current regression, he became silent. He watched television all day. He thought of murder. He smelled. There was a moment in his history, as his mother came home from the hospital, when he watched television rather than visit with her in her sickroom. She came out and said, "Can't you even come in to speak to your mother?" He stayed silent, and later confessed to his half-sister that he wished their mother would die already. Television, silence, murder. The only thing missing in the recapitulation of this tragic scene is how his mother smelled!

In other words, the patient seemed to be re-creating the specific elements of this dire phase of his life, including death-like feelings, sleepiness, and indifference in his therapist. But all of this could not become interpretable until the destructiveness of it really had been survived. The patient's assault may have been his effort to place the therapist beyond his projections; his therapist's call for a consultation may have been her effort to get there, to help him find a usable reality by her first finding a third party who might help her survive his death grip.

Nina Coltart (1986) writes of a similar clinical situation:

> We came to see how much, to his own surprise and horror, this man had needed to live out, and have experienced and endured by another person without retaliation his primary hatred of a genuinely powerful mother. . . . I had given up trying to "understand" this patient, given up theorizing and just sat there day after day without memory or desire in a state of suspension, attending only with an empty mind to him and the unknowable truth of himself, which had shaped his life, until such a moment as I was so at one with it that I knew it for the murderous hatred it was, and had to make a jump for freedom—his as well as mine. (p. 195)

Jumping

The therapist's "jump" may well have been to ask for psychotherapy consultation. I am suggesting that this action at this time in the treatment began the process of change she soon noticed. There is a remarkable moment while the consultation was occurring when, in response to his physically turning away from her and reporting being turned away from by his friends, the therapist asks the patient "if [he] knows something about turning away from people who are seriously ill". To my ear, her approach is stunningly different: calmer, more settled, more "with" the patient. He responds quietly and with vulnerability: "Me. I turned away from my mother when she was ill. I refused to visit her. I told my sister I wished she would just go ahead and die". He fell into a silence that seemed completely different from his earlier provocative withholding.

The therapist eventually picked up on the way in which his mother's illness must have felt like her turning away from the patient. He joined that and spoke of her having lost her will to go on. His own giving up simply followed hers. But the therapist too was struggling with giving up. She too had turned away—toward a consultant— though this turning was in the service of turning back, however painfully, toward her patient. The tone and depth of this exchange suggested to me that the impasse was already resolving.

The therapist noted that, "The consultation provided a third to the deadly stalemate. It provided a holding context through the act of bearing witness to the pain and despair of both the patient and the therapist". I would accent the deeply therapeutic function of becoming a true witness with the patient to the specific emotional events of early family life. It seems accurate to emphasise the "bearing" in all of this, because these truths only become really known emotionally in their actually being relived between patient and therapist. In calling for consultation, the therapist asked for help with her emotional burden, including perhaps her carrying the mother's unacknowledged and projected burden of wanting it all to be over too. Thus, she opened a path for development that the mother–son dyad, in collusion with a father in denial, had foreclosed. Interestingly, it was a path that included a transference father, whose actual function was to feel the burden with her, rather than deny it (Ann-Louise Silver, personal communication).

Psychotherapy consultation differs from psychotherapy supervision. Because it is not ongoing and not embedded in an educational task, consultation is not primarily about mentoring. And, most importantly, it actually makes contact with the patient. It thus functions very powerfully as an actual treatment intervention, the timing of which is in unconscious but direct response to the gathering affective storm between patient and therapist. The consultant is working in this particular treatment moment, and finds himself both as a "third" (Muller, 1996) to the patient–therapist dyad, but also as the "second in combat" (Davoine & Gaudilliere, 2004, p. 153) for the therapist. In these crisis situations, situations of genuine trauma for the therapeutic couple, the principles Davoine and Gaudilliere articulate, derived from First World War military psychiatry and the work of Thomas Salmon, become essential: *simplicity* (no jargon), *proximity* (being with the traumatised person's raw experience), *immediacy* (depending on intuition and on the seeming coincidences within the transference, like perhaps the therapist's experiences as an EMT as they are mobilised by the patient's regression), and *expectancy* (the dimension of hope, of getting better because those at the front wait for you).

To return for a moment to Grinberg's (1997) paper, he writes that, given the confusing welter of theoretical and technical ideas about transference in our literature, "It is difficult not to think that the transference is still our 'cross' owing to the tendency to avoid a committed relationship to it" (p. 5). The cross metaphor belongs to the Freud–Pfister correspondence, and captures not only the burden of the transference, but the notion that working with transference is a chosen role involving suffering on behalf of others. Grinberg summarises what I am calling "taking the transference" in the following way:

> The basis of this attitude would be an acceptance of invasion by these projections and of all the consequences, so as to be able to share and feel on a basis of consubstantiality with the patient the affects contained within them whatever their nature...as if they were part of the analyst's own self. It is a matter of offering one's entire availability. (Grinberg, 1997, p. 11)

Psychotherapy consultation can be one avenue toward a therapist's being able to make and sustain such a difficult offer.

CHAPTER TEN

Psychosis, trauma, and the speechless context

Bridges

Some years ago in London, at a meeting of the International Symposium for the Psychotherapy of Schizophrenia, subtitled "Building Bridges", about 1,000 members gathered to hear a wide array of approaches to the treatment of psychosis. Some presentations seemed extraordinarily interesting and promising; some painstaking and confused; some well meaning, politically correct, pluralistic, and yet disastrous, at least to my hearing, to the sense of the patient as a person. It was in response to the latter that a French friend and colleague said "But what is this 'building bridges' stuff? What if you build a bridge to your enemy? That is not good! We need to blow up some bridges first. Then maybe we can build a few bridges that really hold".

Truth be told, it was from that incendiary comment that I organised a conference on "Psychosis and the Social Context" a few years later. It is a comment whose truth is obvious to any European who knows history, and it is a comment through which this long-time therapist of psychotic patients (and daughter of a resistance fighter) may be mirroring the aggressively self-preservative boundaries of the psychotic and the self-annihilating compromises he or she fears. As you will soon hear, "bridges that work" refers not only to the transference relationship, but also to the language process, which opens a path to foreclosed meaning.

At that same London conference, Michael Robbins, whose intensive psychotherapeutic treatment of psychotic patients over many years has been described in his book, *Experiences of Schizophrenia* (1993), argued that the current approach to the psychotic patient, which sees itself as understanding a disease process, is in actuality enacting the disorder at a socio-cultural level; that is, the treatment approach may reflect socio-cultural countertransference. For example, thought disorder is split off from the person, to be treated as a symptom without meaning—mirroring the schizophrenic's depersonalised splitting of his thoughts from his feelings and from his relationships to people. Similarly, though studies document that the family's degree of denial is a pathogenic factor for high-risk individuals, multiple forces have pushed the treatment culture toward its own denial of interpersonal, developmental factors in the shaping of psychosis and toward seeing the psychotic patient as an isolate—ironically mirroring a primary defensive strategy while it replicates pathogenesis.

And yet to seriously consider psychosis in its social dimension risks our entering into a relationship of considerable anxiety and confusion. Recently, a psychologist who had tested a psychotic patient prefaced her report with a shriek— modulated and professional—but a shriek nonetheless: "It drove me crazy to try and write this!" She then made an amazing statement: "Being with this patient and hearing her responses, I felt I was with something so fierce and precise and hard and there, and yet when I tried to write it, it crumbled and was gone". To me, this preface seemed report enough. In these words, this psychologist captured the power of the psychotic "it", the maddening effort to get "it" into language, and the horror that instead "it" had entered into her.

The conference I organised was born from experiences like that, including two seminars in which I listened to therapists in private practice talk about their work, a surprising portion of which included psychotic patients. Their efforts to be empathically connected to these patients was remarkable, their uneasiness palpable, their confusion profound, and their patients' desire to communicate unmistakable. We are dealing with these patients. We may as well talk about that work unapologetically.

Urgency

Once I found myself sitting on the sandy bank of a New England pond with a Latin-American friend. As some children went into the water and began to paddle and splash, he grew melancholic. He was missing his nine-year-old daughter, who had stayed behind in Chile, and he began to tell me about her. How beautiful she was. She had green eyes shaped liked almonds, and golden hair. Then he told me that he and his wife had adopted her as an infant. When she was five years old, they told her that she had been born to other parents. "And do you know what she did?" he asked me. "She didn't cry. She didn't say a word. She went into our bedroom. She climbed onto our bed and curled up at the foot of it. She lay there, in fetal position, for an entire afternoon.

I have always remembered this story—the sureness with which the child, her world in upheaval, took care of herself. With a knowing as deep as whatever it is that prompts a cat about to give birth to find the inside of a drawer or a pile of hay, she knew she could not go forward without going back. She had to leave the linear movement of time and take her place inside a different rhythm: slow, circular, recursive.

We have all had such moments of true urgency. (Oxenhandler, 1997, p. 65)

The writer is Noelle Oxenhandler, from an early summer New Yorker reflection called "Fallen from grace: How modern life has made waiting a desperate act". Among many wonderful observations, Oxenhandler notes that today's marketplace culture has given us the convenience store, open twenty-four hours a day, seven days a week, the only other institution with these hours being the emergency room. She highlights the irony in this relationship. I begin with this story of withdrawal and silence, of a different kind of knowing requiring a different kind of time, and of a psychic emergency that radically alters a taken-for-granted social context as a way to introduce a story about psychosis, the story of the treatment of a psychotic man.

Hurricane

The patient came for treatment after several years of ongoing psychotic functioning and a long history prior to that of isolation and difficulty sustaining social or vocational activities after college. Around the time of a sibling's graduation, the patient developed appendicitis and underwent an appendectomy that triggered delusional thinking about what was happening to his body, including the idea that he was pregnant and giving birth. Thus began his acute psychosis. His treatment illuminates some of the core struggles and phases of psychotherapy for psychotic patients, as well as the discovery of meaning in their use of the larger treatment context.

In his first psychotherapy session, his therapist "had no idea what (the patient) was talking about". The patient's speech was incoherent and often sarcastic. Instead of being able to use his mind, the therapist found himself with a near uncontrollable urge to urinate. This rather shocking experience of internal pressure disappeared once the session was over. The one moment of clarity from the patient, indeed a moment so clear it felt like the eye of a hurricane, so suddenly and chillingly real the therapist almost could not bear to hear it, came as the patient's statement of what he wanted from his therapy: "Parts of me have died and I want to put them to rest". These parts were "my love and my intellect". The very tentative contract formed between patient and therapist had more to do with learning about how the patient had come to this decision rather than facilitating or challenging it.

The first phase of therapy could be thought of as a process of mutual regulation. Through trial and error, a sense of boundary, space, and optimal distance were established. The therapist's errors, primarily of understanding the limits of his authorisation from the patient, led immediately to disruptions. The patient skipped sessions or erupted with affect, psychotic thinking, or bizarre behaviour. Winnicott's ideas about psychosis turned out to be extremely important. The failure of the holding environment registers as regression in the patient, and, at the beginning, only the therapist will be able to think about this as a two-person phenomenon. Winnicott encouraged us to "watch the operation of these setting factors" (1954a, p. 293) and to note the gradual transition, in fortunate circumstances, from self-holding to being held by the setting, in this context the setting of both the therapy and the residential community in which the patient was living.

With this patient, the therapist learned quickly that questions were felt as disorganising invasions. A commitment to restraint on the therapist's part eventually helped the patient verbalise his corrections: "You don't give me time to know what I feel". What a simple, elegant description of the time needed—in an unobtrusive relational context —to come into being as a person. During this phase, the patient fell into a pattern of whistling to himself as he walked down the corridor to the therapist's office, thereby unconsciously alerting the therapist to be ready for him. This behaviour prepared, in Winnicott's terms, the therapist's object-presenting (1954a), his reliably being there lending itself to the patient's unconscious need for a self-created other; this is the environmental corollary to the development of object relating. At the other boundary, the patient regularly ended the sessions himself. His eventual forgetting to do so and allowing the therapist to share in noting the end of the hour signalled a major movement toward the achievement of secure dependence.

This phase of mutual regulation lasted many months, during which the patient was generally withdrawn in the residential community, occasionally hostile in ways that betrayed his confusion, but also reservedly appealing to others through the quiet reach of his pain. Patients and staff found themselves reaching back to him, often intruding on him. One staff member would often see him on the front porch apparently lost in thought; at some point, she decided no longer to be ignored or ignoring, and so resolutely said "Hello" each time she passed him. He registered the aggression in this form of relatedness, and soon joined it, replying "Hello" to the staff member in a tone of sarcasm, world-weariness, or reluctant playfulness.

The uncanny

A case conference was held on the patient a few months into his treatment, and there a fascinating event occurred. The patient was being interviewed in front of the entire staff by a senior consultant. The consultant's efforts to make contact were completely defeated by the patient's biting hostility and incoherence. He worked harder. Finally, his agony perhaps reflecting the patient's, he said: "What's happened to you?" The patient suddenly answered calmly and clearly: "I've hurt people who didn't deserve it". Again, the eye of the storm. The consultant gently inquired further but to no avail. This moment of contact ended with a sudden return of biting hostility: "Why should I talk to you; X (the consultant's patient) loves you and she's going to die!" After this, the interview became impossible and was soon ended.

When the patient said: "I've hurt people who didn't deserve it", I was stunned. I had just been reading the family history, in which it was reported that a social worker had asked the patient's father, not in the patient's presence, about his life, and he had replied: "I've hurt people who didn't deserve it". This simple, moving phrase contained within it enormous pathos. It referred primarily to his wife, who had become severely depressed and had killed herself shortly after the birth of the patient, upon hearing of her husband's wish for a divorce. What does it mean that this patient brings his father's signifiers, word-for-word, to this major moment of his treatment? And is it not striking that, having done so with the senior male consultant, he instantly attacks him as the quasi-murderer of a woman who loves him? This clinical moment—which seems to illustrate Lacan's (1977) idea that the unconscious is the discourse of the Other—may well capture the defining moment of this patient's life, yet an incomprehensible one, not the least reason for which is that it occurred when he was an infant. And finally, in this list of impossible questions, what if anything is to be made from the uncanny eventuality that this consultant's patient did indeed die, by suicide, a number of months later.

Schizophrenia was first called "dementia praecox": precocious dementia. The etymologies of these two words are interesting. Dementia means "out from" "mind". Mensa was the ancient goddess of thought. This etymological meaning suggests the subject's existence outside of the coverage of the ego or outside Winnicott's primary maternal preoccupation (1956b), which "minds" the baby, minding in the dual sense of providing coverage and imbuing the baby with mental coherence. "Pre-cocious" etymologically takes on almost a synonymous meaning: "pre" meaning "before" and "cocious" meaning "cooked". "Precocious" means "before fully cooked", and its near-synonym, "premature", means "before fully ripened". Matura was the goddess who presided over the ripening of fruits and the name relates to the word "mater" (mother). Both have a Sanskrit root meaning "measurement". All of this suggests that the gestation period, that very basic phase of ripening, represents the primordial measurement of readiness. From a psychological developmental perspective, that meaning of "precocious" which is "not fully mothered" seems to me synonymous with the meaning of "dementia" which is "outside ego coverage".

Even further, I wonder if this name, dementia praecox—derived from the clinically objective assessment of senility-like symptoms in much younger people—does not hide a subjective intuition. Our clinical experience with these patients could easily suggest that they suffer from a *demented precocity*, an urgent, unconscious grasping to get hold of and make sense of, cryptic emotional events occurring prior to the development of a mind with which to grasp them. I think here of Bollas' "unthought known" (1987, p. 277) and of Winnicott's statement that "the patient needs to 'remember' . . . but it is not possible to remember something that has not yet happened, and this thing of the past has not happened yet because the patient was not there for it to happen to" (1974, p. 105). There is an echo here of the patient's statement: "You don't give me time to know what I feel". This is paradox to that edge where the near-nonsensical about something urgent creates enormous tension. I also think here of Freud's declaration—casual, intuitive and completely unelaborated—that "everyone possesses in his own unconscious an instrument with which he can interpret the utterances of the unconscious in other people" (1913i, p. 320).

Water

Davoine and Gaudilliere (1997) write that "traumatic history comes back like a suspended present throughout several generations, for a simple reason: it proceeds from a speechless context . . . no in and out, no past and future, and therefore, no subject" (p. 6). Consider for a moment the history of another psychotic patient. Her maternal grandfather, who was an engineer, drowned in a freak accident on board a submarine. His daughter was ten. Ten years later, his son was killed in naval combat and buried at sea. Ten years later, his wife—after many long and desperate trips to the ocean—drowned herself in her bathtub. The only remaining child had a three-year-old daughter who immediately lost her recently acquired ability, or perhaps willingness, to use the toilet. Bathrooms, bathtubs, water! When this little girl turned ten, her mother's behaviour toward her changed; having dressed her like a doll and carefully groomed her long hair throughout her childhood, her mother began to pull her hair into a ponytail so tightly that the hair fell out. She then cut her daughter's hair quite short, leaving this little girl stunned and humiliated because "I looked like a boy".

About ten years later, as the daughter approached her college graduation, and following a failed and urgent love relationship with a military man, this young woman covered the furniture in her apartment with dust cloths and, in the middle of her school term, went to bed. "I was planning on being there for a long time", she said. When, through the help of friends, she arrived at the hospital for evaluation, she spoke of many delusional ideas, including that it was raining blood. Her exhausted father said that it was time for her to "sink or swim". Death and water recur in this family tragedy with metronomic regularity, fatefully punctuated at a ten-year cadence.

This notion of a "speechless context" precisely describes the enveloping silence of this patient's home life, a silence at the centre of her mother's efficient but deadened care, through which nothing of herself was given or revealed. "People will be annoyed with you if you laugh for no reason", her mother once said to her psychotic daughter. "Are you annoyed?" the daughter responded. "No", said her mother, "but other people will be". In the patient's dream, however, her mother sips brandy, then breaks the glass and comes at her to slit her throat.

This patient recurrently hallucinated in her sessions. Her attitude toward working on her hallucinations seemed identified with her parents' wish for all of this trouble to disappear, reflecting the way in which massive denial and the longing for it all to be over coalesce as, or are recognised as, a death wish in the patient's mind. While her hallucinations were often clearly projective, serving to empty the patient of relationship-disturbing feelings and impulses, another function of her hallucinations seemed directly related to a "speechless context". "You are?" she asked her therapist. "I'm what" he said. "Did you say that you were confused?" said the patient. He had not, but he *was* confused and was considering saying it. This "hallucination" was in fact a pre-cognition, a filling-in of the therapist's silence using the cues of his postural and facial expressions. It could be seen as the patient's reverie, a slightly crazed form of care-taking, an unconscious channel perhaps to her own mother through which she fills the dead space and urgently articulates the mother who cannot articulate herself. It is astonishing to recognise how the unarticulated—Lacan might say "foreclosed"—signifiers of inter-generational catastrophe find their way unconsciously into the speech of the other, in this case, the therapist (Fromm, 2012). In response to the patient's mute and bizarrely flirtatious grimacing, the therapist said: "You look like you're under water". Elaborating on this silent fusion of sex and death, the therapist, again unconsciously, described his grasping for words so that "we don't both drown in the psychosis".

At the front

In their recent book, *History Beyond Trauma* (2004), Davoine and Gaudilliere note that the word, "therapist", derives from the Greek for "the second in combat" (p. 153). They are convinced that psychosis and trauma go hand-in-hand, that the psychotic patient is madly conducting a research into the rupture between his family and the social fabric, a rupture brought about through trauma and betrayal. Their work powerfully links the clinical arena with the historical and the political, and suggests that the patient's psychosis is not at all an attack on the social order; just the opposite, it is a frantic effort to bring a foreclosed social order into existence.

Indeed, they note the ubiquity of military experience in the lives of those early therapists who chose to work with psychotic patients, and, as mentioned in Chapter Nine, they discovered in the work of Thomas Salmon, a First World War psychiatrist, a version of the principles they had long since come to rely on in their work with psychotic patients: *simplicity* (no jargon), *proximity* (being with the traumatised person's raw experience), *immediacy* (depending on intuition and on the seeming coincidences within the transference), and *expectancy* (the dimension of hope, of getting better because those at the front wait for you).

At a conference on psychoanalysis and religion, Davoine (personal communication) posed a question about the difference between belief and trust. Illustrating something about that difference, she said: "My delusional patient asks 'Do you believe me?' and I answer 'I trust you.' " This "I trust you" is a foundational moment in any clinical psychoanalysis, but perhaps it has a more critical place with psychotic patients, especially if we agree with Lacan's description of that condition as a disorder "at the most personal juncture between the subject and his sense of being alive" (p. 153). This evocative definition of madness implies a radical disjunction between two essences of being human: a subjectivity existing in a field of death (Benedetti (1987) and an aliveness outside of any relationship to an encompassing mind.

A chronically and quietly psychotic patient, following the death of her mother "wanted to be psychotic for awhile" and so discontinued her medication. She became threatening, uncooperative, and incomprehensible, and required a high level of containment. When she decided to resume medication, she did so finally feeling "real". Indeed, her breakdown came to seem like a breakthrough. "I want to find my voice. I want to be heard," she said, and she seemed to have integrated anger for the first time. "Of course, I hate my stepmother; she cares nothing for me." She also had advice for her therapist: "If it happens again, tell me you are not my mother." There is indeed a Big History of trauma and betrayal in the generations before her, but in the Little History, this is a patient who lost her mother at a time when her therapist did as well, and a new twosome seemed now to be forming from a field of death *both* parties had now entered (Fromm, 2011).

Davoine and Gaudilliere offer a frame for the treatment of psychotic patients that contains madness within the dyad by recognising its meaning in a potentially dissociated history, including the larger histories shared by both parties. The "I trust you" of Dr Davoine can be seen as the Yes to the subject necessarily engaged with this field of death, the Yes of accompaniment, the "*Oui* (We) *de la Mere*", the Yes because there is a We, even if one party cannot think in those terms and even as the nascent dyad must always ground itself in the "*Nom (Non) du Pere*" (Fromm, 2009; Lacan, 1977). In the earlier patient's story, the central trauma of a mother's suicide is indeed related to betrayal, and the "No" of this particular father seemed to have catastrophically compromised if not destroyed the essential "Yes" this child needed. "I've hurt people who didn't deserve it".

Holding environment

To return now to that story, the next phase of the patient's psychotherapy centred on the articulation of his difficulties being in the evolving treatment relationship. At one point, the therapist suffered a fit of coughing during a session; the patient said to him: "It's okay, go and get some water". The therapist felt this as a gift from the patient, one that crystallised an evolving love between them, one that might provoke, but also through which they might weather, the storms of intimacy. Slowly, the patient explained that he felt that "sacred" parts of his body had been removed during his operation, and he feared that, in the act of speaking, he might literally lose more of his body as well as his mind. Indeed, he feared that he might be pulled into the therapist's body.

Recall now the therapist's uncanny experience of urinary urgency and overwhelming internal pressure during the first session, the delusional pregnancy and surgery that had precipitated his psychosis, and the birth followed by death in his earliest history. Davoine and Gaudilliere write:

> In each case, the catastrophic issues of the great history are woven with the little history of (the patient's) life through transference ... Odd coincidences happen ... They occur at the very beginning of the therapeutic encounter, as if repudiated bits of history had climbed the stage of the analysis ... This outlaw dimension of the 'Real' comes back in a disruptive way ... From this no man's land, the psychotic research presents pieces of a betrayed history, in which very quickly the analyst has to be situated, and must give back, the best he can, his position, so that true speech is possible again. (1997, p. 4)

The patient's merger fears opened up his longing for the mother he had lost a few months after his birth. He felt that with his operation he had lost her "maternal energy" and that without it he was reduced to always running to substitute mothers. He seemed to feel that some fragile connection with his actual mother had been lost in the operation. But he also experienced the mothers who came later as emotionally unavailable, and so "since I needed a mother and only found these fake mothers, I learned to be cold and sarcastic like them". Feeling so deficient and so deprived, the patient was overcome with chronic envy and jealousy, and he pushed people away not only because he wanted them so much, but also because he was so jealous of them. All of this led to pervasive feelings of shame and a powerful tendency toward withdrawal. Eventually his fear of losing himself in his therapist's body, the fantasy unconsciously connected to the therapist's experience in the first session, became, as he felt more grounded in himself, the conscious wish to be held by the therapist. The anxiety then became a worry for his therapist: that the therapist could not stand the patient's intense need for him, nor could he stand the deadness the patient felt inside himself. The neo-Kleinians (Schafer, 1997) might rightly highlight here the shift from the paranoid to the depressive position.

A poignant illustration of this maternal difficulty was captured in a photograph. As he got better, the patient began working at a nursery school, staffed by a Montessori-trained teacher. In a photo taken during a group event, a happy four-year-old is sitting on the patient's lap enjoying the activity going on in the centre of the room. Unlike the other teachers, however, this patient looks uncomfortable and keeps his arms rigidly at his side, an almost unnatural refusal of holding. This problem with contact was mirrored in the packages the patient would occasionally receive from his stepmother, for example, shampoo with no note, apparently a silent message about hygiene without the holding communication that might make this potential injury tolerable. The word "tact" relates to the word "touch", and in this non-communication as well as in this photograph, we see the failure of what Winnicott calls handling leading to personalisation (1954a), or a taken-for-granted, easy relationship between body and self. Fortunately, the teacher could see this problem and worked with her assistant to help him develop greater ease with ordinary physical contact with the children.

In the patient's residential community, he was elected to lead a group whose job it was to bring new people into the community in a welcoming and orienting way. He did a reasonably good job at this, an outcome remarkable not only because of his social difficulties, but also because of a recurrent group dynamic. This group's chairperson is often met by the community's ambivalence toward new patients; they are in fantasy feared, hated, and jealously regarded as the new children who will displace the older children from parental care. Given the fact that this patient was the youngest sibling in his family, and in essence the living sign to the other siblings of the loss of their mother, we can begin to appreciate the enormous power of what looks like his unconscious role re-enactment, a pivotal, intermediary role around which hate of the new and fear of the old are absorbed and enacted. Living this out can be thought of as one form of the patient's *unconscious citizenship* (Fromm, 2000). Among other things, a therapeutic community provides an especially powerful lens as well as a potential space (Fromm, 2009), through which to see and perhaps re-work the issues within this citizenship, for both the individual patient and the community (see also Chapter Thirteen).

Even further, the group dynamic between the psychotic patient and the borderline patient can become available for examined living, including for whatever learning might occur about early family life. It is not unusual that the psychotic patient is regarded with real envy, barely disguised as pity, by the borderline patient. And, in a sense rightly so, because the psychotic patient gets seen—only in part projectively—as the real thing, as obviously suffering, as openly hateful, as the true self locked away behind the borderline's false self. And, of course conversely, the psychotic patient secretly longs for— and is ashamed of lacking—the social ability, the affective coherence, the more or less rational and rationalising speech of the borderline. This too must bear upon this patient's early life: a new baby, hated as a mother-killer and envied because he seemed too young to feel it, who becomes a damaged, uncomprehending child seriously disconnected from subsequent mothers.

It speaks again to the uncanny playing out of necessary dynamics within a therapeutic community that this patient eventually took part in a play put on by the activities department. The play told the story of a reunion of friends, who wind up gossiping, commiserating, and competing about their current lives. Into this superficial pathos comes the character played by the patient, whose hilariously venomous remarks cut through everyone's more hidden motivations and leave the real sadness openly exposed. This character is a sarcastic and compulsive truth teller who nevertheless cannot find the truth of himself, just as the patient's psychosis represents the loss of himself in a chaotic effort to find the truth of the other. These experiences within the treatment setting are risky; they illuminate and potentially strengthen, but they need the backcloth of relationships, including the analytic one, to hold and integrate them. "When I first came here, nothing seemed real to me", a psychotic patient said to her therapist. "Now you seem real to me, and other people are beginning to".

Three dreams

In his therapy, the patient reported a dream. He was leaving an unknown place but had no suitcase. He went to an attic of an empty house, found one, and was packing beautiful antique clothes, some made of lace, and some safety pins. His own interpretation accented his identity as a person who leaves places prematurely, an identity both defined by and secured by separation. In a sense, the suitcase, with its hard exterior, is him. His therapist accented the beautiful and fragile things now inside him, things that evoke another generation's past, and his need to keep them held together so that he can feel like a whole person. The patient accepted this interpretation of their work together quietly, but soon provoked a fight—another hard boundary. I think here of Frances Tustin's (1981) distinction between hard objects and softer, confusional ones, the former serving crude boundary functions for the autistic child. Neither party had noted the attic, even though the patient came everyday to the therapist's top floor office in an old house. This dream illustrates the integrations the patient was making as well as the ongoing anxiety, perhaps in both parties, about recognising their interdependence.

Over many months, a number of events unfolded within the therapeutic relationship, each of which captures an aspect of the treatment of the psychotic patient. The patient slowly introduced the important characters of his life, filling in historical background, with absolutely no reference to his relationship to them or theirs to each other. For the psychotic patient, developmental and relationship history may be the outcome of treatment, rather than its preliminary. Indeed, the "psychotic research" (Davoine and Gaudilliere, 2004) is aimed at an unspeakable, foreclosed history. Especially through dreams, the patient brought in important images from the border of the Real, as Lacan (1977) would say: for example, the deeply resonant image of a baby killer-whale.

Slowly, he allowed sense to the sequence of interaction between him and his therapist. In Bion's (1967a) terms, attacks on linking subsided. For example, his therapist observed that he had gone to sleep in the session after the therapist had announced his vacation. The patient agreed and said that he could not tell the therapist how he felt because he was afraid he (the patient) would hit him. Eventually, like a small child delighting in his power to conjure up the originary myths of his being, he would ask his therapist to tell him again and again various stories about his life, for example, how his parents had gotten together. He cried for the first time in relation to wanting to know his diagnosis. Therapist and patient worked through this by their both reading and talking together about *I Never Promised You a Rose Garden* (Greenberg, 1964). He cried again when he wanted to know the story of his mother, which he and his therapist pieced together in tragic detail—one almost wants to say with safety pins. The patient began to use the pronoun "we".

In the second year of therapy, the patient had a dream. Another patient, with the same name as him, was lying in the road and left for dead; the therapist saved him, and this patient got revenge on the therapist by urinating on his computer (echoing the therapist's very first experience of urinary urgency). This dream also occurred in the context of suitcases, that is, of both parties' thoughts about leaving the treatment programme, the therapist for a major position in a university setting and the patient for a graduate programme to which he had been accepted. His functioning had improved enormously. Indeed, the two things he was trying to bury had revived; his intellectual functioning had risen by twenty-five points and, more problematically, his love, especially for his therapist, had come back to life. In this context of potential separation and its intense pain, revenge for not being left for dead began to make sense.

Carrying these difficult feelings, the patient came to his session and said, "I've got bad news; I'm psychotic again". He drifted into more isolation and scatteredness in the residential community, and he also began to dream that the patient who had committed suicide (and whose suicide he had predicted) was present in his room at night. An "area of death", as Benedetti (1987) calls it, again made its appearance. After his therapist walked out at the end of a patient–staff meeting, the patient went to his room and took a serious overdose. For the psychotic patient, suicide can be an effort to kill—but also to name—that unspeakable thing, that other death for which the patient himself has been the representative. As the patient put it, "I am my mother's sacrificial boy". That other death—in this case, a mother's suicide—has been foreclosed from the symbolic order (Lacan, 1977), leaving the patient only as a deranged witness, who then, like Winnicott's (1974) "Fear of breakdown" patient, searches into the future for this thing of the past—and sometimes finds it, for example, in the suicide of his fellow patient or in his own near-death. "The only possible work is in proximity with the patient", write Davoine and Gaudilliere, ". . . from coincidences of the death area and the analyst's approach of such a zone". (1997, p. 5) Perhaps, the death of his therapist, through the therapist's planned departure, was also such a coincidence for this patient.

Fortunately, he caught himself. Immediately after the overdose, he called for help. He was able to tell his therapist that, when the therapist left the meeting, he felt "I needed you so much", after which he took the overdose. This brought the acute pain about separation, that both patient and therapist were feeling, along with the patient's rage, into the work. Over a number of months, they worked through this pain, and both left for their future lives. The patient said goodbye to the treatment community and began graduate school as well as a new psychotherapy in a nearby city. He continued to function well and to be in touch periodically with his former therapist. Over a long time and a long distance, their connection remained strong.

This treatment illustrates the unfolding of a therapeutic relationship with a psychotic patient, including its phases of mutual regulation, resistances based on merger anxieties, and the centrality of trauma. Such a relational process can be both held and deeply informed by a therapeutic community programme within which important enactments and re-workings may occur. Through these enactments, the psychotic patient as, if you will, a mystified and chaotic signifier within a discourse of an other may find his place in the heretofore, unconscious intergenerational narrative of his family's life (Fromm, 2012). With functioning recovered and a more grounded sense of self, the patient may move on in life, "shrinking to life size" in Sullivan's terms (1940, p. 33), and quietly grieving the family catastrophe that he had in the past simply represented.

But . . .

Several years ago I visited the former concentration camp at Dachau. As I walked down the long, open path of dirt and pebbles leading from the museum, past the barracks, to the crematoria and chapels, the apprehension I had felt in anticipation of this visit turned into something overwhelming. I felt flooded with emotions, sensations, and images. It was a hot, clear, beautiful day. The Bavarian town outside the camp seemed ordinarily quaint and appealing. People went about their lives. But that name, I thought; how could people carry on with that name? As I walked this interminable path, I felt an intensity of feeling—of grief and horror—beyond anything I had known before. I flashed on images from photographs and from the horrific penultimate scene in *The White Hotel* (Thomas, 1981). I began to feel that I was walking on a ground made of bodies and then that the ground itself began to fold up around me, to completely engulf me, though I was still walking. Most shocking to me was the gathering feeling that I was literally unable to speak; no words came to me, but if they had, I felt certain that I would not be physically able to speak them.

This terrifying experience, simultaneously dizzying and enormously weighted, this overwhelmed speechlessness at the scene of catastrophe, changed suddenly through my accidental encounter with words. The words, engraved on a plague in a crematorium, commemorated the murder of four British nurses who had attempted to facilitate the care and rescue of some of the inmates. I will never forget them. "But the souls of the righteous are in the hands of God, and there shall no torment touch them." The profound beauty in these words about a failed rescue rescued me. They forced and released the feelings overwhelming me. In retrospect, I realised the power of that first word "But". It asserted itself as the beginning of the second half of a sentence, the first half of which was silence. It contradicted that silence, the silence of death, of denial, of the Real. It broke my speechlessness.

I found myself remembering this experience as I considered the more familial and psychological disasters of the patients about whom I've been reporting. Like them, I felt engulfed by catastrophe, overwhelmed with feeling, unable to think or speak, in a context—the day, the town—that functioned as a massive denial. Unlike these patients, at least until their treatments, into this silence came an answering other, negating the negation, speaking the word "But". Harry Stack Sullivan once said that: "we are all much more simply human than otherwise" (1940, p. 16). Like our patients, "we have all had such moments of true urgency" (Oxenhandler, 1997, p. 65).

CHAPTER ELEVEN

Dreams represented in dreams

Remembering

A young woman dreamed of a small piece of wire, tied so tightly around her finger that it had cut the skin and blood had begun to flow. The dream meant to her that there was something she needed to badly remember; though it must also be something she wished to forget, in proportion to the pain of her reminder. What might this be? The flow of blood reminds her of her menstrual period and of her female analyst's absent period, absent by virtue of her pregnancy. For many weeks now, the therapy has lost tone, as the patient has attempted to split herself off from the feelings aroused by this fact of her analyst's and her own life. At the same time she has become more depressed, more irritable, more purposeless, and more impelled toward destructiveness in her behaviour. Her dream—or dream fragment—signals a turn in this process.

Perhaps for this patient the wire, like the wire surrounding the concentration camp where her parents first met, symbolises also a pain-filled union: her parents' to each other, hers to her parents, hers to her analyst, her analyst's to her baby—this dream-wire fashioned into a ring. And perhaps the castration motif might eventually claim her attention: what must be *re-membered* is a dreamed *dis-memberment*, this for a patient even more cut off recently from her inner life, soon to be cut off from her analyst, symptomatically given to cutting her body, and forever now cut off from the dead father she both hated and adored.

All of these real or potential meanings come into existence as imaginative elaborations of her dream in conjunction with the whole of her affective life, as its particular personal configurations have accrued in her analysis. But something must be remembered prior to any of this: the dream itself, as much for the meaning of remembering as for the meaning of its content. If the manifest content formulates and expresses the wish to remember, at least the implicit healing or integrative thrust within that wish exists and, even more, is successfully accomplished. The dream, or dream fragment, *is* remembered and brought to the analysis. For it is this dream which could, first of all, have been forgotten, and it is this dream which cuts her sleep, inflicts pain, and in the analysis opens a flow to her inner life.

In other words, the wire reminder *in* the dream is also a reminder *of* the dream; it can be said to represent the dream, insofar as it represents the tipped balance within the dreamer's wish systems toward opening herself more fully and affectively to the analytic process and relationship. If her resistance, at one level, expressed her resentment that she could not, like her analyst's baby, be inside the analyst, the dream and its being remembered allow the analyst to be inside her. One thesis of this chapter is that dreams sometimes contain references to themselves. Put another way, the dreamer sometimes finds it necessary to include in a dream some element that gives representation to the dream itself as an object in the analytic exchange or as the container of powerfully valenced experience.

True self/false self

In *The Offensive Traveller*, V. S. Pritchett (1964) writes:

> By "being offensive", I mean that I travel, therefore I offend. I represent that ancient enemy of all communities: the stranger. Neapolitan girls have crossed themselves to avert the evil eye at the sight of me. . . . And rightly: we are looking on the private life of another people, a life which is entirely their business, with an eye, that, however

friendly it may be, is alien. We are seeing people as they do not see themselves. (p. 4)

How close this is to Winnicott (1963b):

> Starting from no fixed place, I soon came, while preparing this paper for a foreign society, to staking a claim, to my surprise, to the right not to communicate. This was a protest from the core of me to the frightening fantasy of being infinitely exploited. In another language, this would be the fantasy of being eaten or swallowed up. In the language of this paper, it is *the fantasy of being found*. (p. 179)

Both Pritchett and Winnicott concern themselves here with the problem of the stranger, the unknown other, and with the need to establish a privacy for the secure living out of the self. Implicit is the idea of a boundary: for example, the magically protective boundary established by the Neapolitan girls who cross themselves and thus avert a penetrating and perhaps eventually mutual gaze. For Winnicott, boundaries serve primarily to define usable and liveable space (Davis & Wallbridge, 1981), what might be thought of as the climatic or ecological conditions for the development of the self in its various aspects.

More generally, Winnicott's central theoretical preoccupation has to do with the nature of the relationship between the individual and the environment in varying degrees of health and at varying stages of development, including that stage when there is no "between". He found it necessary, as have many if not all psychoanalytic theorists before and since, to postulate a bifurcation of the subject: a shell and a core, a manifest and a latent, a societal self and a central self, an ego organisation and a spontaneous source, a mirror-image and a body-in-pieces. Winnicott (1960) most frequently discussed this duality in terms of the false self and true self. Here is his schematic statement of beginnings:

> The good–enough mother meets the omnipotence of the infant and, to some extent, makes sense of it. She does this repeatedly. A True Self begins to have life. . . . The mother who is not good enough . . . repeatedly fails to meet the infant gesture; instead, she substitutes her own gesture, which is to be given sense by the compliance of the infant. This compliance on the part of the infant is the earliest stage of the False Self and belongs to the mother's inability to sense her infant's needs. (p. 145)

Winnicott describes the true self as "the theoretical position from which come the spontaneous gesture and the personal idea", as evolving "from the aliveness of the body tissues and the working of body-functions, including the heart's action and breathing", as "closely linked with the idea of Primary Process", and as "at the beginning, essentially not reactive to external stimuli, but primary" (p. 148). The true self "does no more than collect together the details of the experience of aliveness; (O)nly the True Self can be creative and only the True Self can feel real" (p. 148).

By contrast, the false self organises as a patterning of reactions to impingement, reactions which early on disrupted the "continuity of being" of the infant and which shifted the locus of a personal centre more to the outside than the inside. Most typically, the false self is a compliant or pseudo-compliant structure, dependent on initiatives from outside itself and more or less skilled in eliciting them. In extreme cases, the false self seems to be the whole of the person; there is some essential lack in the individual's capacity to engage creatively with life, a chronic sense of futility, and "the need to collect impingements from external reality so that the living-time of the individual can be filled with reactions" (Winnicott, 1960, p. 150). Winnicott emphasises that the false self is a defensive organisation; it has, as its functions: (1) the hiding of the true self, perhaps even its disabling and burial, so that no disruption can occur to the static relationship of the false self and its environment; (2) the protection of a secret potential life for the true self with extreme alertness to the danger of annihilation; and (3) "a search for conditions which will make it possible for the True Self to come into its own" (Winnicott, 1960, p. 143).

The false self then, as one of Winnicott's patients describes it, is a care-taker self. It gathers and thrives upon the impingements that might otherwise seduce or attack more vulnerable areas of self-functioning. It is therefore a boundary-establishing structure; it establishes a zone of privacy at the same time that it appeases a needed yet overwhelming environment. The direction of a therapy is toward the handing over of the care-taking function to the analyst; this is what Winnicott means by an organised regression to dependence. Prior to this, there is recurrent testing of the analytic setting and endless possibility for misalliance with the false self. After this delivery (Winnicott offers an implicit birth model, with the false self as midwife for the true self), there is serious risk insofar as the true self is felt to be alive once more, dependent on a living environmental provision, and exceedingly vulnerable to its failure.

This is to some extent the movement of any analytic therapy. The beauty of the psychoanalytic setting is that, in its attention to the need for both frame and medium functions, it divides authority between analyst and patient in such a way as to facilitate a reliable holding and to safeguard an expressive potential. It meets the gestures of the true self in a way designed only to accentuate their inherent shape or, put differently, to recognise them with potential meaning. And it refuses the invitations of the false self for a defensive relationship of prescription and compliance. André Green (1978) has very elegantly described Winnicott's squiggle game in these terms and has emphasised the division of function and authority within the analytic setting. Starkly and schematically defining the locus of initiatives, he writes that, though the rules or frame are set by the analyst, "No analysis is conceivable in which, after the statement of the fundamental rule, the analyst speaks first" (p. 180).

The analyst is thus bound to the function of medium, his total mental and emotional functioning constituting simply a resource available for use. As we know, this nondirective availability generates anxiety and must be repeatedly tested, warded off, or otherwise negotiated. In fact, we frequently encounter clinically people who experience the empty space of the analysis as terrifying rather than frustrating, or calming, or lonely, or demanding, or as an opportunity. It is as though the false self fears being starved out of existence by the analyst's silence, and, to the degree that the person identifies himself only with that defensive aspect of personality, this fear carries the dread of the self's disappearance or annihilation. This is the kind of technical problem that leads Green (1975) to think of the basic analytic task as facilitating "the positive cathexis of the empty space" (p. 17).

Winnicott (1971a) himself makes the following comment about his squiggle game: "One of the aims of this game is to reach to the child's ease and so to his fantasy and so to his dreams" (p. 115). He sees a homology between the blank space of the paper, the play space of the child, and the analytic space, to which Khan (1972a) adds the concept of the dream space. But who makes the squiggle itself and who dreams the dream? Winnicott does not offer us an answer, at least to the latter part of that question, although his comments about the true self qualify also as a description of the dreaming subject: the spontaneous gesture, the personal idea, the work of the body, the link to primary process, the reduced reactivity to external stimuli, and the creative integration of the details of living. Perhaps Winnicott would not have disagreed with Rycroft's (1979) view that dreams are simply intimate and imaginative communications between one part of the self and another: "[T]he dreaming self utters meanings from a timeless, total position . . . while the part of the self that receives dream-messages occupies a preempted, prescribed position localized in a particular time and place, and possesses a preconceived notion of itself which is at risk if it listens seriously to dream-meanings" (p. 148).

But Winnicott, ever reluctant to impinge with interpretations and thus reinforce the tendency of the false self to further dissociate, underplays the meanings of a dream; as Pontalis (1974) comments, for Winnicott, "it is less the *meaning* of the conflict, which can be disclosed elsewhere . . . that is sought for in the dream, than the *capacity* to which it bears witness" (p. 131). Ogden (2005a,b) too highlights the curative value of the dreaming process itself and examines both the obstacles to, and the therapeutic provisions that facilitate, the exercise of this capacity. Winnicott, the happy child grown into paediatrician, seemed always far more attuned to capacities—to be alone, to feel concern, to play—than to drives or faults. It is worth adding here that in the dream one might find not only the subject's capacity to dream, and not only the capacities of the subject evidenced in the dream, but also the subject's assessment of the capacities of the analytic setting. The false self, if viewed as a boundary between the environment and the true self, a variant of Freud's protective shield (1920g), searches its surroundings either for the conditions of compliance or the conditions for delivery.

This is the field sketched by Pontalis in his 1974 paper on "The dream as an object" (further elaborated in his 1981 book):

> Freud, at the same time as he totally revises it, places himself in the tradition of the various seers, secular and religious, where the dream is consecrated to its meaning, thus, to some extent, neglecting the dream as experience, the subjective experience of the dreamer dreaming and the intersubjective experience in therapy . . .. (p. 125)

His central point is this:

As long as one does not appreciate *the function* that the dream fulfils in the analytic process, and as long as the *place* that it fills in the subjective topography remains indeterminant, any interpretation of the *message* of the dream is at best ineffective; at worst, it maintains an unending complicity. (p. 125)

Freud (1923c) struggled with this complicity; he noted, for example, that: "The question of the value to be assigned to dreams is intimately related to the other question of their susceptibility to influence from 'suggestion' by the physician" (pp. 115–116). Rephrased in Winnicott's terms, the false self can find in a particular methodology of analysis an opportunity for collusion and a refuge from more vulnerable aspects of the self. Analytic success can precipitate an escalation of hiding. In 1911, Freud stated that: "All the knowledge acquired about dreams serves also to put the dream-constructing process on its guard" (1911e, p. 95). It is this guardedness or boundary management that will be discussed here.

"I must tell you something"

The patient had a history of major loss—first of person, then of place. She seemed to have felt evicted into premature adulthood by her family's rupture. She suffered acute breakdowns of purpose, cohesiveness, and affect regulation, through which the prominent, enduring aspects of her personality included fierce loyalty, a devoted aspiration toward a perfect lovingness, and a constricting sentimentality. Her early approach to her therapy tended to be diligent and sanitised, the collection of her life's few messy or puzzling details presented for her therapist's benevolent correction. Eventually she made her first trip home; upon her return, on the first day of her second year of treatment, she presented a dream to her therapist.

In the dream, the patient is in a modern vacation house with her family. Suddenly the house is on fire. Then the scene shifts totally as though to another dream. She is at a lunch counter drinking many different liquids at once. A man enters, an old boyfriend, who sits next to her. He does not notice the embarrassing oddity of her many drinks because he is reading the newspaper. She is shocked to notice on its front page a picture in colour of a blazing house and a story about an arsonist. She blurts out that she must tell him something, but then goes to the bathroom. There is no sign designating the women's or the men's room. There is also no lock on either door, and while she is in the bathroom, someone attacks her and attempts to rape her. She escapes and seeks help.

This dream, from one angle and at a manifest level, is an itinerary of the patient's flight. First her home, then her consciousness, then her body are by turns subject to invasion, from which flight is her only recourse. Since there are no signs designating men and women, we are invited to wonder about the identification of the men in the dream, benign or malevolent, with herself and with her female analyst. What might be the potential meaning of this dream, (recognising, of course, that without development of the associative material and the further analytic exchange, such meanings are entirely speculative)? Suppose the boyfriend stands for, as the most immediate displacement, the analyst. From this point of view, the second part of the dream seems an explicit effort to envision, and master or evade, an anxiety within the analytic setting. The patient has a dream, a near nightmare; she then dreams that that dream—represented by the photo and story in the newspaper—will come to her analyst's attention, indeed will be considered newsworthy. She feels either urgently impelled or guiltily compelled—we do not know which—to tell her analyst about this dream. But she does not; instead she withdraws, only to face an assault on her inner space.

We cannot understand this withdrawal without further data from the patient. We can, however, note the movements of the dreaming subject: approaching the other, then receding; filling herself privately, meeting the other, then emptying herself privately. And we can allow the dream to evoke the possible reasons for her decision: anxiety regarding tender feelings toward her analyst (represented as a boyfriend), the hurt related to a breakup, the concern that her analyst will join in a prosecution of an arsonist or will herself make something private into a public matter, the mingled dejection and relief that the analyst fails to see her extreme neediness because of her own interest in the news. Indeed, one could argue that the patient might construe her analyst to be more interested in the dream (and whatever it might represent; e.g., her recent trip home or, at a different level, her drive psychology) than in her, and that she could find relief from painful embarrassment in her analyst's preoccupation. Here is the potential for the patient's feeding her analyst her dreams in order to shield her own solitary and desperate feeding of herself. Within this scenario, her withdrawal becomes a protest: "You have the story, but not the author; the dream but not the dreamer".

My orientation here has to do with the question of why this dream did not simply stop with the burning of the house and her escape from it, why it was necessary to have this second dream at all. Given multiple determination, there can be no simple answer to this question, although Franz Alexander's (1925) hypothesis about dreams in pairs is worth reviewing. Alexander offered examples of dreams that relate to and refer directly to one another without taking up the question of dreams, in general or in particular, being represented in a dream. He demonstrated that pairs of dreams can refer to each other and to the same currently active conflictual wish, and that they usually divide the labour of compromise by paying off the superego in one and allowing a more directly experienced instinctual gratification in the other.

In the example under discussion, the fire and liquid elements may capture the latent conflict: the first dream representing the projected playing out of passion or impulse, the second their being recognised as internal and rather exaggeratedly doused. To this hypothesis we might add an interpretation of the dream pair at the level of the ego's effort toward a curative integration. The first dream represents the problem, the terror, and the fragmenting of a group into its split-off troubled individuals. The second dream represents the solution, the relief, and the reintegration of a group constituted by the patient and the analyst's representative. Finally, we might consider this dream pair as representing the division of dream and dreamer mentioned previously. The first is the dream, in which and from which the dreamer takes flight. The second contains the dreamer, the trace of the first dream in objectified form, and the dreamer's negotiations with the other.

This perhaps is the "subjective topography" to which Pontalis refers (1974). This second dream seems necessary, as the patient's effort to construct, anticipate, and work with, while balancing defensive and communicative needs, the "conditions" of the analytic setting. It seems to be a dream about the place of dreams in the analysis and to represent the patient's tension and ambivalence about delivering herself, at this anniversary moment, to her analyst's care. In

Winnicott's language, the second dream could be seen as illustrating the false self's co-opting of analytic methodology to transform a vehicle of self-revelation into a barrier to analytic impingement. And it does this seductively, playing upon the analyst's potential imbalances of interest, while clinging to the therapeutic relationship rather than the analytic task. Dream is separated from dreamer; the former is offered as an object of interest, but the latter withdraws. Similarly, analyst is separated from analysis; the patient clings to the former and uses a seductive gift to shield herself from the latter. In the dream, her disappearance is hardly noticed.

It is true, however, that the compliant defensive strategies of false self organisation can be played out around any aspect of analytic methodology and that this first dream could have been handled by the patient within the analysis in purely defensive ways. The second dream is thus not necessary for its false self, defensive properties; rather, it is necessary to *represent* the false self, to construct its choices and to test an outcome. Though it is reflexive activity, a stepping back from the simple telling of the passionate story of her first dream, it is not a total withdrawal; at least the patient formulates her experience of her current analytic situation. In reporting the dream, she offers her analyst access to it. The content of the second dream is a holographic model of its context—a mirror reflecting in miniature the patient's experience of, or prediction about, the analysis: for example, that her analyst's attention to what she produced (or how she performed on her trip) would be crushing to her more basic need to be attended to at the level of how she is. This reflects both the true self vulnerability and the false self defensive strategy.

The analytic task is, first of all, to avoid living out in the analysis the defensive programme of the false self, as announced in such a dream. It is not the dream that needs attention, but the dreamer, and the envisioned qualities of the relationship between the dreamer and the dream-receiver. From this particular patient's manifest dream sequence, we might say, perhaps a bit too neatly, that between her history (a home, a fire, a dislocation), and her symptoms (her anality, her gender confusion, her withdrawal and masochism), comes the possibility of language and of the analytic relationship: "I must tell you something". The representation of the dream within this dream comes as an effort to envision, experience and communicate, at one remove, this pivotal moment.

Dreams as objects

The first clinical example illustrated the representation of a particular dream in a second dream. This second example illustrates the representation of dreams as a general category in a particular dream. It concerns a withdrawn, diffusely anxious man, who had felt very troubled and deprived since early childhood. He felt a chronic inner pain relieved, to a degree, through angry, frightening clashes with a girlfriend, whose needs repeatedly excited, then humiliated him. Early in his analysis, to which he adapted with a defensive eagerness, the patient found himself in a rather sudden and diffuse mood of anger toward his analyst. Echoing his initial complaint, he reported that these feelings were experienced with increasing anxiety but remained "out of focus" and beyond his verbal reach. It was as though he were reporting on an intense storm from a radar picture. The analyst commented that between feelings and words there are sometimes images, like those found in dreams, and that perhaps his dreams might help him grasp and understand his current reactions.

In the next session, the patient indeed reported a dream, his first remembered dream in many years. In the dream, he met a student of his and told her that he was angry with her about her recent poor work. She showed him some beautiful photographs. Then, in a different scene, he found a table on which there were many bundles of lovely photographs from his student for many different people. Those marked for him, however, were small and poorly done. He was dejected. He waited until everyone left so that he could then look at the bundles of photographs alone.

The patient's associations took him in the direction of identifying his student with himself, rather than with his analyst. Like his student, he too used his work as a vehicle for passive aggression. Like his student, he felt that his output at his job and in his analysis was inadequate. Like his student, he too had recently served something on a table like the one in the dream; at a recent social event, he had made himself less anxious and fragmented by cooking and serving food, for which he was most appreciated. He also recalled reading a story on the day of the dream about the ghost of a dead child materialising visually in a photograph. On its surface, we also see in this dream the plight of this patient's self-image. His student shows her capability for good work and then that it is reserved for others. His relationship with her, as with others, reflects his own lack, something missing, something perhaps even dead. And further his anger is futile; it is responded to with continued poor work, as though it and he do not exist. Why then even try to bring it into focus?

The dream also unfolds, in a specific way, at the level of the analytic relationship, and it was this aspect of the material that proved most affectively alive for the patient. In the dream, the photographs serve initially to deflect, avoid, buy off, or solve in some other way the confrontation with the patient's anger. Recall that it was the patient's diffuse anger at his analyst that had led the analyst himself to invoke the dream. From this angle, the photographs in the dream—those bundles of images—can be thought of as representations of the dream, and again we find a dream about the place and function of dreams in the subjective situation of the analysis. In this light, potential meanings come into focus: for example, that the patient can indeed speak his anger, but it is the analyst who deflects it by showing him beautiful images; or that the patient will produce many interesting dreams for others, but that what he is left with, what bears his name, what he will take for himself is essentially lacking; or that there is a collusion with the analyst to avoid live anger through defensive feeding and ultimately debilitating productivity; or that any *genuine* examining of his dreams can only be done by the patient alone, after the analyst, in a perhaps narcissistically satisfied state, has wandered off.

The point at issue here has to do with the placing of an object—in the dream, of photographs and in the analysis, of a dream—between two parties, the particular function of which in this example seems to be first of all the blunting of the live feeling, the spontaneous movement between them. Pontalis (1974) would suggest that we take the term *object* in its psychoanalytic sense: the dream as maternal body without whom the patient is lost and anxious; with whom he is shielded, hidden, and submissive. In the figure of the student, there is condensed the dialectic of self with other, most importantly, the analyst, and the dialectic between true and false self. The student represents the analyst, offering the patient dream analysis in the face of his anger; at the same time she represents the patient, producing dreams and denying his anger. The student's false self productivity ultimately leaves him empty, but her blithe nonconformity is also an inspiration and an encouragement.

This patient's false self organisation, so clearly manifest in the eager yet resented compliance with analytic suggestion and in the joining of a substitution of gestures, of products for person, serves to protect both the other whom he needs and the core of himself from being found; there remains, however, a persistent sense of lack, of shame, and of dread. This dream does not clearly illuminate the reasons for the patient's anger at the analyst; the content remains elusive, although the self-representation as a young girl who is looking rather than working might suggest erotic and affectionate feelings as an important factor. Rather, the manifest dream formulates the management of that anger within the analytic situation and predicts the evolution and cost of the defensive playing out of a false self organisation.

Dreaming the unconscious

This patient, a man in his late 20s, had a history of acute psychotic episodes characterised by hallucinations and catatonic phenomena, for which he had been hospitalised briefly on several occasions. At the beginning of an intensive psychotherapy, he presented himself in a most constricted and wooden condition. After a few months, he told his analyst that: "The first move, from psychosis to what I'm like now, is relatively easy. To change beyond this—to really change—will be much harder". He advised patience. A few days before the dream to be reported, the patient had provoked his analyst to caution him sternly against a plan he had mentioned; he had thought that he might visit an old friend in order to "party", making it clear that some drug use was intended. In response to the analyst, to whom the patient had been relating all along as a replica of his authoritarian father, he cancelled his plans. The dream followed shortly thereafter.

In the dream, the patient, his father, and mother are having a mausoleum built. The building is a long white one, and its contents, which include a coffin and medications, create an ambiguity as to whether the person for whom it is intended is already dead or simply very sick. Then, the patient's paternal grandfather is actually dead and in a coffin. Father, mother, and patient are present, and also standing by is a black female servant. In the patient's words, "The seal on the coffin was broken and we had to put a new wire seal on. We found the package, and there were six seals the size of a dime, but one seal could be stretched over the whole coffin". There is then a scene in the parents' bedroom. People are packing things for a trip, perhaps to go to the funeral. The patient packs knives, but can find no forks. "Then it came time to bury the coffin. I said I would help my father carry the coffin. But my father carried it alone. It was very small, about three and a half feet, like [it contained] an emaciated body, and my father would carry it in his hands. But before my father could carry it he had to remove some vases from the top of the coffin. They had herbs and perfumes that had a macabre flavour [*sic*] to them. So I gave them to my mother—no need for them to go to waste. I associated perfumes with my mother".

Later in the session, the patient remembered another aspect of the dream. "During the first part of the dream, someone complained that I wasn't talking enough. I said I had been asking questions about history—my grandfather's history. There was some battle that had to do with Napoleon, and they built a great monument to a hero. It looked like the mausoleum that we had built for my grandfather". The patient then spoke about his grandfather, a lively irascible man, and of his fond memories of spending time on his grandfather's farm. He then associated to the seal. "It was made of rubber, wire, and leather. Almost like it was going to fit over a phallus—a large phallus. Father put it on the first time and it didn't quite work. He likes to dabble at engineering things, but he is not very good at this. I waited for a while, and then said, 'I'll do it. You did it incorrectly'." During the remainder of the session, the patient spoke about his grandfather. He neither offered nor invited interpretative work with the dream, and none was initiated by the analyst.

Obviously this is a complex dream with multiple layers of meaning. One possible interpretation will be explored taking as a cue what may be considered to be the parallel facts that the action of the session revolves around the dream and the action of the dream revolves around the coffin. Suppose the coffin represents the patient's unconscious, including its vehicles or containers, which frequently, of course, are dreams themselves? From this angle, this patient's dream can be seen as representing the psychotic predicament, as articulated by both Winnicott (1947) and Lacan (1977). Indeed, from a Winnicottian perspective, one might think of all psychopathology as arrayed according to how much, and what particular aspects of, psychosomatic functioning must be given up in order to preserve the relationship to the primary object. At the extreme of psychosis, the person has early on come to feel that *any* true self functioning jeopardises this relationship. The true self is thus systematically split off from integration into ordinary functioning with the result that the person feels a primary lack or deadness at the core of personality. Conversely, during psychosis itself, the true self is felt simultaneously as rampantly alive, as not-me, and as actualised in an objectless world, insofar as the object relationships of the false self organisation have been overturned or rendered discontinuous.

This patient's dream represents, within this frame of reference, his sharing with his father, as he perceives it, the wish for the burial of his personality. In clinical descriptive terms, it would be the shared wish for the sealing over of the psychosis, and whatever meanings it contained. This, of course, is the current clinical condition. The action of the dream is literally the effort to seal something for its burial. The patient depicts in the dream a form of foreclosure of what Lacan (1977) would call the paternal signifier. He is not allowed by his father to share in carrying the paternal line. He is not prepared for or allowed to bear the weight of generational succession. He is not accorded the strengthening experience of bearing grief. Rather, he gravitates toward attending to his mother; he offers her a morbid detritus, the leftover herbs and perfumes which themselves seal over the odours of death. Denied access to the paternal signifier, the patient can find no entry into the symbolic order that regulates and assigns places within human interaction. He turns in then on the maternal relationship with its hints of hostility, bizarreness, going to waste, and imaginary denial of the distinction between life and death.

In the dream the patient represents this foreclosure in two ways: first, in his father's refusal of the patient's help and his carrying the coffin alone; second, in the father's unsuccessful attempt to use a condom. The patient thus represents his own existence as a hated accident, his father's inadequacy at "engineering things". His own role becomes a grotesque of paternal lineage; he works to seal and bury finally what his father attempts to foreclose inadequately. As compensation, he envisions a status only in terms of death: the monument to the dead war hero.

The perspective outlined above has clear implications for the analysis. Indeed, the dream itself declares the treatment setting as its primary setting—a long white building, like the one in which the analyst has his office. At the beginning of the dream, the medical trappings suggest that the central character will be a living patient, rather than someone already dead. The action of the dream then proceeds, however, without apparent reference to the analysis, although one could imagine leads toward the transference. Is the patient angry at the analyst, as he seems to be toward his father in the dream, for his unilateral limit-setting and failure to recognise the patient's co-operation? Is the patient's hostilely casual and dismissive giving of the herbs to his mother a reference to postponing his own drug use? Is the patient gleefully castigating the analyst for the latter's fumbling efforts to engineer the patient's life and confine, or seal over, his rambunctiousness? Is the patient's dream an answer somehow to the analyst's complaint that he is not talking enough?

All of these and more are plausible. The last question in particular is important insofar as the patient's answer in the dream has to do with his interest in the paternal line. He sets up an opposition and a paradox: to speak is to risk something within the history of grandfather, father and son; to keep silent, to seal or bury, preserves something. The analyst is therefore most probably represented in the dream, if at all, by the black female servant who can do nothing except simply stand by. This figure is given no active role, nor is one offered to the analyst. Like the coffin carried by his father, the dream is carried by the patient alone. Though some of its more pleasant accompaniments, for example, the memories of grandfather, are shared and elaborated, the dream itself, again like the coffin, remains unopened within the analysis. Rather, the dream-report, like the seal, seems to expand as needed to effectively fill most of the hour and seal out any analytic grappling with the feelings, sensations, memories, and urgencies within the dream. Perhaps, there is even an unconscious mathematics: one effective seal leaves five unused seals, each the size of a dime: fifty cents, fifty minutes in which something that could have been opened stays closed.

This patient's dream may, however, facilitate his analysis by giving representation to his unconscious situation and to the "subjective topography" of his primary object relationships. The analyst cannot therefore proceed blithely toward an opening of something that the patient and others are attempting to close, or toward bringing to life something meant to die. Perhaps the case for defence analysis is simply being restated here, but the importance of such a dream is that it offers an overall view of the emotional landscape and of the effects on the system if one part of it should change. It offers concrete and narratively coherent form to the primary actions of the patient, the primary relationships to be preserved, the methods of that preservation, the available alternatives to it, and the costs of such preservation to the patient's sense of an integrated and vital self.

The analyst too is situated by such a dream and sometimes within such a dream. The range of his actions is bounded by the patient's absolute need to preserve important relationships, including the analytic relationship. The analyst may allow himself to be sealed out for a time, perhaps a very long time, but he does not take part in that sealing. Neither does he open something unilaterally and risk psychosis for the patient or an acute conflict of loyalties. Instead, the analyst can articulate the care-taking efforts and relationship-preserving needs of the false self. Gradually, a dependence on analytic care, which can include bit-by-bit the split-off parts of the personality, becomes a possible alternative to the dissociation-based dependencies within the patient's pathology and life history.

Potential meaning

We come back to Winnicott: true self as a genuine experiencing, a spontaneous movement; false self as environmental alliance, dissociative, preservative, potentially corrupting. Winnicott might encourage us to consider the polarity of dreaming and dream in this light—dreaming akin to playing, which has profound significance for him, and dream as a product for potential use, for transaction, for relating around, as Pontalis (1974) puts it, "no longer a language that is circulating; (but) a currency" (p. 125).

The second patient was justifiably thrilled with his dream—partly because it evidenced to him the existence of an inner life—if something had died during childhood, something also remained alive—and partly because in it he succeeded in giving form to his subjective situation. He was no longer out of focus. In creating the dream as an object, for potentially defensive use, he also created an object out of his dreaming: something tangible, separable, and analysable. Pontalis (1974) comments:

> We can now have a better understanding of why the 'binding' of the
> dream depends on the representable. That which I can see, which I can

represent to myself, is already something that I can hold off: the annihilation, the dissolution of the subject is held aside . . . I can see my dreams and see by means of it. (p. 132)

The three dreams discussed above, which in one way or another seemed to include reference to themselves, reflect the patients' efforts to envision and give form to the subjective conditions of the analytic setting. As such, these dreams represent neither a full and spontaneous giving over to the analytic process, nor simply collusion and concealment; rather, they reflect something in-between, intermediate places from which multiple directions are possible. They are midway between the dream-object used to act something out in the social space of the analysis and the dream-space used to actualise one's personal situation and capacity. They are also midway between an enclosed omnipotent relationship to a fantasised other—the analyst captured and managed in the dream—and a permeable relatedness to a live other: the analyst as one who sees, listens, and whose actions may change the course of envisioned events.

The analyst's function has to do with grasping something of the range of the implicit possibilities the patient may be formulating in the dream about himself, the process—including the process of dream-report and interpretation—and the setting. A transference perspective, in the narrow sense of the analyst as representing an important childhood figure, is less immediately important. Indeed, from this angle, what the dream means in any converging or conclusive way is also less important than what the dream *could* mean, what its potentialities and functions might be in relationship to the analytic setting. It is as though, in Bion's (1962) language, the patient brings into his dreaming preconceptions about the setting that are then either lived out exactly around the finished dream or which spark in the analyst an actual concept about each party's subjective place and function. This kind of recognition, of "thinking out loud" (Ogden, 2005c, p. 24), by the analyst—about possibility rather than truth—introduces play into the situation, extends the boundaries of the analytic space, and offers the patient the leeway to experience himself in the present.

Green (1975) suggests that the analyst creates a "ventilated space" (p. 8), in which potential meaning is offered to the patient, and the extremes of meaninglessness and of absolute certainty are avoided. He speaks of giving "a container to (the patient's) content and a content to his container" (pp. 8–9). In this chapter, contents have been de-emphasised; rather, each of the above dreams has included in the centre of its action a container—a newspaper containing important information, bundles containing photographs, and a coffin. And of course the dreams themselves are containers. I hope to have illustrated how the actions within the dream around these containers illuminate the patient's psychic life and the patient's apprehensions regarding the analytic situation. They forecast possible actions within the analysis around the dream itself as a highly valenced container, and they open up the potential for the analytic setting to become the appropriate container for a mutual, honest, and previously warded-off recognition of the qualities of the patient's relationships, including that with the analyst.

For Winnicott, this is the goal of psychotherapy: to help constitute a potential space for the patient's experiencing. The distillate of his many years of work with severely disturbed patients is contained in his posthumously published formulation that a fear of impending breakdown is, in fact, a fear of a breakdown that has already happened, but that has never been experienced because there was no secure being, no reliable subjective core there to encompass the experience (Winnicott, 1974). Winnicott's concerns always centred around the subject-in-motion, the living self, its being, playing, relating, experiencing; a concept of space follows by definition (Pontalis, 1981). Significantly his only paper having to do with the subject of this chapter is about dreaming, rather than dreams (Winnicott, 1971b). It offers an excellent clinical illustration of the self-atrophy within false self organisation. Winnicott particularly notes the phenomenon of his patient's static, affectless, non-generative fantasying. Through this obsessive mentation, she seemed to create dead times in which to live out the dissociation she had come to identify as herself. Winnicott contrasts this with dreaming, from which she seemed totally estranged.

There is a remarkable moment when this patient awakens in the middle of the night "hectically cutting out, planning, working on the pattern for a dress" (p. 32). Winnicott views this as her defence against dreaming, as her pulling out of her near-dream into wakefulness and depleted busywork, probably in relation to her stated need to possess herself totally and therefore stave off any sense of being possessed by the analytic process and relationship. Winnicott's response is equally remarkable: he goes to the "dream equivalent" (p. 33). He formulates for the patient the meanings her fantasying might have had, had it been dreaming. He seems to tease her with the help he could have been and to reassure her by confirming his uselessness to her in her fantasying activity.

Here is his conceptual summary:

> The fantasying is simply about making a dress. The dress has no symbolic value. . . . In a dream, by contrast . . . the same thing would indeed have had symbolic meaning. . . . The key word to be carried back into the dream was "formlessness," which is what the material is like before it is patterned and cut and shaped and put together. In other words, in a dream this would be a comment on her personality and self-establishment. In a dream it would only to some extent be about a dress. Moreover, the hope that would make her feel that something could be made out of the formlessness would then come from the confidence she had in her analyst.. . . Her childhood environment seemed unable to allow her to be formless but must, as she felt, pattern her and cut her into shapes conceived by other people. (Winnicott, 1971d, pp. 33–34)

In this material Winnicott is working with the concept of potential meaning. It is even tempting, from the point of view of the current presentation, to think of this patient's near-dream as potentially about dreaming and its context of her analysis: at one extreme, creating pattern and fit from formlessness; at the other, making something to wear to the session. Of particular interest is the patient's foreclosure of symbolisation. Winnicott has a great deal to say about the process of symbol formation and its arrest, which is closely related in his theory to transitional object relating. Here it is simply worth noting, following Balmary (1982), that at its linguistic root the symbol differs from the symptom only in terms of the active, integrative attitude of the subject. Winnicott's patient has symptoms that have fallen to her from her childhood and which she accepts now as her lot, her completed though afflicted self. She forecloses nascent symbolising processes because these would confront her with lack: that an other had a place in her formation and that an other must now take part in her growth. From the place of potential other, Winnicott's technique plays this pain against the emptiness of her dissociation.

Freud looked into the dream and found Oedipus: "Born thus, I ask to be no other man, than that I am, and will know who I am" (Khan,

1976, p. 327). But to assume the role of analysand is, to some degree by definition, to become Oedipus: to penetrate the body of one's own source and to claim authority over one's own existence. We might ask what Freud actually saw in his dreams: an unconscious content or the reflection of the position he had taken vis-à-vis the dream? Above all, psychoanalysis from a Freudian perspective accents the primacy of knowing, the Oedipal value—perhaps as Bion (1967b) suggests, an arrogance—on knowing at all costs. Winnicott's concerns precede knowledge. They have to do with the being and becoming of the person, and they describe the collusion of knowing and the terror of being known before the subject's being there to know and be known (Winnicott, 1963b). This chapter has attempted to illustrate these issues around an unusual aspect of dreaming.

CHAPTER TWELVE

Interpretation in psychoanalysis

"V oice and music, music and no music, silence and then voice ... words, memories ... more silence, more breathing together, not rushing, being." The words of that rock and roll bard of Belfast, Van Morrison, from his 1991 album, *Hymns to the Silence*, might as well be the epigraph for Winnicott's brief paper on interpretation (1989a). Given the advice Winnicott offers within it, the paper might also have been called "Interpreting and not interpreting", a parallel to his more well known, earlier paper on "Communicating and not communicating" (1963b). This chapter will offer a number of thoughts about Winnicott's "Interpretation in psycho-analysis" paper, in part because this interesting short work is not widely read and because it provides an opportunity to re-visit interpretation as a central analytic activity, grounded in a particular view of the psycho-analytic process.

Written in 1968, a productive year for the development of his theory, Winnicott begins his paper by telling us that we are reviewing interpretation as one of the "basic principles of the psychoanalytic technique" (1989a, p. 207), and he emphasises the essentially verbal nature of the interpretive exchange. The analyst uses words in response to the words of the patient. Though an enormous amount of the patient's (and the analyst's) behaviour might be classified as non-verbal communication, Winnicott advises us to stick with the patient's words because this is the material that has been actively "offered" (p. 207). In this way, "the patient does not feel persecuted by the observer's eyes" (p. 207).

This last comment reminds me of an observation made by the great English writer, V. S. Pritchett in *The Offensive Traveller* (1964), which I mentioned in Chapter Eleven:

> By "being offensive," I mean that I travel, therefore, I offend. I represent that ancient enemy of all communities: the stranger. Neapolitan girls have crossed themselves to avert the evil eye at the sight of me . . . And rightly: we are looking on the private life of another people, a life which is entirely their business, with an eye, that, however friendly it may be, is alien. We are seeing people as they do not see themselves. (p. 4)

And, once again, that comment has always reminded me of Winnicott's opening statement in his 1963 paper on "Communicating and not communicating" (1963b):

> Starting from no fixed place, I soon came, while preparing this paper for a foreign society, to staking a claim, to my surprise, to the right not to communicate. This was a protest from the core of me to the frightening fantasy of being infinitely exploited. In another language, this would be the fantasy of being eaten or swallowed up. In the language of this paper it is the *fantasy of being found*. (p. 179)

On the threshold of speaking, the right not to communicate! Winnicott follows this startling introduction by saying that "there is a considerable body of literature on the psychoanalytic patient's silences" (1963b, p. 179), but of course, it is his own silence he is authorising. Two of the three patients Winnicott mentions in his paper on interpretation are silent patients. The first responds to Winnicott's interpreting his finger movements with an admonition: "If you start interpreting that sort of thing, then I should have to transfer that sort of activity to something else *which does not show*" (1989a, p. 207, my italics). The second answers with some elaboration to Winnicott's question about the patient's interest in the sport of shooting pigeons, but Winnicott knows that this material was elicited by him, not spontaneously offered to the analysis by the patient. He therefore feels that he cannot use it interpretively, however relevant it might seem. Again and again, Winnicott underlines that we can only give back to the patient something he or she has first and truly given to us. The "interpretive urge" (p. 209) must give way to tactfulness and unresented restraint.

This advice, of course, speaks to the interplay of spontaneous gesture and "answering activity" (in Marion Milner's phrase, 1937) basic to the emergence of true self or to the defensive establishment of false self (Winnicott, 1960). Winnicott felt that the false self could find in any particular methodology of analysis, perhaps especially inter-pretation, an opportunity for collusion with the impinging other and a refuge from more vulnerable parts of the self. I think of Winnicott's guidance here as describing a locus both of authority and of author-ship, which does indeed relate to "basic principles of the psycho-analytic technique". In Chapter One, I outlined those technical principles as the establishment and maintenance of a frame and the analyst's offering himself as a medium.

Briefly, the frame has to do with the boundaries of the analytic situation and the structure for the work. It includes all of those "arrangements" that secure the rhythm, privacy, and constancy of the setting. It implies the analyst's authority, based upon expertise and professional identity; the fundamental rule is a rule of sorts on this basis. The frame anchors the treatment in the reality of roles and prac-tice, all of which is led by the analyst. In Lacanian (Lacan, 1977) terms, the frame situates the treatment in the symbolic order. By contrast, the notion of medium implies the analyst's making available within the space and time of the frame, his total mental and emotional function-ing for the purpose of receiving the range of impressions the patient is trying to convey and to integrate. This is the experiential level of the treatment, the level of transference and countertransference, of process, resonance, and empathic responsiveness. The broader concept of a medium implies materials or a milieu, that exist for the purpose of externalising something, spawning something, transmit-ting something, or contacting something. The transference as medium can carry the connotation of facilitating contact with the dead.

The locus of authority belongs to the patient here. The patient leads in the use of the analyst as medium, and the analyst follows. This relates to Freud's primary discovery that the illness is an illness of the subject, and therefore, the doctor, first of all, structures the analytic situation to receive from the patient, rather than vice versa. Interpretation becomes the broad term for a range of analytic activities having to do with receiving, containing, metabolising, and returning bits of himself to the patient. This is a mirroring function and in Winnicott's words, a "complex derivative of the (mother's) face that reflects what is there to be seen" (1971c, p. 117), and without which, "a mirror is a thing to be looked at but not looked into" (p. 117). As it relates to a mirroring function, Lacan (1977) would situate the analyst as medium in the imaginary order.

Winnicott's primary technical advice is to lend oneself, I would say as a medium, to the process of the patient. "In the simplest form, the analyst gives back to the patient what the patient has communicated . . . letting the patient know that what has been said has been heard, and that the analyst is trying to get the meaning correctly" (1989a, p. 208). If that process includes the patient's silence as "the essential communication", then the analysis "settle(s) back into being a silent one" (p. 210). In his paper, "Fear of breakdown" (1974), Winnicott, at his most eloquent, relates the experience of emptiness to the early childhood experience of "nothing happening when something might profitably have happened" (p. 106), but he also believed deeply that the natural integrative drive was always at work in a person, given a good–enough holding environment, and that, therefore, very often something was profitably happening when nothing appeared to be. About a dream offered by his third patient in the paper on interpretation, Winnicott notes: "The analyst need not do anything about this dream because the work has already been done in the dreaming and then in the remembering and in the reporting" (1989a, p. 211).

A hymn in the silence

This idea of unconscious integrative activity taking place in a context of silence is, in a sense, a uniquely psychoanalytic one. Marion Milner (see Chapter Eight) in her intensely personal autobiographical study *On Not Being Able to Paint* (1957) describes the struggle toward letting go into unconscious creative activity and the requirement of a setting in which it is "safe to be absent-minded" (p. xiii). To give an example from ordinary life, absent-mindedly but audibly, a young man was singing to himself: "Oh great ocean, oh great sea, run to the ocean, run to the sea". He was singing this in the passenger seat of a car as his father was driving him to the airport, where he would board a plane to begin his fall college term abroad. From all indications to his parents in recent weeks, though he was excited about his plan and knew it would benefit him, his latent ambivalence had developed into anxious second thoughts. Indeed, according to his parents, everything in their son now seemed to want to run *from* the ocean, run *from* the sea.

How might we think about this song and this singing at this time? The concept of counterphobia accurately, if in rather sterile language, denotes what the young man is doing, but it does not capture the "knitting" (to use a metaphor from Milner's book) within this musical activity, at least the "knitting" one could imagine in it. Closer might be the *fort-da* moment, in which Freud's (1920g, p. 15) young grandson begins to engage his mother's absence symbolically by throwing and retrieving an object while uttering the German words for "gone" and "there".

The song, by the Irish rock band, U2 (1987) (from an album that his parents had not heard their son play in the previous year or so) is an angry and grief-struck elegy to a young man apparently killed in a political struggle. Its first chorus begins with the line "You run like a river runs to the sea". The meaning of this becomes clearer with the second chorus: "It runs like a river runs to the sea", the "it" referring now to the young man's blood. The third and final chorus, following the line "I'll see you again when the stars fall from the sky", begins "We run like a river runs to the sea". The "we" consolidates the theme of a longed-for reunion and, as well, the suggestion of a flow of tears merging with the flow of blood.

At this point, the song, whose rhythms have all along cut their way into the listener with the edge characteristic of U2, builds to an agonised cry and seems to end. But process follows content, and there is then a return: no more pain or agitation but a hymn, slow and lovely, the first line ("Oh great ocean, oh great sea") sung by the lead singer alone, the second ("Run to the ocean, run to the sea") sung together in chorus. It is as if the great ocean will contain everyone, will bring all of those separated people and disparate selves together, and thereby provide a transcendence of present pain and limitations (Muller, personal communication).

This is a song about loss and reunion, about being alone and being together, about anxiety and prayer. The young man is singing the hymn as a way, one might imagine, of dealing with the developmental task in front of him. In doing so, he is most probably drawing on identifications—that most basic psychological mechanism for staying with someone you are leaving. These identifications might be multiple: with Bono, the macho lead singer of U2, thus with the singer and mourner rather than the lost subject of the song; with the Irish band itself as it supports him, not only in its aggressiveness, but also in its connection to a previous positive experience he had had with a group of students in Ireland; and with his parents through their shared interests in music and travel.

One could imagine two sentences unconsciously going through this young man's mind, one answering and supporting him to accept the other. The first, "You too (U2) must face the pain of separation in your becoming an adult". And the second, "You two (U2) both love this music; you're together!" One last piece of the story: at the moment in the drive to the airport when his father realised what the possible meaning of his son's singing might be, indeed that he thought to even consider its having a meaning, he reported that his son abruptly stopped singing. The father wondered to himself if his son had made his own interpretation of the song, or if the father's way of being, his quiet but possibly felt realisation about his son's singing, had disrupted the young man. If there is anything to this idea, what might have happened to the son's internal process at that point? Did that inner back-and-forth between fear and strength, past and future, alone and together continue silently? In the same terms? If not, did it return?

And if it had really been interrupted, what would be the effect on the "silent doings of ego synthesis" (Erikson, 1956, p. 57)? The father worried that he might have, through the subtle behavioural correlates of his own unspoken mental activity, broken some rhythm and jarred a silence, an unconsciousness, surrounding his son's natural movement toward inner equilibrium. In Winnicott's paper on "Advising parents" (1965a), he wrote that "in health we are constantly engaged in *keeping time with natural processes* . . . (I)f we can adjust ourselves to these natural processes, we can leave most of the complex mechanisms to nature . . ." (p. 119, my italics). Did this father introduce a different beat, so to speak, through his reflections? Had he inadvertently placed an audience before speech that had been addressed confidentially to his son's future self? Had he accidentally turned unconsciousness into self-consciousness?

In Winnicott's terms, the capacity to be alone (Winnicott, 1958), an obviously essential developmental achievement related to the young man's immediate task, develops out of a paradoxical experience: the child's experience of being alone in the presence of another; that is, of becoming, on one's own, absorbed in play and letting the presence of the other fade into the background of support. The child returns from the absorption in play back to his or her immediate interpersonal environment *as though* he or she had actually left it. This is one example for Winnicott of the positive value of illusion and, of course, the value of silence. The young man in our story was singing as though alone, and his father felt his own difficulty in simply letting him be that way, in simply "holding" the situation.

Might this example and the considerations Winnicott introduces about silence, lead us to think of unconsciousness as a kind of setting, like a meditative space, or as a condition, like sleep or bandaging, that provides some form of boundary between the immediacy of life and one's inner experience, and which facilitates organic processes of self-healing—what the Sandler's refer to as "The gyroscopic function of unconscious fantasy" (1986). If psychoanalytic treatment accents coming-to-consciousness in words, might we also argue for, as Winnicott seems to in his paper on interpretation, the therapeutic refusal of such therapeutics.

Of course, my accenting the quieter side of the work, indeed the provision of a context of silence for our patients, is simply an extension of the ordinary provisions of the analytic setting; dream life cannot be contacted in too bright or noisy an environment. Nor do I mean to underplay the potentially problematic aspects of the analyst's silence. In his short paper on "The aims of psycho-analytical treatment" (1962b), Winnicott begins by saying that, in doing psychoanalysis, he aims at "keeping alive, keeping well, keeping awake" (p. 166). The opposite is certainly possible; countertransferential matters of all sorts could lead the analyst toward detachment, sleepiness, even illness, and silence might be the result. In addition, an analyst's silence might reflect a reluctance to interpret for reasons quite different from the father's in the above vignette; rather than "keeping time" with the patient, the analyst might be lost as to what is happening, or fearful of the patient's aggression, or hesitant to speak for a number of other reasons. In the "Aims" paper mentioned above, Winnicott says that he sometimes interprets to let the patient know what he does not know—speech in the service of marking out what is still silent.

What I hope to have highlighted here, however, is the ordinary importance of the analyst's natural provision of an in-tune and generative silence. At stake is the whole question of sublimation as an unconscious healing process (Muller, 1996). In essence, I am suggesting that the provision of space for personally found and personally meaningful activity, a transitional space in a context of silent presence, seems to me to be one of those elusive but essential ingredients for regaining health that only a psychoanalytic perspective, and perhaps especially a Winnicottian one, fully valences.

Being there

As much as the young man's story is a story about his unconscious creative effort to find the courage to "run to the ocean"—and to re-assure himself of a return—it is also a story about a father's dilemmas regarding communicating or not communicating and the strain of providing a silence. In his major paper on communication (1963b), Winnicott becomes radical, even mystical, on this subject: "The central still and silent spot" (p. 189); the individual as "an isolate, permanently non-communicating, permanently unknown, in fact, unfound" (p. 187); "[a]t the centre . . . an incommunicado element" . . . "sacred and most worthy of preservation" (p. 187); and "like the music of the spheres, absolutely personal" (p. 192). This paper contains two of Winnicott's most oft-quoted and, given his opening statement, most personally meaningful paradoxes: "[I]t is a joy to be hidden but disaster not to be found" (p. 186); this counterpoised with the disaster of "being found before *being there* to be found" (p. 190, my italics). It is this latter catastrophe, Winnicott says, that leads to "the hatred . . . of psycho-analysis" (p. 187), and indeed, one can feel Winnicott's guardian hatred for his chosen profession alongside his abiding love in this paper.

Winnicott's interpretive guidance toward waiting and caution has everything to do with the danger of "being found before being there to be found" (p. 190). Analytic interpretation that takes the patient "further than the transference confidence allows . . . suddenly becomes a threat because it is in touch with a stage of emotional development that the patient has not yet reached, at least as a total personality" (1989a, p. 212). Hence, Winnicott's emphasis in the "Aims" paper (1962b) on interpretation that functions to dispel the patient's fear of the analyst's omniscience, the fantasy "that I understand everything" (p. 167). "In other words," he says, "I retain some outside quality by not being quite on the mark" (p. 167). Certainly, his guidance reflects a fierce stance against the analyst's taking on the role of expert in any way, a position he argues vigorously in the "Advising parents" paper (1965a).

This issue of "being there" was a lasting theme for Winnicott. In his posthumously published "Fear of breakdown" paper he writes, "This thing of the past has not happened yet because the patient *was not there* for it to happen to" (1974, p. 105, my italics). In order for it (this "thing" that calls to mind Freud's *Das Ding*) to be experienced, it must be encompassed by an ego, and the development of the ego cannot be taken for granted; rather, it absolutely depends on a special relationship to an other. For the patient's achievement of "being there", a setting must be provided in which a certain kind of object relationship might develop. But again there is a paradox: "[A] good " object is no good unless created . . . yet the object must be found in order to be created" (1963b, p. 181).

"Transference confidence" is the result of the analyst's reliable adaptation to the patient's need in the analytic setting, through which a transitional space is established. It means that the found analyst is felt to have been created by the patient—made into the analyst one needs—and thus, to have become a subjective object. In Marion Milner's words, it means that the "irreducible otherness" (1957, p. 118) of the analyst has nevertheless slid into the "pliability" (p. 118) of a medium. It means that the analyst has accepted the authority of the patient to lead the treatment, in search of the authorship of his or her life. It is "the starting point" (Winnicott, 1963b, p. 192) for "being there", for being alive, and it is the reason that André Green makes the dramatic statement that "no analysis is conceivable in which, after the statement of the fundamental rule, the analyst speaks first" (1978, p. 180). All of this is very near to Lacan's return to Freud's definition of the goals of psychoanalysis: Where It was, there I must come to be (1977, p. 129).

Winnicott's paper on interpretation is dated February 19, 1968. On February 5, 1968, he wrote a short piece on "The use of the word 'use'

"(1989b). These latter remarks take their place in a long-standing preoccupation about how the developmental transition is made from the subjective to the objective object and from fantasy to reality. One can find the kernel of this idea at least as far back as the 1945 paper on "Primitive emotional development," where Winnicott talks of "realization" (p. 149) as the outcome of good–enough object-presenting. It is there as well in "Communicating and not communicating": "The change of the object from 'subjective' to 'objectively perceived' is jogged along less effectually by satisfactions than by dissatisfactions . . . instinctual gratification gives the infant a personal experience and *does but little to the position of the object*" (1963b, p. 181, Winnicott's italics). This train of thought culminates in Winnicott's radical statement in "The use of an object" (1969), a paper also presented "to a foreign society" (The New York Psychoanalytic Society), a paper full of anxious rhetoric, hesitations and pre-emptive strikes, as though Winnicott was again claiming the "right not to communicate". Ultimately this is a paper about survival, which, in a way, Winnicott failed to survive (Kwawer, 1998); his penultimate, very damaging heart attack occurred in his hotel room right after a seriously critical discussion of his presentation. Winnicott's comment was: "The American analysts will kill me one day" (Goldman, 1998, p. 359).

But, in a sense, Winnicott was killing them with this paper, or at least he was mobilising the destructiveness of a very personal, decisively independent statement and throwing himself into living without the illusion—that he himself had helped to cultivate—that all psychoanalysts speak the same language and all would be able to hear him. I want to place this classic paper on "The use of an object" next to Winnicott's more conservative paper on interpretation in order to view them as companion pieces. After all, they were written at about the same time, and Winnicott says fully and with great conviction in the later paper what he has said more succinctly earlier that year in the paper on interpretation:

> . . . (I)t is only in recent years that I have become able to wait and wait for the natural evolution of the transference arising out of the patient's growing trust in the psychoanalytic technique and setting, and to avoid breaking up this natural process by making interpretations . . . it appalls me to think how much deep change I have prevented or delayed in patients *in a certain classification category* by my personal need to interpret. If only we can wait, the patient arrives

at understanding creatively and with immense joy, and I now enjoy this joy more than I used to enjoy the sense of having been clever. I think I interpret mainly to let the patient know the limits of my understanding. The principle is that it is the patient and only the patient who has the answers. We may or may not enable him or her to be able to encompass what is known or become aware of it with acceptance. (1969, p. 711, Winnicott's italics)

This is a powerful statement, but in his next paragraph, Winnicott moves the issue of interpretation beyond the necessary cautions of his February paper. "In contrast with this", he begins, "comes the interpretive work which the analyst must do and which distinguishes the analysis from self-analysis" (1969, p. 711). In other words, simple reliable reflection is essential to the building up of the subjective object and establishes an area of necessary and generative illusion in which the patient comes into his own subjectivity. But something else must take place to get to shared reality. "*This* interpreting (my italics), by the analyst, if it is to have effect, must be related to the patient's ability *to place the analyst outside the area of subjective phenomena*" (p. 711, Winnicott's italics).

Even here, however, the locus of initiative for the discovery of otherness rests with the patient. The patient "places" the object outside, and this is accomplished through destructiveness. The task of the object is to survive in order to come into being as a usable other. Winnicott has "simply", he says, "examine(d) the reality principle under higher power" (1969, p. 714), and in doing so, charted the ongoing interactions of subjectivity and objectivity: the surviving object's "becoming destroyed because real, becoming real because destroyed" (p. 713).

Winnicott does not explicitly take up this complex topic in his paper on interpretation, perhaps because this latter paper is aimed toward "the teaching of students" (1989a, p. 211) (and parenthetically he highlights, in his instructive example of interpretation with his third patient, important technical points, such as the external circumstance of an impending break in the treatment, leading him toward deciding to interpret early, and the need for validation of an interpretation by way of the specific, spontaneous clinical data that follow). There is, however, a central and difficult passage in his paper on interpretation in which Winnicott is trying to address the objection that the reflective process can seem like a "futile" or redundant action by the analyst, and additionally that it might only be an avoidance of the dangers of either getting too far away from or too far into the patient.

> In the limited area of today's transference the patient has an accurate knowledge of a detail or of a set of details. It is as if there is a dissoci-ation belonging to the place the analysis has reached today. It is help-ful to remember that in this limited way or from this limited position the patient can be giving the analyst a sample of the truth; that is to say of something that is absolutely true for the patient, and that when the analyst gives this back the interpretation is received by the patient who has already emerged to some extent from this limited area or dissociated condition . . . In this way the interpretations are part of a building up of insight. (1989a, p. 209)

What is Winnicott saying here? To my reading, Winnicott is describing a subtle level of interaction in which an important partially dissociated element of the self comes into existence in the immediacy of that moment's transference, or one could say, is delivered into being by the patient in the intimate context of the immediate transference. Winnicott's overall dynamic frame of reference here is analogous to Rycroft's (1979) view of dreams: "The dreaming self utters meanings from a timeless, total position . . . while the part of the self that receives dream-messages . . . possesses a preconceived notion of itself, which is at risk if it listens seriously to dream-meanings" (p. 148). The analyst's response to this precarious moment Winnicott calls "acknowledg-ment" (1989a, p. 208), which he suggests, "is perhaps the most im-portant part of an interpretation" (p. 208).

But it seems to me that this simple notion of acknowledgment includes something quite deep and complex. We are, after all, no longer dealing with the analyst's quietly following and reflecting back the closer-to-the-surface process of the patient. We are dealing with something said by the analyst at a certain moment, an interpretive giving back about something deeper in the patient, something emer-gent in the emotional momentum of the transference, a truth at the edge of coming into being. This is the moment when the patient is not talking to the analyst, though he is talking in the transference. Instead, the patient is talking to himself and the analyst is listening. The patient risks being "found" by another in the process of finding himself and, if the interpretation works, a transformative moment occurs.

I think Winnicott is speaking here to the fundamentally important way that *recognition* is embedded in interpretation, in two senses of that word. The first has to do with recognition in the sense of re-cognising. The analyst's words provide what Peter Fonagy calls "mentalization" (Fonagy, Gergely, Jurist, & Target, 2002) or, in Bion's earlier terms, alpha function to the patient's beta elements (1962) or simply thought that is deeply in touch with the patient's raw experi-ence. The whole person referred to by Winnicott at that moment might really be the "plural body" (Davoine & Gaudilliere, 2004, p. 217) of analyst and patient, with the analyst as auxiliary, encom-passing ego. In the process, a hitherto inchoate but crucial part of the patient is brought into the experience of the transference and then, through interpretation, re-transcribed in a different register, one that now involves recognition in speech. In the "Aims" paper (1962b), this is Winnicott's second reason to interpret.

But, in another sense, recognition implies affirmation, acceptance, a fundamental "yes" to the patient (Davoine & Gaudilliere, 2004), a witnessing. In this sense of the term, there is a hint of accepted other-ness in the patient's registration of the analyst. Winnicott, I believe, is describing in this passage those ordinary, remarkable moments of in-between-ness when the patient experiences the analyst as *both* me and not-me, both created and found. The analyst's giving back subtly awakens the patient from a dissociative dream in which a vulnerable aspect of the self has come alive in the transference, but it also returns to the patient the self-of-the-dream, which has been safely held—I would say, "minded" (Fromm, 2004, p. 9)—across this transition by the analyst's capacity for empathic thought. In this bubble of revela-tion in the transference, this dissociative moment of "absolute truth"—a moment, I suppose, in which everything else but the truth must be dissociated—the patient has achieved "being there" and the giving back by the analyst achieves a "being with."

It is this back-and-forth that builds up trust as well as insight and provides a sort of traction to the analysis. It is as though the patient comes to feel that the analyst will be with me where I am and will extend my understanding of myself only in collaboration with me. As Winnicott put it in the "Mirror role" paper (1971c): "When I look, I am seen, so I exist. I can now afford to look and to see" (p. 114). In a sense, Winnicott has argued all along that serious psychopathology can be described as an early dissociation between the experiences of being and of being with, the true self of the former being sacrificed to the false self of the latter. It is this dissociation that Winnicott suggests can be healed through the interpretive process.

The orange dream

There is one last thing I would like to say about Winnicott's paper on interpretation, in the spirit of both playfulness and critique. It has to do with his third clinical vignette. The patient has a recurring dream: "She is starving and she is left with an orange, but she sees that the orange has been nibbled at by a rat. She has a rat phobia and the fact that the rat has touched the orange makes her unable to use the orange" (1989a, p. 210). Winnicott comments on his decision as to whether or not to interpret: "There was an external reason why the analyst could not afford to wait because there was not going to be an opportunity for further sessions. He therefore made the interpretation, thereby running the risk of spoiling the work . . ." (p. 211).

Winnicott interpreted the orange as representing the breast of the good mother whom the patient had lost as a child and the rat as representing the relationship of attack between them. He spoke about the patient's being "stuck", still in touch with what was good about this early relationship but unable to go at it excitedly and make use of it. He reports that: "the patient was able to use this interpretation immediately" (p. 211), and there were clear clinical data to validate the interpretation: specific, affective memories from two developmental eras occurred to her, she felt emotional release, and her clinical condition improved.

But where is Winnicott as a transference figure, or perhaps a countertransference figure, in this dream? In our clinical experience, it is an everyday occurrence that we find ourselves, directly or in disguised form, in our patients' dreams. In my own experience, as described in Chapter Eleven, I sometimes think that the patient's dream contains in it reference to, or representation of, the dream itself as a highly valenced object in the analytic exchange. To find the dream-represented-in-a-dream is to find the patient's unconsciously situating the analytic pair in some kind of configuration and in some action relationship with each other. This point of view has been discussed by Pontalis in his paper, "The dream as an object" (1974).

So what about this orange and this rat? It seems to me that throughout his paper on interpretation Winnicott has been instructing us at most only to "nibble" at the patient's material, lest we spoil it and the patient refuse to touch it. In other words, the relationship of rat, patient, and orange in the dream seems to mirror the relationship of analyst, patient, and dream in Winnicott's paper! The orange, like the dream, could feed the patient, but if the rat touches it—or the analyst touches the dream interpretively—the patient will refuse it. It is as though in the transference she believes the dream is to feed the analyst rather than herself, and she will have no part of it.

I am arguing that, in addition to the meaning this dream has for her early relationship with her mother (a mother whom she lost, as she is about to lose her analyst), this dream has meaning in the here-and-now of the analytic relationship and especially in relation to the interpretive task. Perhaps this recognition, if true, even more strongly confirms the technical advice Winnicott has made central to his paper: be careful about touching something that is not clearly given to you to touch. But what about the patient's ability to, and this is Winnicott's word, "use" the interpretation he actually made? Indeed, one might be hard pressed to find a better example of a patient's being able to use what the analyst has to offer from his independent position and expertise.

It may simply be that levels of relatedness, from subjective to objective, fluctuate or intermingle complexly in the treatment of a patient with a broad developmental range as the background to her difficulties. But what if the caution Winnicott felt about interpreting his patient's dream—a caution worked through respectfully in his decision-making process—actually reflected a countertransferential position, something the patient was doing to Winnicott? What if his caution unconsciously signalled a danger Winnicott felt himself to be in, the danger of the patient's subtle but real destructiveness, mobilised especially when he engaged actively with the material? Again and again, she seems to be saying in her behaviour, here is this orange-dream, but you, Dr Winnicott, may not touch it.

And what if this Dr Winnicott who may not touch the orange-dream represents that part of the patient who was tantalised by, but forbidden from reaching for, the mother over whom she once enjoyed rights but who took herself away from her daughter? Perhaps, in the face of this destructiveness—this quietly intractable, but enacted, unconscious fantasy—Winnicott's deciding on his own to interpret represented survival, the survival of the analytic situation and of Winnicott as a real other with something to offer to the patient. Perhaps, in his interpretation, Winnicott made a daring break—indeed was "placed" by the patient in the countertransference position to make that break— from a locked-in mother–daughter transference–countertransference relationship that permitted neither hungry engagement nor ruthless separateness. As a consequence, the patient seemed able to make that break herself, however briefly, and to take in Winnicott's interpreting from the place of genuine other. Maybe that's why it went so well, why the interpretation could be so fully used.

Of course, I do not know. But it intrigues me to imagine that Winnicott himself went at this dream-orange excitedly, just the way he thought his patient wanted to, but was also terrified to, go at her mother, and that, in a sense, *her* survival of *his* destructiveness might have liberated her, for some bracingly clear period of time, from such an engulfing identification with her mother. One of Winnicott's postscripts to the "Use of an object" paper was written in early 1968 and began with Freud's discussion of Moses. Quite unusually, he talks about fathers: "The father may or may not have been a mother-substitute, but at some time he begins to be felt to be there in a different role, and it is here I suggest that the baby is likely to *make use of* the father as a blue-print for his or her own integration when just becoming at times a unit" (1989c, p. 243, my italics).

This may be the place where Lacan's *nom du pere* (1977) joins the Winnicottian metapsychology—a big topic! What I can only suggest here is that the total clinical situation at the moment of Winnicott's interpretation, which includes the place that the patient has situated him, leads Winnicott to take up his own authority with the patient. He interprets from a position of difference, outside the mother–daughter identification, a place that Lacan argues derives from the position of the father. This is the place of the Third (Muller, 1996), the symbolic order in which a kind of death occurs to the relationship of merger, but life is discovered and perspective found through the medium of speech.

Winnicott's paper on interpretation contains great technical wisdom, a profound respect for the patient and the analytic process, and subtle theoretical possibilities. But Winnicott would be the first to argue against theory, even clinical theory, that is static or absolutist. So, perhaps the lesson of this third vignette is that the analyst's cautious following of the patient's process should sometimes be cautiously held up for examination as well, especially if a patient's dream leads us there.

CHAPTER THIRTEEN

The therapeutic community as a holding environment

Setting factors

A s noted in Chapter Three, in his 1954 paper on regression, Winnicott makes the startling statement that "Freud takes for granted the early mothering situation and . . . it turned up in his provision of a setting for his work" (1954a, p. 284). For Winnicott, it could not have been otherwise; Freud could not have provided, nor could his patients have used, such a deeply holding setting unless early mother–child experiences had been "good enough" and therefore able to be taken for granted. But with more severely disturbed patients, patients for whom regression to dependence is essential to the therapeutic action because the early environment has failed in some way, the treatment setting materialises as a crucial feature.

Winnicott's advice to analysts who might want to treat such patients is to "watch the operation of setting factors; watch the minor examples of regression with natural termination that appear in the course of analytic sessions, and watch and use the regressive episodes that occur in the patient's life outside of analysis" (p. 293). In this chapter, I shall examine a therapeutic community programme as a holding environment, attempt to illustrate the value of some of Winnicott's concepts in understanding unfolding clinical events, and consider the role of the setting as a system, the dynamics of which may lead to "failures" of holding and consequent problematic regression in patients.

The particular therapeutic community programme to be discussed takes place in a completely open and voluntary treatment setting, in which intensive psychoanalytic psychotherapy is supported by a range of clinical services. Patients agree upon admission, in the context of professional assessment of their difficulties, to be responsible for themselves with staff help. They enter a setting with no locks, restraints, or privileging system, and they come and go as they wish. Nor are they required to attend psychotherapy sessions, group meetings, or any other part of the programme. The issue is always their alliance with the treatment, rather than their compliance. The hospital assists patients with their self-management by offering them a sensitive, well-trained staff and by building with them a therapeutic community programme in which they can collectively organise themselves, join the staff in management tasks, and reflect as a group on the community's process.

The open setting

In the regression paper, Winnicott "glance(s)" at Freud's clinical setting and lists what, for him, are some of its obvious features (1954a, p. 285). Winnicott was a theorist of the unnoticed obvious, nowhere more so than in his twelve observations of Freud's clinical setting. His description captures the essential qualities of presence, boundary, and space. For example, the room: "a room, not a passage", "quiet . . . yet not dead quiet", "not liable to sudden unpredictable sounds, yet . . . not free from ordinary house noises", "lit properly, but not by a light staring in the face", "comfortably warm" (1954a, p. 285). Winnicott's setting is not too much this or too little that; rather, it is nicely in-between, both special and ordinary. It offers the reliable solidity and the spaciousness in which movement, play, and spontaneous gesture might arise.

A chronically disturbed patient, when asked, in the middle of a very difficult phase, what it was that made her want to continue treatment in this particular therapeutic community, answered without hesitation: "Because it's on Main Street!" This spontaneous statement startled the staff. It spoke to the way in which the openness of this treatment setting is not simply a physical description. It is also a deep and paradoxical structural intervention for both patients and staff. In a sense, it is a loving refusal on the part of the staff to take care of patients in the traditional way, at least insofar as that tradition includes the exchanging of the patient's resources for the expert's care. In the same way that there is no such thing as a baby (1957, p. 137), says Winnicott, there is no such thing as a patient without a clinician, and no such thing as a chronic patient without a collusive institution.

As a refusing intervention, the open setting can be frustrating, and destructiveness is brought to bear upon it in order to test its survival capacities. But its advantages are many. It provides the space for the patient to find his or her own optimal distance and pace. It also sets up a system of values—for example, values of freedom, responsibility, and negotiation—that can play a powerful part in ameliorating narcissistic pathology. Finally, even though coming to such a setting implies some breakdown in the early care-taking phases of development, it presents even the very disturbed patient with a sharply experienced choice about joining. The holding environment cannot be taken for granted as a one-directional provision of care; rather, it invites patients to join in building that which might take care of everyone and the treatment task itself. This requirement to join—to join an always uncertain enterprise involving self-declaration and the negotiation of differences—is not easy, even though it is therapeutic. It is particularly difficult for people damaged or conflicted in their relationships with others. Hence, the importance of the therapeutic community programme.

The therapeutic community

Winnicott's concepts, like any good theory, help make sense out of the events of daily clinical experience, and therefore are themselves a holding, coherence-gathering environment. I want to suggest further that a residential treatment setting may provide through its various disciplines—psychotherapy, nursing, activities, administration, etc.— a range of environmental provisions to meet and facilitate the early developmental processes Winnicott was so articulate about. With these provisions, problematic object relationships may be played out in a relatively safe social environment. This both distributes the transference, making the weight of unbearable affect more survivable, and it creates the possibility of putting into words the unarticulated but highly charged object relations of the patient's past life.

Before this drama can be played out, however, the patient's capacities to be and be with must be established, and the collective strengths of the community must be developed such that they might anchor a durable social milieu capable of containing regressive moments. Winnicott (1945) spoke of holding, handling, and object-presenting (and later survival) as the environmental provisions necessary to the basic developments of integration, personalisation, and object relating (and later object usage) respectively. The quite ordinary, reliable attentiveness of nursing staff, for example, may become the extraordinary provision of "being there at the right time". The craft studio becomes a space in which to register the developing self over time, which is a holding function, or to use the medium of materials for tentative self-other engagement (Milner, 1957). The psychopharmacologist, in how he talks to a patient about medication, handles, in Winnicott's terms, the relation between self and body. And so on. I do not mean to suggest here a simple schematic such that, for example, personalisation is achieved through the ministrations of a particular department, but rather that these and other daily, accumulating, differentiated provisions from all staff to patients represent symbolic equivalents of those early developmental processes that facilitate the re-establishment of a unit self in a context of others. Conceptualising these provisions helps us notice the crucial developmental issues—and their fate—with which any given patient is struggling.

The therapeutic community enlarges the context of others to include patients as well as all the staff. As a form of psychological treatment, however, it has become increasingly rare in America, along with hospital treatment itself, in the current emphasis on management, financial constraint, and a narrow view of productivity. The promise and the learning beginning in that heady post-war era of Maxwell Jones (1953), Thomas Main (1946), Karl Menninger (1936–1937) and Marshall Edelson (1970) survive now only in a handful of programmes, that rarely come to the attention of today's beleaguered individual practitioners.

And yet all around us we hear about community: community homes for the de-institutionalised patient, strange communities as millennial havens for society's dispossessed, community policing as a major factor in reducing crime rates, community cohesion as distinguishing safe neighbourhoods from unsafe ones, regardless of poverty level, and community affiliations as providing a form of social capital to the democratic process. Indeed, community may be an antidote to the social and perhaps even the structural ailments associated with twenty-first century capitalism: namely, the intrapsychic and inter-generational conflicts associated with greed and envy, the ensuing deprivation of others, including family members, and the effect on superego development, both in terms of conscience and ego ideal.

For seriously disturbed patients, a therapeutic community programme, enriched by a psychodynamic systems perspective, can provide an essential holding environment for treatment as well as a remarkable depth of learning in itself. At the beginning of this therapeutic community's psychoanalytic history, when burgeoning crises with patients were making it clear to senior staff that analytic neutrality was no way to administer a hospital, a "historic decision" was taken "to talk the situation over with the patients" (Christie, 1964, p. 458). This "talking it over with the patients" became the core of the programme. It represents a serious partnership between patients and staff of mutual problem solving and examined living.

Begun in the early 1950s as part of an international movement toward the creation of intentional restorative communities for the treatment of psychiatric patients, this therapeutic community thrived initially on principles related to the ego psychology of the day: the importance of the patients' strengths or conflict-free sphere of ego functioning, the neutralisation of aggression through real tasks and real interaction with people, the importance of social learning, the power of multiple roles to forestall pathological identity foreclosure, and the importance of sublimation through creativity. Winnicott was an ego psychologist as much as he was an object relations theorist (Fromm, 1989a), and many of his developmental interests and conceptual discoveries parallel and coincide with those of Erik Erikson during the ten years the latter theorist was associated with this programme.

In an open setting, the therapeutic community holds by drawing in rather than by holding apart, relying upon each patient's wish, however conflicted or split off, to belong and to develop rewarding relationships. It is a play-space or potential space (Fromm, 2009; Winnicott, 1971e), like Winnicott's room, set off but not sealed off from the world outside the hospital. Within it, patients may play out both the problematic aspects of their personality development and emerging capacities as well.

In this process, projective dynamics inevitably occur; hence the importance of considering symptomatic eruption in group and systemic terms. Acting out by any member of the community not only affects the total community (which is important in its own right); it may also represent something for everyone, something dissociated from conscious dialogue and yet central to understanding the group's having veered off-task in some way. Acting out interpreted in terms of the system restores the holding environment it simultaneously tests (Shapiro & Carr, 1991). This perspective may lead to powerful learning in the here-and-now about the community. It may also lead to powerful learning for the patient (or sometimes for the staff member) who may be carrying an issue for the group, with whatever degree of personal distress and compromised functioning. The therapeutic community could be thought of as an "interpretive democracy", oriented toward finding the meaning within every instance of dissociated unconscious citizenship (Fromm, 2000).

This point of view simply enlarges upon the concept of therapeutic action in "Clinical varieties of transference" (1955–1956), in which Winnicott describes an essential irony in the therapeutic process: reliability of the therapeutic situation brings about the patient's vulnerability to failures in holding, specific failures felt very personally because they echo and open up for examination the early environmental failures of childhood. Such failures in the present, owned and interpreted by the analyst, felt with anger that makes sense by the patient, not only restore, but strengthen, the holding environment while they also deepen an understanding of the patient's total life.

This particular therapeutic community programme is actualised in a series of inter-related small and large groups, the hub of which is the daily Community Meeting, chaired by a patient who is elected for an eight-week term by the patient community. Some of the small groups are task-focused, representing an aspect of the community's functioning (e.g., recreation or integrating new members) for which the patient community has accepted responsibility, given its primary interest in, and greater ability for, these tasks. Other groups take up supportive–reflective tasks; for example, a group of patients vulnerable to substance abuse gathers regularly to support member sobriety and reflect upon the factors within the social environment that might bring about relapse. Moving through the daily life of the community, individual patients not only play out the troubling and unarticulated parts of their personalities, but they also play at the intersection between these troubles and the larger organisational dynamic.

Next

One evening, the community's chef was leaving after working late and noticed in a dark corner of the parking lot a car with the motor running. A patient had rigged a hose to her exhaust pipe and was seriously considering suicide. The chef intervened and walked her to the nurses. The next day, most of the agenda of the Community Meeting was set aside to talk with this patient. She reported "what happened to her", a language which the group defensively joined until a staff consultant commented on the process and re-framed the patient's statement in active terms. Language speaks us more than we speak it; in his comment, the consultant was holding the patient's agency and aggression, while she was inviting the group to join her in disavowing it. A more real discussion ensued. The patient community was upset, moved, and angry at this patient. Her behaviour affected them, from their deep recognition of how traumatic an actual suicide would be, to their admiration for this particular patient's struggles through past suffering, to their upset that this well-liked and thoroughly enjoyed chef might choose not to deal with this kind of stress any longer.

In the course of the discussion, the group's knowledge of this patient led to a reconstruction of the events prior to her action: her insurance company had recently said to her, in effect, "Get going; other people need these dollars". Also, her therapist was away attending to his new baby. Finally, just prior to her gesture, she had asked a staff member (though she had turned down other patients) to meet with her because of her distress. The staff member asked her to wait while she finished the admission work for a new patient. From this coherence-gathering dialogue, itself a holding function, a theme emerged clearly: the patient felt bumped aside by new people—displaced, abandoned, and angry.

This gathering awareness of the context of her action served to seed this patient's psychotherapy with potential for deeper analysis of her early life experiences and the transference. There was more to the issue, however, at the level of the group. It turned out that the agenda item that was set aside for this discussion had to do with the Sponsors Group, a patient-led group whose task is bringing new members into the community in a welcoming and orienting way. The Sponsors Chairperson had planned to confront the patient community with, and lead a discussion about, its recent reluctance to sponsor new patients.

In other words, the patient's angry caricaturing of being disposable in the face of new patients and new children occurred in a context of, and might well have reflected, the group's angry wish to reject those new faces too. When this discussion was eventually taken up, the group recognised that rejecting new patients was really a way of rejecting the changes they felt the treatment setting to be undergoing as it tried to adapt to a newer, financially driven reality of more patients being admitted for shorter lengths of stay. While the group was calling the patient back to conscious citizenship, it was also recognising her action as already reflecting a kind of unconscious citizenship (Fromm, 2000) in the sense of its unconsciously representative nature as a protest against unwanted change. Further, once this dynamic became clear, the staff took more seriously the community's problems with rapid admissions as well as its own contribution to this enactment. Each of these levels of understanding constitutes a deeper level of holding for the individual patient and for the community.

No

Tall, strong, competent, and aggressive, this patient's longstanding instability in her work and relational life had long since led to the diagnosis of borderline personality disorder. After some time in the community programme, she was elected to the position of treasurer in the committee that coordinates and funds patient recreation projects. Another part of the treasurer's role, for reasons lost in the programme's history, was membership on the patient–staff group that tries to deal with social problems in the patient community. Soon after being elected, this patient aggressively protested aspects of her job, especially participating in the social problems group. After discussion, the relevant patient chairpersons agreed to review job descriptions, but this was not enough for her. She refused to come to any meetings and to provide funds for ongoing projects until her demands were met, thus bringing a portion of the community's recreation to a temporary standstill.

After a number of efforts to engage her individually and in the appropriate meetings had failed, this was brought to the Community Meeting for resolution. When full discussion and efforts at honest reflection with all relevant parties made no headway, the community, in the face of an escalating threat from this patient, voted to replace her in her role. A new treasurer was elected and the patient was required to turn over the relevant funding materials. She had been amazingly blind to the impact of her rages and her denigration, then horrified and humiliated that the community had, in essence, voted to go on without her.

At that climactic Community Meeting, patients spoke to her about how bullying and intimidating she had been. Her first response was that they were lying, that no one was truly afraid of her, and that the nursing staff did not see her as intimidating. One nurse then spoke caringly but honestly: "I agree with these patients. You have been angry and threatening lately. Last night, when you told me that if I left your side, you couldn't be responsible for yourself, I felt like I was being held hostage. I'm surprised you don't see yourself as threatening. I guess you need to know that sometimes you do come across that way". Other patients and staff added their own recent perceptions, reminding the patient of other aspects of herself they had come to know besides her anger. The meeting then shifted abruptly from a tense, confrontational tone to a more conciliatory one, in which the patient began to talk about her loneliness and how friendless she had become. Later, at the evening coffee hour, patients made informal overtures to her. She joined them and soon thereafter began to help with the technical aspects of a play the community was producing.

During her subsequent treatment in and out of the treatment setting, this patient did not again enact her difficulties in this extreme way. Instead, this experience in the therapeutic community assumed the status of a symbolic event for her, to which she referred frequently in her psychotherapy whenever she found herself wanting to impose her psychological needs on external reality. Her immediate reaction, which sustained itself over time, was enormous relief that she was not necessarily the overwhelmingly powerful and destructive person she feared herself to be, and she came to understand this sense of herself as evolving from a control-or-be-controlled dynamic originating in her early life.

Getting to this level of understanding and acceptance required that the patient's therapist remain firmly situated in empathic connection with her while also in symbolic connection with the community. The patient's defensive tendency was toward splitting the therapist from the community and re-creating a dyadic relationship more sympathetic and yielding than her relationship with the intransigent community. These two relationships came to be seen by the patient as representing aspects of her early life experience, including sharply split experiences of her mother and later of the parental couple. The therapist's interpretation of this triangular dynamic, including the pressure to choose sides rather than choose understanding, eventually helped the patient see the family basis for her intense feelings, but only after the concrete community situation had been held and lived through empathically.

Disturbed patients regularly threaten destructive acting out, but they are also quite sensitive to the limits of those around them. Though they recurrently flirt with those limits in order to discharge affective tension and to substantiate a sense of self, they also find ways, as this patient did, to modulate their feelings in order to preserve their relationships and their membership in the community. In the interplay between patient and community, defensively dis-integrated elements of the patient's personality are held by the process in sharp relief and made more consciously available for potential re-integration. This patient's roles on the recreation committee and the social problems committee involved giving (money and attention respectively) to others. Not only could this large woman not stand to fit in with already established procedures, she apparently could not bear the envy that the giving aspect of her job stimulated in her.

The fallout from these difficulties had real effects on others, putting into the group the conflict the patient was experiencing. Would they be able to hold the tension, to consider her issues, to imagine granting her special request, to reflect upon what all of this might mean for them, and to face aggression without dissociation? These questions highlight the link between holding and containment (Ogden, 2005d). A primary role for community programme staff is to help the total community hold this difficult situation and to facilitate the containment process: that is, to help the group direct its attention to unfinished business, to assist in the articulation of both resistance and task, to make sense of one's own feelings, to counter pressures toward group fragmentation, and to establish a "continuity of situation" through to whatever resolution the group might make (Stern, Fronn, & Sacksteder, 1986, p. 30).

The working through of this kind of episode in the community programme pre-supposes the total community's capacity to absorb aggression and yet maintain differentiated relationships (informal alliances, a range of perspectives) with the disturbing patient. Sometimes, as this one did, it ends with a reparative gesture of the patient and a deeper confidence in all concerned that the community can handle the problems that may arise. As Winnicott (1969) understood, it is no small accomplishment for the community and no small joy for the patient to find that the object of the patient's destructive assault has survived, has held all concerned through an emotional storm, and is genuinely available to be re-joined. The psychic outcome for the patient may well be a variation of that decisive experience Winnicott refers to in the context of the object's survival, namely, that the omnipotently destructive self, alone in a world of projections, evolves toward a potently reparative self in a world of others.

There is, however, another set of questions to be asked about this episode. Why a crisis in the community's "chief financial officer" at that time? Why did the community elect a person so determined to say "No" in roles that also required saying "Yes"? Why was there tension at the link between social problems and recreational projects? Did this patient represent something beyond her own personal difficulties in the current community or organisational dynamic?

On this level of examination, the patient's situation might not have come to so dramatic and risky a climax had we been able to find ourselves in her. By this I mean that it may have been no accident that issues of money and envy came to the fore in the person of this patient. Managed care in America was making its first serious inroads into psychiatric treatment. A number of patients had suffered abrupt terminations of their funding. Marked differences had erupted into the community's consciousness between those patients whose funding was private and relatively secure, and those patients whose funding was through insurance and suddenly quite insecure (see also

Chapter Five). Envy was inevitable around these issues of money, and recreation seemed a luxury.

All of this led not only to anxiety in the patients, but also to strong differences within the staff about how to respond to the gathering crisis. This patient's declarations within her treasurer role that "I've got the power because I've got the money," and "If you let me go, I'll do something destructive" captured the enormous strains, fantasies, and clinical dilemmas the staff was struggling with during this time. This broadens the issue of survival to the level of the treatment frame and the mission itself. From a psychoanalytically informed, organisational perspective, we could perhaps have seen this patient's disturbance as both a symptom of, and a consultation to, the survival processes of the institution itself.

Democracy

In his paper on democracy, Winnicott (1965b) makes the point that "a democracy is an achievement at a point of time of a society that has some natural boundary. Of a true democracy . . . one can say: In this society at this time there is sufficient maturity in the emotional development of a sufficient proportion of the individuals that comprise it for there to exist an innate tendency towards the creation and re-creation and maintenance of the democratic machinery" (pp. 157–158). Winnicott adds:

> The essence of democratic machinery is the free vote . . . The point of this is that it ensures the freedom of the people to express deep feelings, apart from conscious thoughts. In the exercise of the secret vote, the whole responsibility for action is taken by the individual, if he is healthy enough to take it. The vote expresses the outcome of the struggle within himself. (p. 157)

The issues of the external world are "made personal" (p. 157) through gradually identifying oneself with all parties to the struggle, thus making it a true internal struggle, and resolving the struggle, for better but quite possibly for worse, in a decisive and necessarily depressive moment.

In contrast to the "mature" individual who is able to "find the whole conflict within the self" and is therefore "capable of becoming depressed about it" (p. 158), Winnicott describes first those individuals with an antisocial tendency, born of deprivation and eventuating in a ruthless and aggressive claim against authority and second, the "hidden antisocial" (p. 158), insecure in his personal identity and borrowing on the authoritarianism around him to keep an internal peace. For Winnicott, the "whole democratic burden" (p. 159) falls on that crucial critical mass of relatively mature individuals. He finds an anti-democratic tendency in many of society's institutions, cautioning "the doctors of criminals and of the insane . . . to be constantly on guard lest they find themselves being used, without at first knowing it, as agents of the anti-democratic tendency"(p. 160). What nurtures the democratic tendency? Winnicott simply refers to "ordinary good homes" (p. 160), focusing only on the possible interferences of society with the good sense and natural authority of parents.

How does this apply to a therapeutic community? To the degree that the therapeutic community is built upon democratic principles— principles such as the belief that each person's voice matters, the conviction that finding one's authentic voice is therapeutic, and the recognition that participation in decisions by which one is affected is both just and healthy—it relies upon the collective maturity of embattled, deprived and insecure people. To the degree that the therapeutic community exists within a medical model, it is vulnerable to the hidden antisocial or authoritarian tendencies involved in the localisation and control of illness. And yet, one could also make the case that a therapeutic community programme that facilitates the living out of democratic principles is inherently therapeutic and its successes increase the collective maturity of the whole.

Winnicott once quipped that an adult is a person with a point of view. A democratic frame of reference invites a person toward discovering his or her point of view, toward declaring it publicly, toward listening to the points of views of others and, in doing so, toward learning more, and surrendering or standing one's ground. It faces its members with problems of difference, conflict, and compromise, with moments of decision that both join and separate one from others, and with the requirement to re-join, after the battle so to speak, in order to carry on something larger than the self, namely, the total community's life. This terrain—between one-ness and two-ness (on the way to third-ness)—is the political equivalent of that developmental territory leading up to the depressive position, which Winnicott linked with severe personality disorders (see Chapter Two).

Patients in this kind of therapeutic community programme are challenged in the place they most need to develop, that is, toward taking authority in a world of others rather than simply being subject to the authority of others or attempting to dominate them. The open setting for a therapeutic community structurally recognises the separate authority of the patient group, the authority of a citizen-consumer rather than a quasi-employee, and rather than a patient role in which authority is simply surrendered to the staff. It requires a partnership between an authorised patient group and a receptive staff group in order to maintain its functioning and maximise the treatment benefit. It also requires staff leadership to hold this authority differentiation, to work with it, and to lead reflection about democracy-eroding intergroup dynamics.

Cultural crisis

At a Community Meeting, a young, first generation, Korean-American woman challenged the candidacy of an older man who was running for an eight-week term as Community Chairperson, a position of considerable authority in the community programme. She confronted him with his overtures toward a new female patient and the dangers of romantic entanglement while in treatment. She justified her insistent questioning by saying: "It's not that I don't want you to become chairperson. It's that I want you to really want it, to love it, to not be put off by anything that I or anybody else could say to you".

The consultant to this large meeting found himself commenting on a theme in the discussion that linked to cultural differences. The candidate was arguing what could be heard as an American position. There was the community's need for leadership, but there was also this man's own "pursuit of happiness" with this new female patient; he emphasised the good job he could do for the community, but also how this job would be "good for (his) therapy". His challenger was speaking with passion against this divided self, from a place where role and person could be imagined to be one, where giving oneself over to the role might occur so completely that it would be distracting, trivialising, and irrelevant to wonder about one's own therapy as in any way separate from this commitment to community. From this perhaps more Eastern place, "loving it" meant not concerning oneself at all with any notion of personal desire as separate from the community's.

This issue resonated deeply in the patient's life history. Her life had been shaped by events before she was born. Her father had sent his first child back to his home village because he and his wife could not care for an infant while they were completing their law degrees in the city. Later, during the patient's early childhood, her mother's rage and guilt at having acquiesced to this separation led the father to forfeit his place with his second child and to give her over to a now fiercely possessive mother. The patient's adolescent struggle to separate could only be seen by her mother as an evil betrayal by her daughter or as an evil infiltration by American culture bent on taking away her second child. Thus, along with her ferocious but deeply guilt-inducing autonomy struggle, the patient also felt an enormous wish and fear about surrender.

The Community Chairperson position eventually served an important compromise function for her. During the next term, to everyone's surprise, this quite young woman firmly declared her candidacy and took up the position with more natural authority than anyone in recent memory. She unambivalently surrendered herself, not to another person, but to what is best in the American system, and she found in her learning about authority a way of becoming clearer about her life in her family.

As though a microcosmic study in Erikson's *Life History and the Historical Moment* (1975), she led the entire community through a fascinating period. Because of the discharge of a number of more experienced patients, newer patient leadership was struggling to develop, some patient offices were not filled, and some functions, that patients had performed ably, were left undone. Staff became anxious, unconsciously longed for their older culture of long-term treatment with less frequent patient turnover and began, again unconsciously, to direct patients as though they were employees. This patient as Community Chairperson felt this possessiveness based on a potentially lost culture keenly, and she stopped it through an amazing clarity about the distinction between patient and staff authority. In Bion's (1961) terms, she brought a powerful unconscious "valency" (p. 116) from her family dynamic to the community, that became available as a resource in the face of an unconscious democracy-eroding staff-patient process. Perhaps representing the Third (Muller, 1996), which derives from a paternal function, the staff consultant firmly supported the effort to hold the distinction between staff and patient authority.

Instead of complying with staff need and losing the patients' authority in the process, the Chairperson addressed her constituency. She realised that they had lost touch with whether or not they wanted these endangered community functions, and she had the strength to let them go, rather than to cajole or coerce people toward keeping them going for the sake of tradition. She led the community in risking that many age-old community practices would not survive, in order to find what the community might actually want to survive from within itself. In a sense, she led a process that Winnicott (1945) once called "realiza-tion", that is, the developmental process through which necessary illu-sions—in this case, the patients' illusion that the community is *only* a play-space and the staff's illusion that the community carries out *their* dreams—admit an appreciation of external reality.

Soon the patient community *felt* the value of these community functions and took them up again in a more vital way. And the staff too, with considerable gratitude, rediscovered their appropriate roles as partners to the patient enterprise. This was true cultural renewal. In leading it, this patient seemed to have reworked important family issues for herself, as she was also helping the community. For exam-ple, one meaning of suicide in this patient's life, as she came to realise in her psychotherapy, related to an extreme claim to her own personal authority, an effort to kill a false self adaptation (Winnicott, 1960) and to discover what might survive as her true desire. She insisted, almost at the cost of her life, on truly being let go of by her mother (and on her own letting go of her mother) so that a felt and chosen connection to her culture and to her mother might have a chance to develop from within. We see here personal crisis meeting community crisis in which a particular person seems to have been called unconsciously to a role and a crucial task: namely, redressing the total community's shift toward false self adaptation by rediscovering what, if anything, within the prevailing tradition might be actively joined as true.

Sanity and bonding

Analogous to Winnicott's (1965b) notion of the "ordinary good home", the therapeutic community has been defined as "a structure of belonging within which might exist the possibility of the individual's finding his or her own way" (Cooper, 1991). When a psychotic patient who had been transferred to a closed hospital during an acute regression was speaking at the Community Meeting about his possible re-admission, he responded to a patient's question about what he hoped to gain from his return by saying "sanity and bonding". Given the quality of the group's discussion with him, what he meant seemed clear. Indeed a patient spoke of her walks with him and how she could tell during her conversations that when she understood him, he got anxious. "It can be scary getting close to people," she said, and he agreed. This exchange is precisely sanity and bonding. The fact that it came so naturally, and was joined so movingly, in this patient-to-patient interaction speaks to one aspect of the texture of the "ordinary good" community.

Winnicott's concept of "potential space" (Fromm, 2009; Winnicott, 1971e) is relevant to this work. The, one might say, "ordinary good" interpretation at the Community Meeting of the prospective patient's anxiety about closeness was made by another patient. New patients, new staff, and professional visitors at the Community Meetings regularly have the experience of asking themselves, "Was that a staff member or a patient who said that?" This is a powerfully and helpfully de-centring moment, in which patients become in their daily participation what others think of as staff. They can then sometimes come to appreciate, with whatever mixture of exhilaration and chagrin, that patienthood is a role, not an intrinsic aspect of person—a realisation basic to the process of taking authority.

Conversely, as part of the therapeutic community programme, staff take the daring step of attempting to make freely available for interpretation *their* unconscious organisational enactments. They too belong in this deep sense. They take part in the conscious give-and-take of the community's democratic process, helping patients achieve the kind of capacities for living Winnicott was so attentive to, while they also surrender themselves to an "interpretive democracy" in which anyone—patient or staff—can facilitate the community's development by contributing toward making sense of it. They thus attempt to free themselves from rigid and "hidden antisocial" role attributes, recognise *in vivo* the "psychological equality" (Kennard, 1998, p. 27) of all human beings, and add their weight to the critical mass of maturity necessary for a truly democratic, therapeutic process.

A holding environment both enriches the developmental process and contains its various elements toward their eventual integration. "The operation of setting factors" (Winnicott, 1954a, p. 293) can be considered as an effort to understand the systemic dynamics of the holding environment. Winnicott argued that a reliable setting invites patient regression to early failures of the environment, which must be accounted for as part of making sense of the patient's experience. The data of this chapter suggests that this accounting may go beyond the understanding of the enactments within the psychotherapeutic dyad and include an understanding of the particular organisational dynamic with which a given patient has become psychologically implicated. This is another aspect of the essential "examined living" practice of any successful therapeutic community.

REFERENCES

Alexander, F. (1925). Dreams in pairs and series. *International Journal of Psycho-Analysis, 6*: 446–452.

Antonovsky, A. (1978). The thinking cure. *Contemporary Psychoanalysis, 14*: 338–404.

Balint, M. (1968). *The Basic Fault*. London: Tavistock.

Balmary, M. (1982). *Psychoanalyzing Psychoanalysis: Freud and the Hidden Fault of the Father*. Baltimore: Johns Hopkins University Press.

Benedetti, G. (1987). Illuminations of the human condition in the encounter with the psychotic patient. In: J. Sacksteder, D. Schwartz, & Y. Akabane (Eds.), *Attachment and the Therapeutic Process: Essays in Honor of Otto Allen Will, Jr.* (pp. 185–196). Madison, CT: International Universities Press.

Bion, W. R. (1961). *Experiences in Groups*. New York: Basic Books.

Bion, W. R. (1962). A theory of thinking. *International Journal of Psycho-Analysis, 43*: 306–310.

Bion, W. R. (1967a). Attacks on linking. In: *Second Thoughts* (pp. 93–109). New York: Jason Aronson.

Bion, W. R. (1967b). On arrogance. In: *Second Thoughts* (pp. 83–92). New York: Jason Aronson.

Bird, B. (1972). Notes on transference: universal phenomenon and the hardest part of analysis. *Journal of the American Psychoanalytic Association, 20*: 267–301.

Bleger, J. (1966). Psycho-analysis of the psycho-analytic frame. *International Journal of Psycho-Analysis, 48*: 511–519.

Bollas, C. (1982). On the relation to the self as an object. *International Journal of Psycho-Analysis, 63*: 347–359.

Bollas, C. (1987). The unthought known: early considerations. In: *The Shadow of the Object* (pp. 277–283). London: Free Association.

Bollas, C. (1999). Borderline desire. In: *The Mystery of Things* (pp. 127–135). London: Routledge.

Bollas, C. (2002). *Free Association*. Cambridge: Icon.

Bruch, H. (1978). *The Golden Cage: The Enigma of Anorexia Nervosa*. Cambridge: Harvard University Press.

Christie, G. (1964). Therapeutic community and psychotherapy: the Austen Riggs Center. *The Medical Journal of Australia, 1*: 457–460.

Coltart, N. (1986), 'Slouching towards Bethlehem' . . . or thinking the unthinkable in psychoanalysis. In: G. Kohon (Ed.), *The British Middle School of Psychoanalysis: The Independent Tradition* (pp. 185–199). New Haven and London: Yale University Press.

Cooper, R. (1991). Can therapeutic community be planned? *International Journal of Therapeutic Communities, 12*: 261–266.

Cooperman, M. (1969). Defeating processes in psychotherapy. Paper presented at a meeting of the Topeka Psychoanalytic Society, Topeka, Kansas, 27 March 1969.

Davis, M., & Wallbridge, D. (1981). *Boundary and Space*. New York: Brunner/Mazel.

Davoine, F. (1989). Potential space and the space in between two deaths. In: M. G. Fromm & B. L. Smith (Eds.), *The Facilitating Environment: Clinical Applications of Winnicott's Theory* (pp. 581–603). Madison, CT: International Universities Press.

Davoine, F., & Gaudilliere, J.-M. (1997). Schizophrenia and historical catastrophes. Paper presented at the 12th International Symposium for the Psychotherapy of Schizophrenia, London.

Davoine, F., & Gaudilliere, J.-M. (2004). *History Beyond Trauma*. New York: Other Press.

Deutsch, H. (1942). Some forms of emotional disturbance and their relationship to schizophrenia. *Psychoanalytic Quarterly, 11*: 301–321.

Edelson, M. (1970). *Sociotherapy and Psychotherapy*. Chicago: University of Chicago Press.

Erikson, E. (1956). The problem of ego identity. *Journal of the American Psychoanalytic Association, 4*: 56–121.

Erikson, E. (1961). The roots of virtue. In: J. Huxley (Ed.), *The Humanist Frame* (pp. 145–165). New York: Harper.

Erikson, E. (1964). *Insight and Responsibility*. New York: Norton.

Erikson, E. (1970). Autobiographic notes on the identity crisis. *Daedalus*, 99: 730–759.

Erikson, E. (1975). *Life History and the Historical Moment*. New York: Norton.

Erikson, J. (1976). *Activity, Recovery, Growth: The Communal Role of Planned Activities*. New York: Norton.

Farber, L. (1966). *The Ways of the Will*. New York: Basic Books.

Ferenczi, S. (1928). The elasticity of psycho-analytic technique. In: *Final Contributions to the Problems and Methods of Psycho-Analysis* (pp. 87–101). London: Hogarth, 1955.

Fonagy, P. (1991). Thinking about thinking: some clinical and theoretical considerations in the treatment of a borderline patient. *International Journal of Psycho-Analysis, 72*: 639–656.

Fonagy, P., Gergely, G., Jurist, E., & Target, M. (2002). *Affect Regulation, Mentalization and the Development of the Self*. New York: Other Press.

Freud, A. (1976). Changes in psychoanalytic practice and experience. *International Journal of Psycho-Analysis, 57*: 257–260.

Freud, S. (1905e). Fragment of an analysis of a case of hysteria. *S.E.*, 7: 7–122. London: Hogarth.

Freud, S. (1911e). The handling of dream-interpretation in psycho-analysis. *S.E.*, 12: 91–96. London: Hogarth.

Freud, S. (1913i). The disposition to obsessional neurosis. *S.E.*, 12: 317–326. London: Hogarth.

Freud, S. (1915c). Instincts and their vicissitudes. *S.E.*, 14: 117–140. London: Hogarth.

Freud, S. (1920g). *Beyond the Pleasure Principle*. *S.E.*, 18: 7–64. London: Hogarth.

Freud, S. (1923c). Remarks on the theory and practice of dream-interpretation. *S.E.*, 19: 109–121. London: Hogarth.

Fromm, M. G. (1978). The patient's role in the modulation of countertransference. *Contemporary Psychoanalysis, 14*: 279–290.

Fromm, M. G. (1989a). Winnicott's work in relation to classical psychoanalysis and ego psychology. In: M. G. Fromm & B. L. Smith (Eds.), *The Facilitating Environment: Clinical Applications of Winnicott's Theory* (pp. 3–26). Madison, CT: International Universities Press.

Fromm, M. G. (1989b). Photography as transitional functioning. In: M. G. Fromm & B. L. Smith (Eds.), *The Facilitating Environment: Clinical Applications of Winnicott's Theory* (pp. 279–314). Madison, CT: International Universities Press.

Fromm, M. G. (2000). The Other in dreams. *Journal of Applied Psychoanalytic Studies, 2*: 287–298.

Fromm, M. G. (2004). Psychoanalysis and trauma: September 11 revisited. *Diogenes, 23*: 3–19.

Fromm, M. G. (2009). Potential space and maternal authority in organizations. *Organisational and Social Dynamics, 9*: 189–205.

Fromm, M. G. (2011). 'We are all more human than otherwise': psychoanalytic treatment of psychotic patients. *The American Psychoanalyst, 45*: 17–19.

Fromm, M. G. (2012). *Lost in Transmission: Studies of Trauma Across Generations*. London: Karnac.

Fromm, M. G., & Smith, B. L. (Eds.) (1989). *The Facilitating Environment: Clinical Applications of Winnicott's Theory*. Madison, CT: International Universities Press.

Fromm-Reichmann, F. (1959). *Psychoanalysis and Psychotherapy: Selected Papers*. Chicago: The University of Chicago Press.

Ghent, E. (1992). Paradox and process. *Psychoanalytic Dialogues, 2*: 135–159.

Goldman, D. (1998). Surviving as scientist and dreamer. *Contemporary Psychoanalysis, 34*: 359–367.

Gorney, J. (1979). The negative therapeutic interaction. *Contemporary Psychoanalysis, 15*: 288–337.

Green, A. (1975). The analyst, symbolization and absence in the analytic setting (on changes in analytic practice and analytic experience). *International Journal of Psycho-Analysis, 56*: 1–22.

Green, A. (1977). The borderline concept. In: P. Hartocollis (Ed.), *Borderline Personality Disorders: The Concept, the Syndrome, the Patient* (pp. 15–44). New York: International Universities Press.

Green, A. (1978). Potential space in psychoanalysis: the object in the setting. In: S. Grolnick & L. Barkin (Eds.), *Between Reality and Fantasy* (pp. 169–189). New York: Jason Aronson.

Green, A. (1999). *The Work of the Negative*. London: Free Association.

Greenberg, J. (1964). *I Never Promised You a Rose Garden*. New York: Holt, Rinehart, & Winston.

Greenson, R. (1974). On transitional objects and transference. In: *Explorations in Psychoanalysis* (pp. 491–496). New York: International Universities Press, 1978.

Greenson, R., & Wexler, M. (1969). The nontransference relationship in the psychoanalytic situation. In: *Explorations in Psychoanalysis* (pp. 359–386). New York: International Universities Press, 1978.

Grinberg, L. (1997). Is the transference feared by the psychoanalyst? *International Journal of Psycho-Analysis, 78*: 1–14.

Hauser, S. (2006). *Out of the Woods: Tales of Resilient Teens.* Cambridge, MA: Harvard University Press.

Hughes, R. (1981). *The Shock of the New.* New York: Alfred A. Knopf.

Jones, M. (1953). *The Therapeutic Community.* New York: Basic Books.

Kennard, D. (1998). *An Introduction to Therapeutic Communities.* London: Jessica Kingsley.

Kernberg, O. (1975). *Borderline Conditions and Pathological Narcissism.* New York: Jason Aronson.

Kernberg, O. (1984). *Severe Personality Disorders.* New Haven: Yale University Press.

Khan, M. (1960). Regression and integration in the analytic setting. In: *The Privacy of the Self* (pp. 136–167). New York: International Universities Press, 1974.

Khan, M. (1963). Silence as communication. In: *The Privacy of the Self* (pp. 168–180). New York: International Universities Press, 1974.

Khan, M. (1969). On symbiotic omnipotence. In: *The Privacy of the Self* (pp. 82–92). New York: International Universities Press, 1974.

Khan, M. (1971). The role of illusion in the analytic space and process. In: *The Privacy of the Self* (pp. 251–269). New York: International Universities Press, 1974.

Khan, M. (1972a). The use and abuse of dream in psychic experience. In: *The Privacy of the Self* (pp. 306–315). New York: International Universities Press, 1974.

Khan, M. (1972b). Dread of surrender to resourceless dependence in the analytic situation. In: *The Privacy of the Self* (pp. 270–279). New York: International Universities Press, 1974.

Khan, M. (1976). The changing use of dreams in psychoanalytic practice. *International Journal of Psycho-Analysis, 57*: 325–330.

Khantzian, E. (1999). *Treating Addiction as a Human Process.* Northvale, NJ: Jason Aronson.

Kirshner, L. (2011). *Between Winnicott and Lacan: A Clinical Engagement.* New York: Routledge.

Kohut, H. (1977). *The Restoration of the Self.* New York: International Universities Press.

Knight, R. (1953). Borderline states. *Bulletin of the Menninger Clinic, 17*: 1–12.

Kris, A. (1982). *Free Association: Method and Process.* New Haven: Yale University Press.

Kwawer, J. (1998). On using Winnicott. *Contemporary Psychoanalysis, 34*: 389–395.

Lacan, J. (1977). *Ecrits: Selected Writings of Jacques Lacan*. New York: Norton.

Langs, R. (1976). *The Bipersonal Field*. New York: Jason Aronson.

Lewin, B. (1954). Sleep, narcissistic neurosis, and the analytic situation. In: *Selected Writings of Bertram D. Lewin* (pp. 227–247). New York: Psychoanalytic Quarterly, 1973.

Lewis, J. (1991). Systems, stress and survival: psychiatric hospitals in the 1990's. Presentation at the National Association of Private Psychiatric Hospitals Annual Meeting, 30 January 1991.

Luepnitz, D. (2009). Thinking in the space between Winnicott and Lacan. *International Journal of Psycho-Analysis, 90*: 957–981.

Main, T. (1946). The hospital as a therapeutic institution. *Bulletin of the Menninger Clinic, 10*: 66–70.

Mehler, J. A., & Argentieri, S. (1989). Hope and hopelessness: a technical problem. *International Journal of Psycho-Analysis, 70*: 295–304.

Menninger, W. (1936–1937). Psychoanalytic principles applied to the treatment of hospitalized patient. *Bulletin of the Menninger Clinic, 1*: 35–43.

Milner, M. (1937). *An Experiment in Leisure*. London: Chatto and Windus [published under the pen name of Joanna Field].

Milner, M. (1952). Aspects of symbolism in comprehension of the not-self. *International Journal of Psycho-Analysis, 33*: 181–195.

Milner, M. (1957). *On Not Being Able to Paint*. New York: International Universities Press.

Milner, M. (1969). *The Hands of the Living God*. New York: International Universities Press.

Modell, A. (1963). Primitive object relationships and the predisposition to schizophrenia. *International Journal of Psycho-Analysis, 44*: 282–292.

Modell, A. (1968). *Object Love and Reality*. New York: International Universities Press.

Morrison, V. (1991). See me through, Part II. *Hymns to the Silence* (CD). New York: Polygram Records.

Muller, J. (1992). Transference and Lacan's subject-supposed-to-know. *Phenomenology and Lacanian Psychoanalysis* (pp. 37–46). The papers of the 8th Annual Symposium of the Simon Silverman Phenomenology Center. Pittsburgh: Duquesne University.

Muller, J. (1993). Walking or falling into the wild. The 6th Erik H. Erikson Lecture at the Austen Riggs Center, Stockbridge, Massachusetts.

Muller, J. (1996). *Beyond the Psychoanalytic Dyad*. New York: Routledge.

Needham, J. (1969). *The Grand Titration: Science and Society in East and West*. Toronto: University of Toronto Press.

Ogden, T. (2005a). On not being able to dream. In: *This Art of Psychoanalysis* (pp. 45–60). New York: Routledge.

Ogden, T. (2005b). This art of psychoanalysis: dreaming undreamt dreams and interrupted cries. In: *This Art of Psychoanalysis* (pp. 1–18). New York: Routledge.

Ogden, T. (2005c). What I would not part with. In: *This Art of Psychoanalysis* (pp. 19–26). New York: Routledge.

Ogden, T. (2005d). On holding and containing, being and dreaming. In: *This Art of Psychoanalysis* (pp. 93–108). New York: Routledge.

Oxenhandler, N. (1997). Fall from grace. In: *The New Yorker*, 16 June 1997.

Parsons, M. (1990). Marion Milner's 'answering activity' and the question of psychoanalytic creativity. *International Review of Psycho-Analysis, 17*: 413–424.

Peraldi, F. (2010). La pere silencieux. In: G. Chagnon, M. Hazan, & M. Peterson (Eds.), *Penser la Clinique Psychanalytique* (pp. 47–69). Montreal: Liber.

Phillips, A. (1996). *Terrors and Experts*. Cambridge: Harvard University Press.

Plakun, E. (1991). Prediction of outcome in borderline personality disorder. *Journal of Personality Disorders, 5*: 93–101.

Podro, M. (1990). 'The landscape thinks itself in me': the comments and procedures of Cezanne. *International Review of Psycho-Analysis, 17*: 401–408.

Pontalis, J.-B. (1974). Dream as an object. *International Review of Psycho-Analysis, 1*: 125–133.

Pontalis, J.-B. (1981). *Frontiers in Psychoanalysis: Between the Dream and Psychic Pain*. New York: International Universities Press.

Pontalis, J.-B. (1993). *Love of Beginnings*. London: Free Association.

Prelinger, E. (2004). Thoughts on hate and aggression. *The Psychoanalytic Study of the Child, 59*: 30–43.

Pritchett, V. S. (1964). *The Offensive Traveller*. New York: Knopf.

Rangell, L. (1975). Psychoanalysis and the process of change; an essay on the past, present, and future. *International Journal of Psycho-Analysis, 56*: 87–98.

Rayner, E. (1991). *The Independent Mind in British Psychoanalysis*. Northvale, NJ: Jason Aronson.

Robbins, M. (1993). *Experiences of Schizophrenia*. New York: Guilford.

Rodman, F. R. (Ed.) (1987). *The Spontaneous Gesture: Selected Letters of D. W. Winnicott*. Cambridge, MA: Harvard University Press.

Rosen, V. (1955). The reconstruction of a traumatic childhood event in a case of derealization. *Journal of the American Psychoanalytic Association*, 3: 211–221.

Rosenfeld, H. (1979). Difficulties in the psychoanalytic treatment of borderline patients. In: J. LeBoit & A. Capponi (Eds.), *Advances in Psychotherapy of the Borderline Patient* (pp. 187–206). New York: Jason Aronson.

Rycroft, C. (1979). *The Innocence of Dreams*. London: Hogarth.

Sacksteder, J. (1989). Personalization as an aspect of the process of change in anorexia nervosa. In: M. G. Fromm & B. L. Smith (Eds.), *The Facilitating Environment: Clinical Applications of Winnicott's Theory* (pp. 394–423). Madison, CT: International Universities Press.

Sandler, J., & Sandler, A. (1986). The gyroscopic function of unconscious fantasy. In: D. Feinsilver (Ed.), *Towards a Comprehensive Model for Schizophrenic Disorders* (pp. 109–123). Hillsdale, NJ: Analytic.

Schafer, R. (Ed.) (1997). *The Contemporary Kleinians of London*. Madison, CT: International Universities Press.

Searles, H. F. (1975). The patient as therapist to his analyst. In: *Counter-transference and Related Subjects* (pp. 380–459). New York: International Universities Press, 1979.

Searles, H. F. (1976). Transitional phenomena and therapeutic symbiosis. In: *Countertransference and Related Subjects* (pp. 503–576). New York: International Universities Press, 1979.

Searles, H. F. (1986). *My Work with Borderline Patients*. Northvale, NJ: Aronson.

Shapiro, E. (1997). The boundaries are shifting: re-negotiating the thera-peutic frame. In: *The Inner World in the Outer World* (pp. 7–25). New Haven, CT: Yale University Press.

Shapiro, E., & Carr, A. W. (1991). *Lost in Familiar Places: Creating New Connections Between the Individual and Society*. New Haven, CT: Yale University Press.

Shapiro, E., Zinner, J., Shapiro, R., & Berkowitz, D. (1989). The influence of family experience on borderline personality development. In: J. S. Scharff (Ed.), *Foundations of Object Relations Family Therapy*. Northvale, NJ: Jason Aronson.

Stern, D., Fromm, M. G., & Sacksteder, J. (1986). From coercion to collab-oration: two weeks in the life of a therapeutic community. *Psychiatry*, 49: 18–32.

Stone, M. (1986). *Essential Papers on Borderline Disorders: One Hundred Years at the Border*. New York: New York University Press.

Sullivan, H. S. (1940). *Conceptions of Modern Psychiatry*. New York: Basic Books.

Symington, N. (1986). The last lecture. In: *The Analytic Experience* (pp. 320–331). New York: St. Martin's Press.

Thomas, D. M. (1981). *The White Hotel*. New York: Viking.

Tustin, F. (1981). *Autistic States in Children*. London: Routledge & Kegan Paul.

U2 (1987). One tree hill. *The Joshua Tree* (CD). New York: Island Records.

Vaillant, G. (1992). The beginning of wisdom is never calling a patient a borderline. *Journal of Psychotherapy Practice and Research*, 1: 117–134.

Volkan, V. (1981). *Linking Objects and Linking Phenomena*. New York: International Universities Press.

Will, O. A. (1964). Schizophrenia and the psychotherapeutic field. *Contemporary Psychoanalysis*, 1: 1–29.

Winnicott, D. W. (1941). The observation of infants in a set situation. In: *Collected Papers: Through Paediatrics to Psycho-Analysis* (pp. 52–69). New York: Basic Books, 1958.

Winnicott, D. W. (1945). Primitive emotional development. In: *Through Paediatrics to Psycho-Analysis* (pp. 145–156). New York: Basic Books, 1958.

Winnicott, D. W. (1947). Hate in the countertransference. In: *Through Paediatrics to Psycho-Analysis* (pp. 194–203). New York: Basic Books, 1958.

Winnicott, D. W. (1948). Reparation in respect of mother's organized defence against depression. In: *Through Paediatrics to Psycho-Analysis* (pp. 91–96). New York: Basic Books, 1958.

Winnicott, D. W. (1951). Transitional objects and transitional phenomena. In: *Through Paediatrics to Psycho-Analysis* (pp. 229–242). New York: Basic Books, 1958.

Winnicott, D. W. (1952). Psychoses and child care. In: *Through Paediatrics to Psycho-Analysis* (pp. 219–228). New York: Basic Books, 1958.

Winnicott, D. W. (1954a). Metapsychological and clinical aspects of regression within the psycho-analytical set-up. In: *Through Paediatrics to Psycho-Analysis* (pp. 278–294). New York: Basic Books, 1958.

Winnicott, D. W. (1954b). Withdrawal and regression. In: *Through Paediatrics to Psycho-Analysis* (pp. 255–261). New York: Basic Books, 1958.

Winnicott, D. W. (1955–1956). Clinical varieties of transference. In: *Through Paediatrics to Psycho-Analysis* (pp. 295–299). New York: Basic Books, 1958.

Winnicott, D. W. (1956a). The antisocial tendency. In: *Through Paediatrics to Psycho-Analysis* (pp. 306–315). New York: Basic Books, 1958.

Winnicott, D. W. (1956b). Primary maternal preoccupation. In: *Through Paediatrics to Psycho-Analysis* (pp. 300–305). New York: Basic Books, 1958.

Winnicott, D. W. (1957). Further thoughts on babies as persons. In: *The Child and the Outside World* (pp. 134–140). New York: Basic Books.

Winnicott, D. W. (1958). The capacity to be alone. In: *The Maturational Processes and the Facilitating Environment* (pp. 29–36). New York: International Universities Press, 1965.

Winnicott, D. W. (1960). Ego distortion in terms of true and false self. In: *The Maturational Processes and the Facilitating Environment* (pp. 140–152). New York: International Universities Press, 1965.

Winnicott, D. W. (1962a). Ego integration in child development. In: *The Maturational Processes and the Facilitating Environment* (pp. 56–63). New York: International Universities Press, 1965.

Winnicott, D. W. (1962b). The aims of psycho-analytical treatment. In: *The Maturational Processes and the Facilitating Environment* (pp. 166–170). New York: International Universities Press, 1965.

Winnicott, D. W. (1963a). The development of the capacity for concern. In: *The Maturational Processes and the Facilitating Environment* (pp. 73–82). New York: International Universities Press, 1965.

Winnicott, D. W. (1963b). Communicating and not communicating leading to a study of certain opposites. In: *The Maturational Processes and the Facilitating Environment* (pp. 179–192). New York: International Universities Press, 1965.

Winnicott, D. W. (1965a). Advising parents. In: *The Family and Individual Development* (pp. 114–120). New York: Basic Books.

Winnicott, D. W. (1965b). Some thoughts on the meaning of the word democracy. In: *The Family and Individual Development* (pp. 155–169). New York: Basic Books.

Winnicott, D. W. (1969). The use of an object. *International Journal of Psycho-Analysis, 50*: 711–716.

Winnicott, D. W. (1971a). *Therapeutic Consultations in Child Psychiatry*. New York: Basic Books.

Winnicott, D. W. (1971b). Transitional objects and transitional phenomena: clinical material. In: *Playing and Reality* (pp. 1–25). New York: Basic Books.

Winnicott, D. W. (1971c). Mirror-role of mother and family in child development. In: *Playing and Reality* (pp. 111–118). New York: Basic Books.

Winnicott, D. W. (1971d). Dreaming, fantasying, and living. In: *Playing and Reality* (pp. 26–37). New York: Basic Books.

Winnicott, D. W. (1971e). The location of cultural experience. In: *Playing and Reality* (pp. 95–103). New York: Basic Books.

Winnicott, D. W. (1974). Fear of breakdown. *International Review of Psycho-Analysis*, 1: 103–107.

Winnicott, D. W. (1989a). Interpretation in psycho-analysis. In: C. Winnicott, R. Shepherd, & M. Davis (Eds.), *Psycho-Analytic Explorations* (pp. 207–212). Cambridge, MA: Harvard University Press.

Winnicott, D. W. (1989b). The use of the word "use". In: C. Winnicott, R. Shepherd, & M. Davis (Eds.), *Psycho-Analytic Explorations* (pp. 233–235). Cambridge, MA: Harvard University Press.

Winnicott, D. W. (1989c). The use of an object in the context of *Moses and Monotheism*. In: C. Winnicott, R. Shepherd, & M. Davis (Eds.), *Psycho-Analytic Explorations* (pp. 240–246). Cambridge, MA: Harvard University Press.

INDEX